Interdisciplinary perspectives on modern history

Editors
Robert Fogel and Stephan Thernstrom

The politics of community

The politics of community
Migration and politics in antebellum Ohio

KENNETH J. WINKLE
University of Nebraska, Lincoln

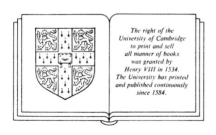

The right of the
University of Cambridge
to print and sell
all manner of books
was granted by
Henry VIII in 1534.
The University has printed
and published continuously
since 1584.

CAMBRIDGE UNIVERSITY PRESS

Cambridge
New York   New Rochelle   Melbourne   Sydney

Published by the Press Syndicate of the University of Cambridge
The Pitt Building, Trumpington Street, Cambridge CB2 1RP
32 East 57th Street, New York, NY 10022, USA
10 Stamford Road, Oakleigh, Melbourne 3166, Australia

First published 1988

Printed and bound in Canada

Library of Congress Cataloging-in-Publication Data
Winkle, Kenneth J.
The politics of community: migration and politics in antebellum
Ohio / Kenneth J. Winkle.
p.   cm.
Bibliography: p.
ISBN 0-521-34372-0
1. Ohio – Politics and government – 1787–1865. 2. Migration,
Internal – Ohio – History – 19th century. 3. Political participation –
Ohio – History – 19th century. I. Title
F495.W65   1988
324.9771'03–dc19   87-20733
                    CIP

British Library Cataloguing in Publication applied for.

For Allan G. Bogue

Contents

Tables and figures

Figures

Preface

Studies of antebellum political behavior tend, quite naturally, to focus on patterns of partisanship that helped to provoke the Civil War. Such studies have painted a clear picture of antebellum ideology, party organization, the sources of partisan allegiances, political realignment, the emergence of the slavery issue, and the deepening sectional crisis. When I began this examination of popular political life in antebellum Ohio, however, I wanted to look first at patterns of participation, establishing the outlines of Ohio's eligible and active electorate, before moving on to an analysis of partisan issues and behavior. Initially, that task seemed simple and straightforward. Traditional interpretations of political participation on the eve of disunion had emphasized the liberality of the franchise after a generation of suffrage reform, especially in the North, unequaled rates of voter turnout, and the aggressive commitment of political parties to mass participation.

In fact, the foundations of political participation in antebellum Ohio proved far more complex than this traditional framework had led me to expect. Near the beginning of my research, I came across poll books – individual-level records of voting – and I tried to link them to the U.S. census to determine the social, economic, and ethnic sources of popular participation. The results were troubling. To my surprise, most of the voters recorded in the poll books were not listed in the U.S. census: they were migrants. This unexpected discovery led me to a vast literature in social history dealing with the often surprising geographical mobility of nineteenth-century Americans. While conducting this initial study of voter turnout, I therefore realized that a thorough analysis of popular participation in antebellum Ohio demanded an accounting of the geographical mobility of the electorate and its impact on political behavior. A number of impressive studies in political history had previously noted the substantive and methodological importance of migration among nineteenth-century voters. As I continued my research, however, I found that the political implications of migration were vast and that they permeated the legal, partisan, and popular foundations of antebellum participation. Migration, in short, was an important ingredient in the welter of political rules, practices, and organizations that antebellum Americans thought of as democracy.

My new interest in the impact of migration on political behavior shifted my focus away from dramatic political events at the state and national levels to the common behavior of individual voters and the social context of popular politics within communities. Political participation began here, at the local level, where the restless migration of the period made its greatest impact. I found, too, that the political effects of migration appeared only fleetingly in the sources that represent the mainstay of nineteenth-century political history – aggregate voting returns, newspapers, and private letters – and therefore often remain hidden from view. My goal, however, was to keep the individual voter in center stage. As a result, I have drawn most heavily on public documents and quantitative records, which provide a clearer likeness of actual voters, in drawing this portrait of local political life.

In sum, this book explores the relationship between migration and politics not to explain the more visible political events of the Civil War era but to present an important part of the less visible social context within which those events arose and took their shape.

I am both surprised and pleased by the number of scholarly debts I acquired while researching and writing this book. During the early stages of research, teachers, colleagues, and friends at the University of Wisconsin-Madison encouraged my interest in this subject and challenged me both to expand its scope and to sharpen its focus. The staffs of a number of libraries and archives went beyond the call of duty in searching out, cataloging, and making available local records, some of which were unaccessioned and yet were indispensable to my research. These libraries and archives include Wayne State University Archives, the Ohio Historical Society, Kent State University Archives, the University of Cincinnati Archives, Bowling Green State University Archives, the University of Akron Archives, Ohio University Archives, the Newberry Library, and the State Historical Society of Wisconsin. Additionally, several county clerks kindly turned over their attics to me in my search for local records.

While I was writing the dissertation that eventually became this book, several colleagues and friends read and commented on various drafts of individual chapters. They include Neil Basen, George C. Brown, and Ralph Kloske of the University of Wisconsin-Madison; Donald J. Rogers of the University of Hartford; Lois N. Magner and Linda L. Peck of Purdue University; Ruth Crocker of

Auburn University; John M. Glen of Ball State University; Philip V. Scarpino of Indiana University-Purdue University at Indianapolis; Robert S. Salisbury of the Université d'Orléans; and Philip R. VanderMeer of Arizona State University. David Ward and John B. Sharpless of the University of Wisconsin-Madison; Ronald P. Formisano of Clark University; William G. Shade of Lehigh University; Earl J. Hess of the University of Georgia; and Paul Burch of Purdue University read all or substantial portions of the manuscript at a later stage and offered many helpful suggestions.

During the publication of this book, the editors at Cambridge University Press offered crucial advice and encouragement. In particular, Frank Smith has been remarkably generous with his time during the past three years and has invariably offered sound and thoughtful suggestions. The editors of the Interdisciplinary Perspectives on Modern History series provided crucial encouragement and welcome advice. Finally, I discussed some of the issues and evidence that appear in Chapters 5 and 6 in an article, "A Social Analysis of Voter Turnout in Ohio, 1850-1860," in *The Journal of Interdisciplinary History*, 13 (Winter 1983), 411-35.

My greatest scholarly debt, however, belongs to Professor Allan G. Bogue, my dissertation director at the University of Wisconsin-Madison. Professor Bogue was a constant source of encouragement, guidance, and good humor. He combines two of the most valued traits in an adviser – an insistence on rigorous scholarly standards but also the willingness to listen to and encourage innovative ideas. All those who know Professor Bogue's scholarship and character will appreciate his impact on my education as a historian.

Any errors of substance or method that have survived such counsel must remain, of course, mine alone.

Introduction

This study examines the impact of migration on political participation in antebellum Ohio. The idea that migration, in one form or another, helped to shape American political behavior and institutions is as old as the westward movement itself. In a guide for migrants published in Cincinnati in 1848, for example, John Mason Peck observed that "Migration has become almost a habit, in the West. Hundreds of men can be found, not fifty years of age, who have settled for the fourth, fifth, or sixth time on a new spot." Peck went on to portray wave after wave of frontiersmen passing westward, taming a wilderness, and learning a new way of life from their experiences. This and similar contemporary descriptions of the impact of westward migration on both individuals and their society later emboldened a generation of historians, Frederick Jackson Turner and his students most prominent among them, to focus on the westward movement as an important, even crucial agent in shaping the character of American political life. Today, few historians would argue along with Turner that "The existence of an area of free land, its continuous recession, and the advance of American settlement westward, explain American development." But the impact of westward migration on American politics, and particularly the Turnerian portrait of "individualism, economic equality, freedom to rise, democracy" in the new West, remains a persistent theme within American historiography.[1]

The impact of migration on American political development during the nineteenth century has been a perennial subject of controversy, but that continuing debate has recently acquired new urgency. Approaching the subject of migration from an entirely different direction, a school of "new" social historians, employing quantitative methods, has pointed to internal migration as a central feature not only of the new West but of nineteenth-century society throughout America. A host of quantitative "community studies" makes abundantly clear that migration – whether from east to west, from country to city, or from Europe to America – played a dominant role in shaping nineteenth-century social, economic, and cultural life. Social historians' discovery that the frontier was not unique for its

1

restless migration has not halted the venerable search for some link between migration and national development but has actually reinvigorated it. It is now clear that frequent migration was a "habit" among many more Americans and a problem within many more communities than Turner and his disciples ever imagined.[2]

At the same time, the new social historians have amassed an array of ever more sophisticated historical tools for measuring migration and examining its impact on nineteenth-century behavior and institutions. Migration studies are now crucial to our interpretation of nineteenth-century social organization and development. Political historians, however, have been slower to incorporate the conclusions and the methods of migration research into their own studies of nineteenth-century political behavior, to assess the impact of such pervasive migration on nineteenth-century politics. Quantitative community studies that focus on migration represent a largely untapped body of substantive and methodological insights into nineteenth-century social and economic behavior that political historians overlook at their own peril. The new body of migration studies, in short, poses a substantive and methodological challenge that political historians can no longer ignore.[3]

Indeed, modern migration studies arose in the first place from historians' initial attempts to give Turner's frontier thesis a rigorous empirical meaning, to ground the frontier experience in a broader historical context. As early as 1935, for example, James C. Malin, a leading critic of Turner, examined persistence and migration in five Kansas rainfall belts, noting distinct "cycles" of migration that corresponded with general cycles of economic boom and bust. Malin drew on aggregate records of residence to establish a link between migration and economic development even after the frontier had passed. The idea of such a general relationship between rates of migration and levels of economic activity held up remarkably well as the number of community studies that focus on migration swelled during the succeeding half-century.[4]

Although historians continued to overlook the full extent of geographical mobility for many years, the restless mobility of nineteenth-century Americans became stunningly apparent with the application of the geographical case study to historical research. Beginning in the late 1950s, agricultural historians working in the Midwest produced a flurry of rural population studies that made not only theoretical but crucial methodological contributions to the study of American migration. William L. Bowers, Mildred Throne, Merle Curti, Peter Coleman, and others produced important case studies of geographical mobility among actual individuals in nine-teenth-century Iowa, Wisconsin, and Illinois. Those case studies, Curti's most prominent among them, found much of their inspiration in the continuing controversy over the validity of the Turner thesis. Succeeding migration or "persistence" studies have tended to focus on uncovering both the extent and the sources of geographical mobility, rather than its political consequences. Virtually all of these studies of individual-level migration have identified wealth, occupation, and age as the most important sources of geographical mobility. During the nineteenth century, persistence was apparently a privilege that belonged only to the wealthiest and most highly skilled Americans. Westward migration continued unabated well beyond the frontier stage, and the cityward migration and foreign immigration that joined it reflected, in general, a constant search for economic opportunity.[5]

The greatest impact of the rural population studies was not, however, to settle the debate over the Turner thesis at all but to lend many aspects of that controversy sudden national importance. In 1964, when Stephan Thernstrom produced the first study of geographical mobility within an eastern city, it became quite apparent that restless migration was a national phenomenon throughout the nineteenth century. Thernstrom set the pattern for a spate of urban community studies by applying the case-study approach to urban populations. Still, most of the early urban case studies focused on social rather than geographical mobility. Only more recently have historians come to consider both varieties of migration – geographical and social – as national phenomena that were intimately related. It is now clear that "moving out" and "moving up" were largely expressions of a common impulse – the search for economic opportunity – and may in fact have been interdependent. From this national perspective, the frontier was only one expression of that ceaseless search for economic opportunity that was a central feature of life throughout nineteenth-century America. Westward migration was indeed only one of many means to that end, only the most conspicuous of many varieties of migration.[6]

By beginning with the conclusions and methodology of quantitative community studies, political historians can examine the political consequences of widespread and frequent migration during the nineteenth century. Even a cursory review of migration studies shows that restless migration was a phenomenon not only of the frontier but of long-settled communities throughout America and throughout the nineteenth century. Migration studies routinely uncover rates of persistence from just under 25 percent to just over 50 percent between decennial censuses. Further, it has become clear that decennial rates of migration tell only part of the story, because they conceal the movement of migrants between census years. In fact, annual rates of migration were typically two to three times higher than we would have expected, judging from decennial rates alone. Every year, a significant minority of Americans became migrants, and a majority may have moved during each decade. We can now ask the same questions about American political behavior in general that we have long applied to the frontier, questions about the relationship between wholesale migration and patterns of participation, partisan organization, the distribution of political power, political stability, the development of local political institutions, and the rise of a more egalitarian political system.[7]

The mid-nineteenth century is a good starting place to look for the impact of migration on political participation. By almost any standard, the mid-nineteenth century saw the emergence of modern participant politics in America. After 1840, state legislatures and constitutional conventions gradually revoked property and taxpaying qualifications, and by 1860 most states had embraced the principle of universal white manhood suffrage. At the same time, nationally competitive parties began devising new campaign strategies designed to create strong grassroots organizations, generate deep partisan commitments, and mobilize voters. Later, especially during the 1850s, party leaders eagerly embraced emotional sectional and cultural issues, such as slavery and immigration, to attract even more voters to the polls. In this environment of flexible suffrage rules and heated partisan competitiveness, eligible voters trooped to the polls in record numbers.[8]

Further, historians have come to characterize the mid-nineteenth century as an era of "boundlessness," an age of cultural as well as physical expansion. A popular feeling of "boundlessness," which John Higham associated with the rise of Jacksonian democracy, appeared after 1815 in response to a new sense of national security that was accompanied by rapid technological advance, political democratization, a revival of evangelical Protestantism, and a novel romantic philosophy. Such boundlessness was centrifugal, breeding territorial and economic expansion, along with a diffuse popular restlessness, a multitude of perfectionist reform movements, and a sudden wave of westward migration. Colonial culture had emphasized a communal organization of society that prevented or at least tempered individualism for the sake of family, congregation, and community. Historians have recently noted the organization of colonial society into "closed corporate communities," but they have also outlined a general retreat from communalism and a corresponding rise of individualism as the eighteenth century came to a close.[9]

Antebellum philosophers idealized the new America as "an individual standing alone, self-reliant and self-propelling." The antebellum legal environment simultaneously sought to foster economic growth and cultural expansiveness by releasing individual initiative from the shackles of communal responsibilities. Nineteenth-century jurisprudence reflected a new confidence and national aggressiveness that took the community for granted and stressed economic opportunity for individuals. The same decades that brought the most aggressive westward expansion and the highest levels of political participation in American history also witnessed Americans' weakest legal and cultural commitment to their communities. Such a cultural, social, and economic boundlessness gave widespread migration free rein in shaping the outlines of an emerging system of participant politics. In fact, some historians have linked the Civil War itself to that cultural expansiveness, as an "excess of democracy" weakened institutional restraints and bred political instability.[10]

Traditionally, students of electoral participation have emphasized the most dramatic changes in the American voting universe, focusing on the impact of high levels of popular participation on parties and policies during these decades of expansion, most particularly during the Civil War era. They have made important advances in analyzing election returns to sort out a wide variety of political, social, and economic influences on political behavior. But our understanding of the demographic foundations of this awakening of political involvement and of the sources of popular participation at the local level remains meager. In particular, historians are beginning to exploit individual-level electoral data to show more precisely how an array of social and demographic variables acted within political systems to encourage or discourage political participation. By focusing on individual participants in the political process, these individual-level studies reveal vividly the fluid mobility of the antebellum electorate.[11]

The American political system has quite obviously come to grips with the demands of a modern, mobile electorate. Today, fairly uniform and equitable residence requirements, generally convenient registration procedures, absentee ballots, and even standard forms of personal identification such as the driver's license accommodate a mobile society and bar relatively few migrants from the polls. All these adaptations to a migratory electorate were un-known, however, during the antebellum decades. They developed only gradually during the nineteenth century as the political system came to grips with frequent migration. Residence requirements were a much more controversial political issue before the Civil War, and migration put voters at a considerably greater political disad-vantage. During this formative period of popular politics, we might therefore expect high levels of migration to find their first political expression and to leave a deep impression on emerging political institutions and behaviors.[12]

This study is a comprehensive examination of the relationship between politics and internal migration, migration within the Unit-ed States, during these formative years. Historians have long noted the influence of heavy European immigration on the content and conduct of nineteenth-century political life. Indeed, a growing body of ethnocultural studies has convincingly demonstrated an impor-tant relationship between voters' ethnic and religious backgrounds and their partisan affiliations. This study does not discount such ethnocultural aspects of antebellum political life but focuses on the personal experiences of migrants and persisters rather than on their inherited, ethnocultural characteristics. This study argues, in short, that migration as a social process made an important impression on migrants' political behavior quite apart from their national, regional, or religious heritages. It seeks to sort out the impact of migrants' common experiences, as migrants, on their political behavior. Such a behavioral approach means simply that this study emphasizes the actual experiences of migrants and persisters and the impact of those personal experiences on their political behavior and attitudes. Evidence suggests that Ohioans reacted more strongly to the sheer numbers of internal migrants who passed through their state and their communities than to those migrants' ethnic origins. Only 11 percent of Ohioans were foreign-born in 1850, whereas almost 40 percent were interstate migrants. Indeed, Ohio did not alter suf-frage rules for the foreign-born between 1809 and the Civil War but experimented continually during the same period with suffrage re-quirements for internal migrants. In practice, native-born migrants and foreign immigrants appear to have undergone very similar ex-periences, as migrants, on their way to the polling place, despite any differences in the way they behaved once they arrived there. The experience of migration exerted its greatest influence not on partisanship but on patterns of participation. The impact of migra-tion on patterns of political participation and the voters' actual experiences as migrants, rather than their ascribed attributes, therefore take precedence in this study.[13]

The present study of migration and politics therefore emphasizes the political and social behavior of individuals rather than focusing on the behavior of aggregated ethnic, religious, or occupational groups. Almost by definition, migration studies examine the behavior of individuals. Any examination of the impact of migration on political behavior, therefore, must also begin with individuals. Such a focus diverts attention away from national political events as a point of departure and highlights political processes at the local level, encouraging a "bottom up" approach to political history. Concentration on the impact of migration on politics can thus provide insights into the inner workings of community politics, including local patterns of power, the theory and application of suffrage rules, local party organization, and actual election practices.

This study draws heavily on individual-level sources, many of which have never before been examined. It employs quantitative records of political and social behavior among individuals, where necessary, as well as written expressions of attitudes, opinions, and especially personal experiences. When possible, the study permits individual migrants and persisters, voters and policymakers to speak for themselves. For these reasons alone, this is a case study, surveying the impact of migration on local politics within a single state. Indeed, many of the chapters focus on single counties, and some of them highlight individual townships because of the precise, individual-level analysis that is often required to unravel subtle relationships between migration and politics. Figure I.1 shows the five local study areas on which much of this study focuses. The local study areas include communities located within five of Ohio's six geographical regions to ensure broad coverage of statewide trends.

The first two chapters survey patterns of migration in antebellum Ohio. Chapter 1 draws on census data and the observations of contemporary commentators to explore the impact of the westward movement on patterns of settlement. The chapter reveals a far-reaching transition from rapid settlement during the 1830s and 1840s to more sedate growth in population and, in eastern Ohio, actual population decline during the 1850s. Ohioans' cheerful approval of migration disappeared as the line of most rapid settlement moved ever westward through and beyond the state. Urban growth, new transportation routes, and foreign immigration took on new prominence as the westward movement into Ohio came to a close.

Figure I.1. The five local study areas and Ohio's regions.

Chapter 2 is a county-level case study of migration that focuses on voters and sorts out long-distance migration from merely local moves. The chapter surveys the interaction of transportation, economic activity, urban growth, and migration within a local electorate. Records of residence among individuals reveal that population growth and decline within a single county rested on the net balance between immigrants and emigrants over long distances and not on local-level migration. Even local patterns of settlement depended most heavily on rates of migration over long distances. This evidence suggests that migration was a near-universal experience in antebellum Ohio and that most voters, at one time or another, were long-distance migrants.

The next four chapters examine the impact of these patterns of migration among voters on various aspects of political participation – suffrage, electoral practices, voting, and local political leadership. Chapter 3 examines the impact of migration on suffrage. An examination of case law and statutes demonstrates that increasing levels of migration after 1815 provoked a new judicial conception of legal residence in Ohio that made it easier, in theory, for migrants to gain suffrage in their new communities. Reacting to their experiences with migration, Ohioans gradually altered their state's suffrage rules during the nineteenth century to accommodate increasing numbers of internal migrants. Reflecting national legal trends, Ohio jurists gradually broadened rules of suffrage for internal migrants, giving migrants more freedom to move without suffering legal disabilities and to participate in their communities even as relative newcomers. At the beginning of the century, voters had to depend on their communities to grant them rights of suffrage, but by the end of the Civil War voters were free to participate in communities of their own choosing. These new rules of suffrage awarded migrants important new political rights.

Resisting this theoretical liberalization of suffrage rules, however, the state's legislators continued to restrict suffrage for migrants in practice. In the wake of migration, the legislature had to draw explicit rules of legal residence to sort out legal from illegal voters. A new election law, passed in 1841, defined legal residence in Ohio for the first time but then permitted a local board of election judges to apply those rules on election day. As a result, a minority of persisters could use residence rules to control access to the ballot box and screen newcomers. The mobility of the majority of voters therefore lent exaggerated political power to a small minority of settled persisters. These electoral practices that discriminated against recent migrants are the subject of Chapter 4.

Chapter 5 discusses the impact of new suffrage rules, new electoral practices, and patterns of migration on voting. Aggregate electoral data can conceal complex patterns of participation that reflect the restless geographical mobility of voters during the period. The combination of increasing migration and a broadening suffrage produced sometimes dizzying rates of turnover among voters at the local level. Most voters cast only one or two ballots in a community before moving on again. At the other extreme, only a relative hand-ful of voters persisted in a community over an entire decade. The typical voter was therefore both a migrant and a short-term partici-pant in local political life.

Chapter 6 discloses that turnover within the local electorate was not random. A wide variety of demographic influences – fertility, aging, mortality, and migration – helped to determine which voters persisted and participated at the local level and which did not. Mi-gration, however, was the dominant demographic influence on pat-terns of local political participation. Persisters tended to be wealthier, more occupationally skilled, and older than emigrants from the community or recent immigrants to it. They were therefore overrepresented at the ballot box over the long run and in local office. In the midst of migration, this relatively stable "core commu-nity" of economically successful persisters used new suffrage rules and political practices to dominate leadership roles and therefore acquired unusual political authority. These persisters provided po-litical stability within their communities.

Chapter 7 is a case study that reconstructs the attitudes and be-havior of over 100 voters in a single election to test the conclusions of previous chapters. The case study provides a detailed portrait of an actual election in one Ohio county. It shows how, in practice, interactions between migrants and persisters, guided by suffrage rules and electoral practices, helped to shape the political life of antebellum Ohio communities.

This study, in short, examines the impact of high levels of migra-tion on political behavior, and especially on patterns of political participation, within antebellum communities. In drawing a com-prehensive portrait of the local electorate before the Civil War, this study focuses on the everyday social environment in which more dramatic political events took place. It argues that a host of some-times hidden social and demographic factors joined more visible political events and institutions during the antebellum period in shaping the contours of local political life.

1   *The tide of emigration*

Like Americans in general, most Ohioans moved frequently during the nineteenth century, over long distances as part of the westward movement or in shorter moves within their own state. The antebellum decades were a period of buoyant economic growth, fueled by westward expansion, rapid advances in transportation, the rise of modern commercial cities, and an aggressive entrepreneurial ethos. Patterns of migration were therefore bound up with much broader social, economic, and cultural trends. In a complicated circular relationship, migration, westward expansion, urban growth, economic opportunity, and new transportation routes all contributed to and rested upon one another. Migration of some kind was a nearly universal experience before the Civil War, but it was not, of course, a uniform experience. Migration was often a very personal decision, and the characteristics and circumstances of specific individuals – their age, occupation, wealth, nationality, and even their personalities – influenced their decisions about when, where, and whether to move.

John Klippart was probably typical, but he was much more explicit than most migrants when explaining his reasons for moving, which he did frequently. Klippart, in fact, moved four times in one year. In 1846, Klippart was a teacher in a common school in Canton, Ohio, where he was born. At age 24, Klippart decided to leave teaching for a career in trade, to earn more money and start his own business. But he could find nothing in Ohio – "times here were hard," as he put it – and so both economic opportunity and a spirit of adventure drew him westward to St. Louis. In St. Louis, Klippart looked for a position selling dry goods but could not find one. So he turned instead to teaching French, which he had studied to see him through hard times such as these. Disappointed in business, Klippart moved a second time, agreeing to teach school on a plantation in Tennessee. But disliking slavery and having satisfied his desire to see Tennessee, he moved back to Ohio, this time to Wayne County. Klippart moved a fourth and final time in 1846 for a more personal reason, to marry the sweetheart he had left behind in Canton. Klippart's journey included a half-dozen different kinds of migration –

westward, interstate, rural-to-urban, urban-to-rural, return, and intrastate – all in one year. Back in Ohio, the self-educated Klippart stayed put for the rest of his life and developed into one of the state's leading agriculturalists, publishing the famous manual *The Wheat Plant* in 1860.[1]

But only the most articulate migrants left such complete records of their personal migration histories. The great majority of migrants left personal information only in government records such as the U.S. census, and these quantitative documents reveal only the broadest outlines of their movements. Important social and economic trends, however, such as migration from east to west, from country to city, and from Europe to America, dominated patterns of migration and therefore permit a rough but revealing portrait of the most frequent itineraries of nineteenth-century migrants.[2]

The westward movement dominated patterns of migration in antebellum Ohio. Ohioans liked to picture their state as a "gateway" between the East and the West. Ohio lay astride two important routes of westward travel, the Ohio River and the Great Lakes, and a third route of less importance, the National Road. The state's southern boundary, the Ohio River, was the major westward route before the opening of the Erie Canal. It carried hundreds of thousands of southerners into southern Ohio and westward into southern Indiana, southern Illinois, and the new Southwest of the lower Mississippi Valley. After the Erie Canal opened in 1825, Lake Erie, Ohio's northern boundary, surpassed the Ohio River as a route of westward expansion. Lake Erie carried settlers primarily from New England and the middle states (New York, Pennsylvania, and New Jersey) into northern Ohio and the upper Midwest. The National Road bisected the state and carried settlers into the interior before the opening of Ohio's own canal system.[3]

Ohio's boosters recognized the geographic position of their state as "the center of the great current of American travel, transport and emigration" and promoted the region as the "great natural gateway between the Eastern and Western States." As a result of its location and fertile farmland, Ohio was indeed the fastest growing state in the Midwest for half a century. Between 1800 and 1850, Ohio claimed an average population increase of almost 400,000 every decade. Population growth is the result of two distinct phenomena: natural increase and net migration. Natural increase is simply the difference between births and deaths. Net migration is the difference between immigration into an area and emigration from it. When immigrants outnumber emigrants, net migration is positive, and population increases. Before 1840, the primary source of population growth in Ohio was net migration. Net migration accounted for more than half of all population growth between 1800 and 1840 – 87 percent from 1800 to 1810, 72 percent from 1810 to 1820, and 31 percent from 1820 to 1830. The 1830s were the decade of peak settlement in Ohio, the years of greatest growth during the nineteenth century. During that decade, Ohio gained over 580,000 new residents, over one-third of whom were westward migrants. Growth tapered off after 1840, however. Emigrants began to outnumber immigrants, and natural increase replaced net migration as a source of population growth.[4]

During these years of settlement, Ohioans gloated about their state's rapid growth and viewed westward migration as an "immense tide," an "immense stream," a "perennial stream," a "great current," or a "tide of emigration."[5] Ohio did indeed benefit from a tide of internal migration that sent millions of Americans moving from state to state, generally westward, before the Civil War. Even apart from the arrival of millions of European immigrants, internal migration – movement within the United States – was common. Movement between geographical units as large as states cannot be susceptible to exact measurement, but patterns of interstate migration can be helpful in illuminating broad regional trends. Figure 1.1 depicts patterns of interstate migration elicited from the U.S. census of 1850. Figure 1.1 illustrates the movement of migrants from their state of birth to their state of residence in 1850. Such a crude index as interstate migration does not reveal actual migration paths, intervening destinations, length of residence, return migration, or movement within states. Further, Figure 1.1 does not capture the movement of interstate migrants who died before 1850. The resulting "snapshot" of interstate migration presents a very conservative portrait of actual migration streams, but it does summarize the interstate movements of everyone living in America in 1850.[6]

Not surprisingly, even so conservative an index as interstate migration captures the impressive geographical mobility of antebellum Americans. One-fifth of all native-born Americans were living outside their state of birth in 1850. All told, 6,027,118, or 30 percent of all Americans living in 1850, were either native-born interstate migrants or foreign-born immigrants. As the state's boosters liked to point out, Ohio did indeed straddle antebellum America's busiest channel of westward migration. In 1850, there were 1,056 possible migration streams among the 33 states and territories. Figure 1.1 provides a summary of patterns of interstate migration by diagram-

Figure 1.1 Interstate migration streams of 50,000 or more migrants, 1850.
Source: DeBow, *Statistical View,* 114–18.

ming the 17 interstate migration streams that each included 50,000 or more migrants. While those 17 migration paths accounted for fewer than 2 percent of all possible migration streams, they contained over two-fifths of all interstate migrants. The 17 streams depicted in Figure 1.1 summarize the dominant pattern of interstate migration at midcentury.[7]

Most interstate migration, northern as well as southern, was westward. But there were regional differences. Westward migration was most prevalent in the North. Twelve of the 17 largest migration streams originated in northern states, and northern migrants tended to travel farther than did southern migrants. New York alone sent 50,000 or more westward migrants to five states before 1850, stretching from Pennsylvania westward to Wisconsin. The largest southern migration streams reached only into adjacent states. Not only did more northern than southern migrants move west, but the northern frontier gained population at the expense of the South. While the Upper South, Virginia and Kentucky, sent 50,000 or more migrants to two lower midwestern states, Ohio and Indiana, there were no compensating southward streams. Interstate migration in both North and South was predominantly westward, but northerners met southerners most often in the Midwest and not in the new Southwest.[8]

Ohioans were important participants in this tide of westward movement. In 1850, Ohio stood in the middle of the great northern stream of migration that flowed westward from Vermont to Wisconsin. Before 1850, the state received 50,000 or more migrants from New York, Pennsylvania, and Virginia and sent at least that many to two western states, Indiana and Illinois. Eight of the 17 largest migration streams involved Ohio. Each of them sent an average of 100,000 migrants to, from, or through the state. At any moment, therefore, Ohio could claim an impressive proportion of America's westward migrants. In 1850, almost one-fourth of the nation's interstate migrants had been born in Ohio or were living there.

Before midcentury, Ohio could and did depend on westward migrants to fuel population growth. Ohio joined only New York and Pennsylvania as both an origin and a destination of major migration streams. But unlike those two eastern states, as late as 1850 Ohio was still experiencing net immigration, receiving more migrants than it was sending westward. One in seven interstate migrants lived in Ohio in that year. Ohio had received, in fact, 2.5 times as many interstate migrants as it had given up. Before midcentury, Ohio was the leading beneficiary of a tide of emigration that was washing westward from the Atlantic to the Mississippi.[9]

In 1850, almost four of every ten Ohioans were in-migrants. Most of the newcomers, 71 percent, were American-born. Predictably, Ohio's immediate neighbors to the east were the most generous contributors to the state's population. Pennsylvanians represented more than a quarter of Ohio's newcomers, while about one-fifth were Virginians or New Yorkers. Overall, almost one-half of Ohio's in-migrants were northerners and only one-fifth were southerners. Germans were the dominant foreign immigrant group, 15 percent of Ohio's newcomers. Irish represented another 7 percent; 3.4 percent were English by birth.

As late as 1846, the state's commissioner of agriculture crowed with satisfaction about "Gathering to ourselves the industrious and enterprising from other states and nations." Indeed, Ohio had claimed more interstate migrants than any other state in 1850. But, ominously, the state's 295,000 emigrants put Ohio in fourth place, behind New York, Pennsylvania, and Virginia, as a contributor of migrants to the westward movement. In keeping with the national trend, 84 percent of Ohio's emigrants went west before 1850. Ohio was an important stepping-stone between the East and the West. As one observer pointed out in 1833, at the peak of immigration, "Western Pennsylvania has scattered its sons over Ohio, while the latter has peopled Indiana and Illinois." Two-thirds of Ohio's westward migrants were indeed settled in Indiana in 1850, generally in the northern part of that state. Another one-fifth lived in Illinois. Michigan, Missouri, and Wisconsin together claimed 13 percent of Ohio's emigrants.[10]

The line of peak settlement was shifting westward, bringing fewer easterners and southerners into Ohio and sending more Ohioans westward. The state was maturing, and population density and land prices were increasing. "While the grandfather smokes his pipe in the wide hall of a Kentucky double cabin," wrote one observer, "his son follows the plough in Ohio, and his grandson opens a new farm in Indiana." New farms to the west were beckoning a third generation of westward migrants to the Mississippi Valley and beyond.[11]

After 1850, the westward movement began to work against Ohio for the first time. Ohio's boosters were accustomed to bounding growth and counted primarily on the westward movement for half a century to stimulate economic progress. In 1857, for example, Ohio's commissioner of statistics argued that "population is regarded, by all economists, as the first element of strength and wealth." His elaborate "law of growth" therefore included immigration as a vital element of progress. "Growth" meant above all growth in population. But the commissioner stated a second law of growth that he recognized as far less attractive. "Population," he warned, "is migratory." After 1850, this second law of growth threatened to subsume the first one. By 1860, Ohio was losing population to the westward movement for the first time.[12]

The line of peak settlement passed through Ohio during the 1840s and 1850s, into Indiana, Illinois, and Iowa. After a half-century as the fastest growing midwestern state, Ohio abruptly fell to fifth place behind Illinois, Iowa, Wisconsin, and Indiana. During the 1850s, Ohio's population grew by only 18 percent, which represented less than even the level of natural increase, down from 62 percent during the 1830s and 30 percent during the 1840s. Eighty-six percent of the growth during the 1850s occurred solely through natural increase, representing Ohio-born children ten years or younger in 1860. The westward movement was now draining away more settlers than it was bringing to Ohio, and the state began to suffer the effects of net emigration. Ohio's commissioner of statistics soon found himself grudgingly reporting an immense migration not into the state but out of it.[13]

Ohio faced a crisis of depopulation during the 1850s. Between 1850 and 1860, in fact, Ohio gave up more emigrants than any other state, jumping ahead of New York, Pennsylvania, and Virginia as the biggest loser of westward settlers. Illinois, Iowa, Wisconsin, and Indiana were now growing faster than Ohio ever had, filling up with migrants not only from the East and the South but from Ohio as well. In just ten years those four states together duplicated all the growth that Ohio had accumulated over its first 50 years. Illinois alone grew 50 percent faster than Ohio had during its decade of fastest growth. Worse yet, from Ohio's point of view, an impressive number of those new Hoosiers and Hawkeyes had their roots in Ohio. In 1860, 37 percent of all interstate migrants to Indiana were from Ohio, as well as one-fourth, one-fifth, and one-tenth of interstate migrants to Iowa, Illinois, and Wisconsin, respectively. All told, nearly one-fourth of all native-born migrants to those four states were transplanted Ohioans. By midcentury Ohio was, indeed, as the frontier historian Frederick Jackson Turner later described it, "a hive from which swarms of pioneers sought new homes."[14]

The 1850s therefore presented a new challenge to Ohioans, who had counted on a steady stream of newcomers from the East to fill their cities and stimulate their maturing economy. They had always recognized that they were living in, as one of them boasted during the 1830s, "one of the most emigrating states in the Union." But now, instead of a boast, that message was a warning. Before 1850 a leading beneficiary of the westward movement, Ohio was suddenly its biggest benefactor. As the secretary of state, William Trevitt, pointed out in 1855, "The tide of emigration is supposed to be setting against us."[15]

Rural regions were hit hardest by the new "spirit of emigration," because Ohio's cities continued to grow long after the line of settlement passed westward. The "tide of emigration" drew off many younger farmers and left bitter farmers in its wake. Cheaper land and transportation in Illinois and Iowa fostered a new wheat and corn belt further west, and Ohio agriculture peaked in 1850 and then declined. Rural depopulation, as it was labeled, brought both bewilderment and resentment. In 1857, John M. Millikin, president of the Ohio Board of Agriculture, adopted a tone of unappreciated generosity as he recounted his state's contributions to westward settlement. "For the last thirty years our capital and our population have been heavily drawn upon to improve and to populate the new States and Territories of the west," he complained. "Those who have left us for more western homes, constitute a portion of our most intelligent, industrious and enterprising population." Westward migration was now hurting Ohio. Another farmer watched an emigrant train leaving for Illinois and then lamented that "These are the kinds of materials we can least afford to spare from Ohio."[16]

Those who stayed behind felt both resentment and wonderment when they saw others moving on. "Day by day are we convinced of the foolishness displayed by men here in Ohio," a farmer complained, "in selling out comfortable homes and moving West for the purpose of bettering their condition." Ohio farmers argued from bitter experience that emigration was detrimental to both farming and farmers. The new movement west seemed so sudden and irrational that many called it a "mania" or a "fever." Still others traced the abrupt emigration to unthinking greed, "the love of acres and gain." "As soon as a farmer finds himself in possession of two or three hundred dollars," complained two Coshocton County farmers, "he puts it into his pocket; and very frequently borrows a similar amount of his neighbor, 'takes the cars' goes [sic] west, and buys land for his sons or himself." Just as rootlessness was detrimental to the farmer as an individual, according to the prevailing sentiment, so was it damaging to the farming community. "A wandering disposition is, in a high degree, prejudicial to the development of the best traits of man's nature," wrote a Franklin County farmer in 1860, "and it is alike unfavorable to improvement and progress in the cultivation of the soil." A farmer owed it to himself and his neighbors to stay on his farm, improve it, and cast his lot with his community. "How long this spirit shall continue," wrote two farmers to the Ohio Board of Agriculture in 1855, "it is impossible to tell, but it is retarding the improvement and prosperity of this part of Ohio; and we are well satisfied, that most of those who embark in this enterprise, do it their injury."[17]

Settled farmers tried hard to put the best face on rising rates of emigration. Some of them insisted that the high quality of Ohio's newcomers more than compensated for the increasing number of migrants heading west. Frederick Kuhne, who wrote a history of Ohio agriculture in 1859, discounted the economic impact of westward migrants because they were "more than replaced by a superior class of farmers" from New England, New York, Pennsylvania, and other eastern states. John Klippart, too, wrote to the Board of Agriculture in 1860, to argue that rural emigration simply proved that Ohioans were superior farmers. "That farming in Ohio is profitable," he wrote, "may be inferred from the fact that in many portions of the State the agricultural population is decreasing; the cause of which may be attributed to intelligent and successful farmers purchasing adjoining tracts from smaller farmers." Klippart, who had become a leading authority on Ohio agriculture, recognized that regions of intensive, commercial agriculture supported fewer and fewer farmers as they matured. Klippart felt sure that "many would prefer to remain in the immediate neighborhood of their nativity," as he ultimately did, "than to emigrate." But land ownership was too alluring to laborers who could count on only seven or eight months of work every year.[18]

Many young men, the most frequent migrants during the nineteenth century, were also drawn westward during the late 1840s by the Mexican War and the California Gold Rush. Klippart expressed his disapproval. "The discovery of gold in California," he complained, "seduced from rural life and converted into a Californian, every one who had the means, the inclination and the health to encounter the incidents and dangers of a voyage thither." Closer to home, the expanding railroad network of the 1850s not only made travel more convenient but also provided new employment for rural youths. "One great impediment to perfect farming," Hugh Gamble of Richland County wrote in 1856, "is the lack of laborers in the field, while our extensive public and company works are progressing." Klippart agreed that "Railroads have made a more extensive demand for employees upon our rural population than did the entire Mexican War." But probably many more young men gave in to the allure of Ohio's growing cities. "Very many farmer's [sic] sons acquire such a disrelish for the occupation of their fathers," wrote an eastern Ohio farmer, "that as soon as they are old enough, they leave for some town or city." Cityward migration within Ohio joined the more apparent westward movement as an impediment to farming. Young men who were "raised farmers," one farmer concluded, "would be better off to follow that occupation, than to throng to our cities and villages."[19]

By 1860, in fact, urbanization had taken over from the westward movement as a focus for migration in Ohio. With the ebbing of the westward tide and with economic maturation, internal population shifts associated with rural depopulation, urban growth, and new transportation routes took on new prominence. Most apparently,

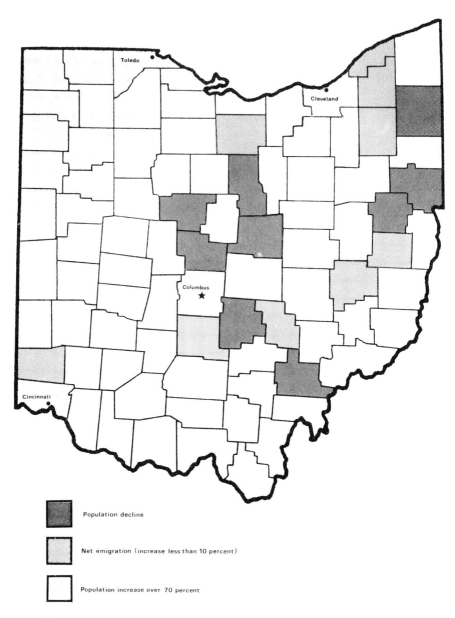

Population decline

Net emigration (increase less than 10 percent)

Population increase over 70 percent

Figure 1.2. Population growth and decline in Ohio counties, 1840–50. *Source:* DeBow, *Seventh Census,* 817–18.

there was an internal population shift from east to west during the 1840s and 1850s. Figure 1.2 depicts the pattern of population growth and decline in Ohio during the 1840s, the last decade of growth through migration. Figure 1.2 reinforces the image of a tide of migration washing across Ohio from east to west. By 1840, rapid settlement was largely restricted to the Maumee Valley, the counties of northwestern Ohio that represented the state's last frontier. The Maumee country opened up to the commercial grain trade only in 1845 with the completion of the Miami Canal, which set off feverish farm making. Thousands of new settlers poured wheat flour, corn whiskey, and pork products through Toledo, which became Ohio's fastest-growing city. Growth exceeded 70 percent throughout the Maumee Valley and actually reached 132 percent in the extreme northwest corner of the state. Here farmers routinely reported that "our county is settling fast" or "our county is filling up fast." Urban growth represented a secondary source of population increase during the 1840s. Outside the Maumee Valley only the counties containing Ohio's largest cities – Cincinnati, on the Ohio River, Cleveland, on Lake Erie, and Columbus, on the National Road – displayed increases in population rivaling those of the unsettled Northwest.[20]

But the first signs of population decline tempered this rapid or moderate growth throughout most of the state. Between 1840 and 1850, nine counties scattered throughout eastern and central Ohio lost population. These were the first counties west of Pennsylvania to experience population loss. Another nine counties grew by less than 10 percent. Sluggish growth in these counties reflected net emigration. Clearly, the line of peak settlement had moved through most of Ohio by 1850. In its wake, rural areas, especially those in the "old wheat belt," were reaching their peak and beginning to decline, and only the largest cities were still growing impressively.[21]

The 1850s brought an acceleration in this pattern of sluggish growth and population decline (Figure 1.3). During the 1850s, population fell in 15 counties in eastern Ohio. Low increases occurred in another 23 counties, representing every region of Ohio except the Maumee Valley, which alone continued to support bounding settlement. Overall, population loss or sluggish growth affected more than twice as many counties during the 1850s as during the 1840s. A westward-moving line of peak settlement straddled Ohio during the 1850s, bringing rapid settlement before it and depopulation in its wake.

Population decline was the result of overpopulation in rural re-

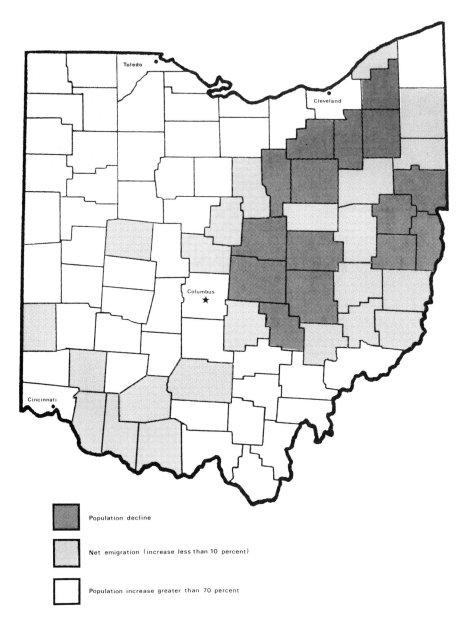

Population decline

Net emigration (increase less than 10 percent)

Population increase greater than 70 percent

Figure 1.3. Population growth and decline in Ohio counties, 1850–60.
Sources: DeBow, *Seventh Census,* 817–18; Kennedy, *Eighth Census,* 64–73.

gions and its attendant economic and social problems. Counties losing population during the 1850s recorded a population density of 54 people per square mile at the start of the decade. The counties in the Maumee Valley that were still growing registered a population density of only 15 per square mile, less than one-third the state's average. Farmers were actually abandoning land in the Muskingum Valley, while the number of farms rose 70 percent and farm size increased in the Maumee Valley. The line of settlement that drained migrants westward now straddled the state and provoked internal population shifts. The western half of Ohio was still growing while the eastern half was losing population.[22]

Urban growth gained new importance as the line of rural settlement moved westward. During the 1850s, in fact, 60 percent of all population growth in Ohio occurred in cities and towns. Just as the westward movement controlled the balance of migration to and from Ohio before midcentury, rapid urbanization, abetted by foreign immigration and new railroads, dominated patterns of settlement after 1850 and brought different kinds of migration to the fore.[23]

The Ohio River was the traditional focus of urban growth before the opening of the Erie Canal. Settlement gradually moved northward along the principal tributaries of the Ohio – the Muskingum, Hocking, Scioto, and Miami rivers. Ohio built its own canal system after the Erie Canal began channeling agricultural products from the Great Lakes region to the East Coast. The Ohio canals ran north and south, feeding produce from the multiplying farms of the state's interior into both Lake Erie and the Ohio River. But the canals benefited northern Ohio and especially the Lake Erie ports most heavily. When the canals opened, northern Ohio was far less settled than the Ohio Valley and much better situated to take advantage of the Erie Canal. The Ohio canals therefore fueled tremendous growth in the Lake Erie port cities, especially Cleveland and Toledo, the canal termini.[24]

In the interior, crossroads along Ohio's canals not only boosted urban growth but actually encouraged the founding of new canal towns. At the same time, the establishment of new routes of transportation northward to the lake provided, for the first time, a comprehensive trade system that could compete with the older Ohio River marketing network, which was centered at Cincinnati and, ultimately, at New Orleans. The canals attracted thousands of migrants to northern Ohio and, as a result, benefited the Lake Erie ports, with their connections to Buffalo and New York City, at the

Figure 1.4. Ohio counties containing 40 percent or more interstate or foreign migrants, 1850. *Source:* DeBow, *Statistical View,* 284–85, 290–91.

expense of Ohio River towns. The Erie Canal therefore diverted trade from the Ohio River to Lake Erie, and Cleveland and Toledo gradually extended their hinterlands southward along the canals. Internally, the canal traffic drew a new concentration of light manufacturing, such as flour milling, to towns and cities along the canals.[25]

The Ohio canal system, in short, spurred the development of commercial agriculture in northern Ohio and created a new system of commercial towns and cities. Figure 1.4 depicts the concentration of migration along the canals, on Lake Erie, and across northern Ohio. Figure 1.4 identifies Ohio counties that contained 40 percent or more interstate migrants or foreign immigrants in 1850. Immigration was heaviest around Lake Erie. South of the Maumee Valley and the Western Reserve, impressive levels of immigration attended growth in important canal towns. The five southerly counties containing 40 percent or more newcomers boasted growing cities and lay astride Ohio's canals. Columbus and Zanesville were important junctures on both the Ohio Canal and the National Road. Dayton and Sidney were beneficiaries of the completion of the Miami Canal in 1845. Cincinnati was both the state's largest city and its fastest growing, and it stood at the junction of the Miami Canal and the Ohio River. The canal system dominated patterns of urban growth before 1850.[26]

Ohio's canal counties, as sites of urban growth and commercial agriculture, grew much faster than the rest of the state. Counties bordering on a canal grew by 39 percent during the 1840s, while the population of all other counties increased by only 26 percent. In addition, the canal counties, as the most densely urban areas of Ohio, attracted many foreign immigrants. In 1850, 18 percent of the residents of the canal counties were foreign immigrants, compared to only 7 percent in the rest of the state. Cities throughout Ohio, in fact, attracted more than their share of interstate migrants and foreign immigrants. The counties containing Ohio's 20 largest cities held 44 percent interstate migrants, as compared to only 35 percent elsewhere. And more than one-half of those urban newcomers were foreign immigrants, compared to only one-fifth in rural areas. Cincinnati alone claimed over one-third of Ohio's German immigrants. As Ohio's commissioner of statistics pointed out, "the merchants, mechanics, and artizans [sic] of our now fast growing cities and towns are largely derived from the Eastern States."[27]

But this network of growing canal towns and cities was relatively short-lived. It was upset suddenly after 1850 by the railroads. The Ohio canals and the growing cities they supported provided an efficient marketing network for much of the state. Most farmers hauled their produce over generally short distances to canal towns, which served as regional marketing centers. As a farmer in Paulding County boasted in 1849, "We have two fine canals passing through our county, which takes [sic] every article of produce to a place of shipping or selling," generally on Lake Erie. But a broad crescent of counties from southwestern to northern Ohio lacked a reliable water link with either the lake or the Ohio River. They relied instead on the Sandusky River and subsidiary plank roads to market their produce at the lake port of Sandusky. Indeed, while farmers in counties adjacent to the canals expressed general satisfaction with the state's marketing facilities, those in peripheral areas were increasingly dissatisfied. They needed cheaper and more reliable routes to Lake Erie and the Ohio River to compete with farmers in the more prosperous canal counties.[28]

Farmers in peripheral areas turned to the railroad to bring economic development. Railroad transport permitted integration into Ohio's growing commercial economy. A farmer from hilly and landlocked Highland County, for example, wrote that "The fruits of Highland are quite equal to the fruits of any of the surrounding counties, and when our railroad to Cincinnati is completed, will form an article of export." A Holmes County farmer echoed that sentiment and complained that "A railroad is much needed through our county." In such peripheral areas, railroad transport signaled the initial commercialization of agriculture and, more ambitiously, promised seemingly limitless social and economic opportunities. Railroads in southern Ohio, for example, could not only relieve the river counties from dependence on the Ohio River but also establish contact with "the whole railroad world."[29]

Ohio's emerging railroad network at first complemented and only later competed with the existing river, lake, and canal system. The city of Sandusky chartered the state's first railroad in 1832 after failing to win inclusion in the state's canal network. Completed in 1845, the Mad River and Lake Erie Railroad, like Ohio's canals, ran north and south to feed produce from interior farms into Lake Erie and the Ohio River. The Mad River and Lake Erie connected Sandusky on the lake with Xenia in the Miami Valley. Through its link with the Little Miami Railroad, running southward to Cincinnati, the Mad River and Lake Erie connected the river with the lake and answered the transportation needs of western farmers who had felt left out of their state's canal system. Ohioans went on to lay 2,371 miles of track during the 1850s, much of it financed by internal towns and counties seeking market outlets. By 1860, Ohio possessed 16 completed railroads and 2,946 miles of track, three-and-one-half times as much track as canal channel, in fact the most trackage in the entire nation.[30]

Ohio farmers were seldom disappointed with their new railroads, which generally stimulated agricultural improvement. Railroads encouraged commercial production in settled regions and farm making further to the west, and many observers reported new farms and urban growth in their wake. John Goodin, a Hardin County farmer, wrote with satisfaction that "Since our railroad markets have opened, our farmers are more stimulated, and larger crops are put in." James Denniston wrote from Preble County that "the railroad has more than tripled the amount of business done at Eaton, in the exportation of produce, and gives to the place a business appearance, not frequently to be found in inland towns." Even the mere expectation of a railroad link might encourage agricultural development through anticipatory settlement. A farmer from Darke County, on the Indiana line, observed that "our population is increasing rapidly, and the prospect of a rail road to Dayton has advanced the price of lands and given a new impulse to the farmers." A Columbiana County farmer summed up his neighbors' profound faith in the new railroads: "In short, 'the good time coming,' long and anxiously looked for by our farmers, has come at last."[31]

But increasing railroad competition threatened the profitability of the once-coveted Ohio Canals. Beyond lowering tolls along the canals, Ohio's Board of Public Works could not hope to compete with the cheaper, more reliable, and more extensive private railroad net. The early rail lines tapped the state's interior much more efficiently than canals ever could and terminated at the traditional canal junctures with the lake and the river. In 1851, for example, the Board of Public Works complained that the new railroad network was not only competing with the canals but actually diverting canal traffic where the two networks met. The railroads lowered their rates at such important canal cities as Cincinnati, Toledo, Dayton, Cleveland, Columbus, and Newark to lure traffic away from the canals. Because the Board of Public Works followed suit, both railroad rates and canal tolls favored Ohio's largest cities. By competing with the canals, the new railroads boosted the largest canal cities but doomed many smaller canal towns to extinction.[32]

The growing railroad network, in fact, provoked a largely new pattern of urban growth in Ohio. The railroads upset the state's traditional marketing system that was centered on the Ohio River, Lake Erie, and their connecting canals. The earliest railways served largely as adjuncts to the existing water routes, running north and south and feeding produce over short distances into Lake Erie and the Ohio River. But during the 1850s the intrusion of major eastern lines shifted commercial emphasis from north-south to east-west routes. By the end of the decade, four Ohio railroads belonged to the New York Central system, the Baltimore and Ohio controlled another four, and the Pennsylvania Railroad had planned or acquired five additional Ohio railroads terminating at Pittsburgh. The increasing east-west orientation of Ohio's rail network, along with its overland connections with New York, Pittsburgh, and Baltimore, profoundly altered the western economy and imposed a new pattern of urban growth that eventually obscured the traditional lake-river rivalry. The overland routes, in short, supplanted the lake and the river as links with the East. After 1854, the single Baltimore and Ohio connection with the Ohio River alone prompted a reversal of Cincinnati's grain markets from the south to the east. In general, the eastern rail lines accelerated the shift in trade that had begun with the opening of the Erie Canal, benefiting northern towns and the Lake Erie ports at the expense of Cincinnati. The Lake Erie ports grew 173 percent during the 1850s, four-and-one-half times faster than the Ohio River cities.[33]

The new railroad network, which reached almost all of Ohio's 88 counties by 1860, helped to diffuse urban growth and commercial agriculture throughout the state. In the process, the railroads largely bypassed the old canal towns and quickly imposed a new pattern of urban growth upon the Ohio countryside. By providing east-west links among the most important canal stops, the new railroads reinforced the locational advantages of Ohio's largest cities. But they also stimulated the growth, even the founding, of many smaller towns all along their tracks. In 1853, for example, 163 towns and cities lay along Ohio's canals. Fully 94 percent of these canal towns were excluded from the new railroad net. Similarly, 94 percent of the new railroad towns were integrated into regional trade routes for the first time. By 1853, the transition from canal to railroad had stimulated a whole new city system that put 153 canal towns and their rural hinterlands at an economic disadvantage while boosting an additional 141 railroad towns.[34]

Urban growth rather than westward settlement dominated Ohio's economy during this emerging railroad era. Population growth was no longer the province of river valleys or waterways. The canal counties grew considerably faster than the rest of the state during the 1840s, but after 1850 situation on a canal made no impact at all on population growth.[35] The canal counties had not really lost a locational advantage – all the other counties had gained one. The new, tightly knit railroad network erased regional differences in migration and growth that were formerly grounded in stages of settlement or access to waterways. During the 1850s, Ohio's population increased by only 18 percent. At the same time, the state's 20 cities – incorporated places of 2,500 or more residents – grew by a more spectacular 50 percent. They alone accounted for almost one-third of Ohio's population growth. Rural towns grew by an even larger 62 percent. The state's rural population, however, grew by only 9 percent. Cities and towns dominated population growth, while farming communities suffered net emigration.[36]

In the wake of the westward movement, urban growth and rural decline came to the fore. Ohio's migrants were now just as numerous as ever, but they were qualitatively different from their grandparents. Most of them were moving from the farm to the city, from Europe, or out of Ohio further westward. The westward passage of the line of settlement during the 1840s and 1850s, the growing cities that emerged in its wake, new routes of transportation, and foreign immigration combined to stir up powerful currents of movement into, out of, and within the state.

2 *An electorate in motion*

A popular view of nineteenth-century society maintained that farm families were much more firmly rooted than were city people and that country living was therefore less hectic and more stable than urban life. In 1855, for example, Mrs. Josephine Bateham, editor of the "Ladies' Department" of the influential agricultural journal *The Ohio Cultivator*, told her readers that

> One of the great blessings of rural life . . . is, there is less frequent occasion for removals; indeed, few farmers' families as such, except for those bound for "the West," ever make a greater change of residence than from the old log home to the new "frame." But in the city, the moving day which comes every year or two . . . is the spectre that haunts a large portion of the population.

Nineteenth-century rural society, as Mrs. Bateham viewed it, was far more stable than urban life. Country dwellers, and especially farm families, tended to stay put, moving up instead of out (to the new "frame") because upward social mobility minimized the need for emigration. Urban migrants, on the other hand, were quite different from rural migrants. In cities, "removal" occurred much more frequently, and it involved more residents. A rather sinister "moving day" shadowed the less settled city dwellers, many of whom actually moved "every year or two." Finally, yet a third kind of migrants, westward, mingled with urban and rural migrants, but they were so familiar to her readers that Mrs. Bateham mentioned them only in passing, in a cursory aside.[1]

Most recent students of American migration would agree wholeheartedly with Mrs. Bateham's assessment of urban mobility during the mid-nineteenth century: it was very high. But according to her traditional portrait of nineteenth-century rural society, we might expect to find impressive patterns of migration only in large and fast-growing cities – in Ohio, such cities as Cincinnati, Toledo, and Cleveland. This chapter dispels that impression by focusing on a mostly rural area and revealing as much or more migration in country towns and townships as in big cities. Indeed, the conclusions of a large number of historical studies leave little doubt that nineteenth-century society in general was extremely mobile. Numerous case studies have documented low rates of persistence in American communities of every variety, rural as well as urban, throughout the nineteenth century. The discovery of high levels of migration within long-settled rural regions was in fact one of the biggest surprises to emerge from American social history in recent decades. A thorough examination of the role of migrants in local politics requires an assessment of how many voters moved in both town and country, where they moved, and how frequently they migrated.[2]

This chapter focuses on patterns of migration and their sources among 2,500 eligible voters in one local study area, Shelby County in the upper Miami Valley. This study reconstructs streams of migration from quadrennial enumerations of eligible voters (white adult males) that were compiled in Ohio townships in 1851 and 1855. The enumerations were required by statute to facilitate quadrennial reapportionment of the Ohio legislature and are simply lists of names. The enumerations contain the names of all eligible voters residing within a given township on a given date, and they therefore represent records of legal residence in Ohio townships. Unlike the U.S. census, the quadrennial enumerations include only eligible voters and recur every four rather than ten years. They therefore make it possible to examine the movements of all eligible voters in an entire county over a four-year period.[3]

Shelby County, located in the upper Miami Valley, straddled the Greenville Treaty line that marked Ohio's last frontier. The county was created in 1819 and has maintained its present boundaries since 1828. Sidney, the county seat, was nestled in the western bank of the Great Miami River, which flows south toward Cincinnati. Surveyed in 1820, the city was incorporated in 1834. Shelby County's rapid urban growth and agricultural development during the 1840s and 1850s mirrored that of the Miami Valley as a whole. The Miami Valley continued to benefit from both the westward movement and urbanization long after eastern Ohio had begun losing population. Already the most densely populated region of Ohio, the Miami Valley added almost 110,000 residents during the 1850s, an increase of 23 percent – higher than the state's overall increase of 18 percent. The region's growth in urban population was twice that rapid during the 1850s. The valley's five largest cities, including Sidney, grew by 46 percent between 1850 and 1860, and during that decade of growth over one-third of the region's residents were already living in cities and towns. Urban growth, in both large cities and rural towns, was the hallmark of economic development in the Miami Valley, as throughout Ohio, during the 1850s.[4]

Both urban growth and rural development depended heavily on the improvement of transportation links and the commercialization of agriculture. Urban growth in the Miami Valley arose from locational advantages along the region's major transportation routes. During three generations, urban concentrations advanced gradually northward from the Ohio River – first along the Miami River, then along the Miami Canal after 1828, and finally, after 1845, along a new railroad network. Towns prospered or languished according to their situation within each successive transport network. Sidney, for example, grew up in a curve of the navigable Miami River and survived by attracting a feeder canal during the 1840s. During the 1850s, however, many flourishing towns lost trade and population to new junctions along Ohio's railroads. Here again, Sidney successfully achieved incorporation into a new transport network, attracting a railroad very early, in 1851. The city attracted two rail lines, the Cleveland, Columbus and Cincinnati Railroad in 1851 and the Dayton and Michigan Railroad in 1856.[5]

The arrival of the railroads and the region's integration into a growing northern economy stimulated commercial farming and, indirectly, the growth of towns and cities. During the 1850s, this sustained agricultural development meant the opening of 5,000 new farms in the Miami Valley, and commercialization provoked even more intensive agriculture. Mean farm size fell during the decade from 124 to 116 acres, while the proportion of improved acreage on the typical farm rose from 55 to 62 percent. Meanwhile, Ohio's entrance into the commercial grain trade brought a sudden shift in the valley from corn to wheat culture, and the value of farmland jumped 66 percent to $46.90 an acre in 1860. Overall, the 1850s brought a transition in economic focus from local hinterlands to regional markets. As a result, sustained growth rewarded only those few cities, such as Sidney, that were most advantageously situated on regional transportation routes. After 1850, these were generally railroad towns.[6]

As a result of all the economic changes that were transforming the Miami Valley, Shelby County experienced rapid population growth and sudden shifts in population. This chapter examines growth, persistence, and migration within all 14 of Shelby County's townships, but divides the county into three geographical areas – Clinton Township, at the center of the county; an inner ring of six rural townships immediately surrounding Clinton Township; and an outer ring of seven additional rural townships (Figure 2.1). Clinton Township contained the city of Sidney, the county seat and the

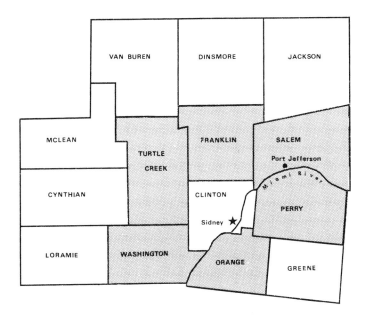

Figure 2.1. Shelby County.

area's largest town. Sidney had 1,302 residents in 1850, representing
two-thirds of Clinton Township's residents and four-fifths of Shelby
County's urban population. This single "urban" township was surrounded by rural settlement and therefore provides an opportunity
to examine a medium-sized city's attraction for rural migrants. The
inner ring of six rural townships is shaded in Figure 2.1.[7]
  According to Mrs. Bateham's traditional view of nineteenth-century society, we might expect to discover more transient voters in
Clinton Township, which was urban, than in the 13 rural townships
and to find them moving more frequently. Given the tremendous
importance of cities and towns in Ohio's maturing economy, we
might also expect Clinton Township to grow most rapidly as well.
Population growth was indeed a common experience in Shelby
County during the early 1850s (Table 2.1). The county's population
of white adult males increased by almost one-quarter over just four
years, from 1851 to 1855. But even in the midst of general economic
development, population growth was far from uniform, varying
widely among the county's 14 townships. In general, urban growth
did in fact outpace rural settlement, although two rural townships
grew even faster than Clinton Township. Overall, however, Clinton

Table 2.1. *Population change and persistence in Shelby County, white adult males*

Township	Total, 1851	Total, 1855	% change	% persistence
Clinton	298	459	+ 54.0	43.3
Inner Ring:				
Franklin	40	164	+ 17.I	51.4
Turtle Creek	171	265	+ 55.0	42.1
Washington	224	256	+ 14.3	43.8
Orange	191	219	+ 14.7	43.5
Perry	170	222	+ 30.6	46.5
Salem	262	231	- 11.8	39.3
	1,158	1,357	+ 17.2	43.8
Outer Ring:				
Jackson	154	218	+ 41.6	60.4
Van Buren	80	159	+ 98.8	22.5
McLean	169	185	+ 9.5	26.6
Loramie	294	280	- 4.8	37.8
Greene	226	248	+ 9.7	42.9
Cynthian	178	240	+ 34.8	49.4
Dinsmore	142	197	+ 38.7	49.3
	1,243	1,527	+ 22.9	42.0
Shelby County	2,699	3,343	+ 23.9	42.9

Source: Quadrennial enumerations of white adult males, Shelby County, Ohio, 1851 and 1855.

Township grew three times as fast as the inner ring of rural townships surrounding it, and urban growth in Sidney, within Clinton Township, accounted for all of that divergence. Interestingly, growth within the outer ring of rural townships slightly outpaced that within the inner ring, suggesting at the outset that proximity to the city of Sidney inhibited rural development during the 1850s.

Changes in population were quite variable in the study area, ranging from a loss of 12 percent to a gain of 99 percent among the 14 townships. This variation suggests that county-level rates of population growth and loss are not reliable indicators of growth and decline within individual localities. Further, students of migration have found it quite dangerous to employ rates of growth and decline as indicators of migration and persistence. In spite of a wide variation in rates of growth among the 14 townships, rates of persistence ranged only from 22 to 60 percent. This relative uniformity in rates of persistence is a well-known phenomenon. It suggests that rates of persistence in a region show little, if any, relationship to net changes in population. The 14 townships displayed fairly uniform rates of persistence in spite of wide differences in local growth and decline. In fact, overall rates of persistence in Clinton Township, the inner ring of rural townships, and the outer ring were virtually identical, ranging from 42 to 44 percent. In short, communities suffering population loss, those maintaining a stable population, and those growing impressively may all share the same rate of persistence.[8]

This seeming paradox has a simple solution. Population growth usually fluctuated according to local rather than regional economic conditions throughout nineteenth-century America. Population growth usually signified heavy immigration into an area, not high rates of natural increase or low rates of emigration. Natural increase, of course, varied little from place to place. More surprisingly, however, rates of *emigration* were also quite uniform. Most migrants were "pulled" out of their homes rather than "pushed" out of them. Emigrants tended to respond to "pull" factors, such as the West or growing cities, that were very general, representing the combined attractiveness of all possible destinations. Such general pull factors did not vary much from place to place and so neither did rates of emigration and persistence.[9]

Immigrants *to* an area, by contrast, were responding not to the general pull of an entire region but to the attractiveness of a specific destination. As a result, rates of immigration were much less uniform than were rates of emigration. Figure 2.2 displays a "migration profile" of the 14 townships in Shelby County to illustrate this point. The horizontal axis records the rate of emigration from each township, and the vertical axis records the rate of immigration into each of them. A township that experienced equal rates of immigration and emigration would fall on the diagonal line, signifying a stable population. Townships lying below the line suffered more emigration than immigration and thus lost population. Townships lying above the diagonal grew, attracting more immigrants than emigrants.[10]

Figure 2.2 shows that rates of emigration from the 14 townships varied much less than rates of immigration into them. Eligible voters left these townships at fairly uniform rates, in spite of great differences in population growth. Voters moved *into* the 14 townships at widely varying rates, however, and it was therefore the differences in rates of immigration that produced differences in overall population growth. There was, in fact, an almost perfect correspondence between rates of immigration and rates of growth among the 14 townships but almost no relationship at all between emigration and

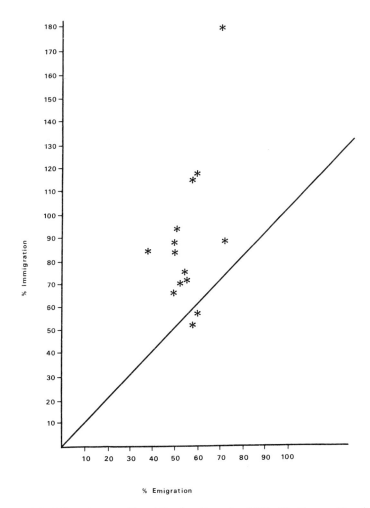

Figure 2.2. Migration profile of Shelby County, 1851–55. *Source:* Quadrennial enumerations of white adult males, Shelby County, Ohio, 1851 and 1855.

population growth or decline. Growth itself was therefore more the result of high levels of immigration than low levels of emigration.[11]

Another important lesson of the "migration profile" is that even communities that lost population could experience high rates of migration. They could welcome dozens or even hundreds of newcomers and still lose population simply by suffering more emigration than immigration. By the same token, population stability did

Table 2.2. *Migration streams among seven townships, percent*

	Destination, 1855:							
	Clinton	Franklin	Turtle Creek	Orange	Washington	Perry	Salem	Outside System
Origin, 1851:								
Clinton	43.3	0.7	0.3	1.0	0.7	0.3	1.0	52.7
Franklin	2.1	51.4	3.6	1.4	0.7	1.4	2.9	36.4
Turtle Creek	2.3	0.6	42.1	0.6	1.8	0	0	52.6
Orange	2.6	0.5	0	43.5	4.2	0	1.0	48.2
Washington	0.4	0	0.9	0.9	43.8	0	0.4	53.6
Perry	2.9	1.8	0.6	0.6	0	46.5	2.4	45.3
Salem	4.2	0.8	0.4	0	0	5.3	39.3	50.0

Source: Quadrennial enumerations of white adult males, Shelby County,Ohio, 1851 and 1855.

not necessarily signify an absence of migration, only equal numbers of immigrants and emigrants. As long as a township fell on the diagonal line in the "migration profile," its population remained constant, without any reference at all to rates of migration. A practical lesson is that we cannot substitute rates of population growth – or urban versus rural status – for some index of migration into and out of an area. Even townships that lost population could experience impressive levels of immigration and emigration. So did seemingly sleepy rural communities, in contrast to Mrs. Bateham's view.[12]

Migratory voters were therefore ubiquitous in the study area, leaving the 14 townships at fairly uniform rates but entering them much less uniformly. Considerable numbers of voters moved through all the townships, even those whose populations appeared stable on the surface or declined. On average, only 43 percent of all voters remained in their townships of residence over those four years, 1851 to 1855.

By presenting each of the 14 townships separately, however, the preceding discussion of migration has disclosed nothing about the subsequent behavior of emigrants, the distances they traveled, or their destinations. Through more extensive linkage, the quadrennial enumerations permit an analysis of migration between contiguous townships, retaining local-level migrants to reveal the movements of eligible voters within Shelby County. Initial examination of the quadrennial enumerations revealed virtually no migration between Clinton Township and the outer ring of rural townships between 1851 and 1855. The outer townships, therefore, were not part of Clinton Township's "migration hinterland," and the following analysis need not consider those potential migration streams. Instead, Table 2.2 reveals streams of migration that included Clinton Township and the inner ring of rural townships. Pooling the enumerations of these seven townships and linking them across four years (1851 to 1855) reveals 49 local migration streams and seven streams of emigrants who left the county entirely.[13]

Table 2.2 presents rates of persistence and migration among 1,427 eligible voters based on township of residence in 1851. (It reveals, for example, that 2.1 percent of white adult males living in Franklin Township in 1851 lived in Clinton Township in 1855.) Table 2.2 therefore contains three distinct groups of cells. Rates of persistence in each township appear in the seven diagonal cells while rates of long-distance emigration occupy the last column. The remaining 42 cells record all short-distance migrants, those who migrated locally to one of the six other townships in the study area.[14]

As Table 2.2 makes clear at a glance, the bulk of emigration from Shelby County was long-distance. Most emigrants presumably moved westward or to a more distant city. This preponderance of long-distance emigrants confirms the operation of general pull factors strongly attracting migrants away from the 14 townships uniformly. But Table 2.2 also discloses streams of local migrants that have generally been obscured by the more visible westward movement. An important minority of voters moved only locally. Between 1851 and 1855, only 43 percent of the area's 1,427 eligible voters persisted in their townships of origin. Another 49 percent moved out of the area entirely, leaving 8 percent who were local migrants. Focusing on migrants only, 12 percent of all emigrants moved to one of the other six townships in the study area (Table 2.3). At least 8 percent of all eligible voters and one-eighth of all migratory voters, therefore, moved locally between 1851 and 1855.

Interestingly, rates of local migration were not uniform through-

Table 2.3. *Local migration by township, 1851-55*

	All emigrants	Local migrants	% local migrants
Franklin	68	17	25.0
Turtle Creek	99	9	9.1
Washington	126	6	4.8
Orange	108	16	14.8
Perry	91	14	15.4
Salem	159	28	17.6
	651	90	13.8
Clinton	169	12	7.1
All townships	820	102	12.4

Source: Quadrennial enumerations of white adult males, Shelby County, Ohio, 1851 and 1855.

out the study area but varied widely among the seven townships. These local movements can tell us something about why voters moved as they did. Initial analysis revealed that emigrants left Clinton Township and the inner ring of rural townships at virtually the same rate. An analysis of local versus long-distance migration suggests, however, an urban-rural difference in the *distance* of emigration (Table 2.3). In general, residents of Clinton Township were more likely to leave the study area entirely. In other words, urban and rural voters were about equally likely to leave their townships of origin between 1851 and 1855, but urban residents were almost twice as likely to leave the county. Urban emigration was not quantitatively different from rural emigration, but it was qualitatively different. Clinton Township did not lose more than its share of eligible voters, but those it did lose tended to move farther than did rural emigrants.[15]

This difference in the distance traveled by urban and rural emigrants undoubtedly reflects the important impact of urbanization on patterns of migration. The predominant direction of migration during the nineteenth century was from the country to the city. Clinton Township contained over one-half of the area's artisans, merchants, and professionals. These practitioners of urban occupations were, of course, more likely to move to another city than into the country, and they were therefore more likely to travel longer distances. As a result, although they did not emigrate in greater proportions than did the farmers and farm workers of the countryside, they were more likely to leave the county entirely.[16]

Table 2.4. *Migration to adjacent townships, 1851-55*

	To adjacent township	To nonadjacent township
Franklin	70.6 %	29.4 %
Turtle Creek	88.9	11.1
Washington	83.3	16.7
Orange	81.2	18.8
Perry	71.4	28.6
Salem	96.4	3.6
Mean	83.3 %	16.7 %

Source: Quadrennial enumerations of white adult males, Shelby County, Ohio, 1851 and 1855.

A traditional "gravity" model of human migration links the volume of particular migration streams to both intervening distance and the population density of areas of origin and destination.[17] According to that model, levels of migration should increase over shorter distances. This was true in the study area (Table 2.4). Levels of migration to adjacent townships exceeded rates of migration to nonadjacent townships in every instance. Voters who did not leave the area entirely tended to move to an adjacent township. We might also expect the city of Sidney, because of its population density, to play a special role in shaping patterns of migration within its own hinterland. Sidney was indeed a powerful magnet for long-distance migrants. The city attracted more than its share of long-distance migrants relative to the rural townships. Long-distance migrants to the study area settled in Clinton Township more often than population alone would warrant. Again, Sidney was a center of local commerce and manufacturing, and men who were artisans, merchants, and professionals presumably would have preferred to move to this urban center.[18]

Clinton was already the area's most densely populated township, and the city of Sidney was growing much faster than its hinterland. Sidney therefore grew by attracting more long-distance migrants than did the rural townships surrounding it. In fact, like other Ohio cities, Sidney contained far more than its share of both interstate migrants and foreign immigrants. In 1850, only one-third of all eligible voters in Clinton Township were Ohio natives, compared to just over one-half in the rural townships. Similarly, over one-fifth of Clinton Township's adult men were foreign-born, compared to a mere 8 percent in the rural townships. Clinton Township, in fact, contained more foreign immigrants than the other six townships combined. This part of the traditional view – cities as a focus of interstate and foreign migration – finds confirmation in the study area.[19]

Clinton Township also held the same attraction for local migrants, receiving one-third of all rural emigrants who remained in the immediate area. Thus, not only did Clinton Township attract more than its share of long-distance migrants, but it also received relatively more local migrants. Interestingly, the urban township's attraction for migrants was stronger within its own hinterland than beyond it. Thirty-two percent of all local migrants settled in the urban area, but only 28 percent from outside Shelby County did so. Sidney's attraction for migrants was therefore inversely related to intervening distance, confirming another assumption of the traditional gravity model.[20]

But whereas Clinton Township attracted more long-distance and short-distance migrants than did the six rural townships, it could not hold most of the migrants it attracted. The six rural townships managed to keep their residents longer than did Clinton Township. Linking the quadrennial enumerations of 1851 and 1855 with those of 1859 shows that although four-year rates of persistence were nearly identical in both urban and rural townships, eight-year rates diverged sharply. Eight-year rates of persistence were 28 percent in the six rural townships but only 19 percent in Clinton Township. The rural townships attracted fewer migrants but kept them longer, compensating, in part, for their lower levels of immigration. Quite simply, population turned over more slowly in the country than in the city.

At least 8 percent of all eligible voters moved locally between 1851 and 1855. Those local migrants represented 12 percent of all emigrants. Urban and rural voters emigrated in equal proportions, but the urban emigrants tended more often to leave the immediate area. Migration streams were defined in part by distance, and local migrants tended to settle in an adjacent township. But at the same time, long-distance migrants, and especially foreign immigrants, favored the single urban township over the rural townships as a destination. And local migrants displayed an even greater preference for Clinton Township. All the townships' electorates grew through immigration, and Clinton Township's grew fastest because it attracted the most immigrants, long-distance immigrants in particular. Finally, migrants to the rural townships were fewer, but they persisted longer on average than did urban voters.

How, then, did the three streams of migrants identified by Mrs.

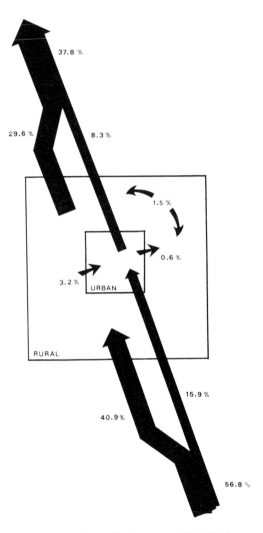

Figure 2.3. Migration hierarchy: All migrants, 1851–55. *Source:* Quadrennial enumerations of white adult males, Shelby County, Ohio, 1851 and 1855.

Bateham – urban, rural, and westward – combine in Shelby County to set this local electorate into motion? Figure 2.3 considers all 2,543 migrants in the seven-township study area – immigrants, emigrants, and local migrants – to present a local "migration hierarchy." Long-distance migrants were far and away the most numerous members of the local electorate. Long-distance migration streams were also the most important contributors to population growth in both urban and rural townships. Long-distance migrants outnumbered local migrants in every instance. As a result, the growth of the area's pool of eligible voters largely reflected its "favorable balance" of long-distance migration. When a township attracted more long-distance immigrants than emigrants, its population grew. Local migrants made only a small impact on rates of growth and decline. At the same time, a disproportionately large share of long-distance immigrants settled in the single urban township. Clinton Township's balance of long-distance migration was therefore more favorable than that of the rural townships, and its population grew faster during the four-year period. Rates of growth and decline reflected patterns of long-distance rather than local migration.[21]

Streams of long-distance migrants, moving both into and out of the area, contained 95 percent of all identifiable migrants. Obviously, the study area depended on long-distance migrants for overall population growth. Local migration streams could never have produced the net rates of growth experienced throughout the county during the 1850s. Still, the local migration system did contribute to urban growth by producing a small net shift in population from the rural hinterland to Clinton Township. Rural-to-urban migration was over five times as common as urban-to-rural movement, and fully 10 percent of Clinton Township's growth resulted from local migration. In the face of widespread long-distance migration and bounding urban growth, Clinton Township still drew one-tenth of its new voters from its immediate rural hinterland. But despite only a small compensating trickle of urban-to-rural migrants, only two of the rural townships actually lost population. Long-distance migration into the rural townships more than replaced the migrants lost to Sidney, and urban and rural growth were, in general, complementary.[22]

We can now assess Sidney's impact on its rural migration hinterland. In general, Sidney did not prevent growth in the rest of Shelby County. Growth within the inner ring of rural townships was, however, somewhat lower than that within the outer ring. Clinton Township did benefit from local migration, but rural emigrants represented only one-tenth of the urban township's new voters. At the same time, three-fourths of the migrants from the adjacent rural townships were long-distance emigrants from the area. In short, rural-to-urban migration within Shelby County represented a mere eddy within a tide of long-distance migration to, from, and through the region. The Shelby County seat did not depend on its immediate

Table 2.5. *Agricultural development in Shelby County, 1849-59*

	Clinton, 1849	Inner Ring, 1849	Inner Ring, 1859
Number of farms	37	664	642
Total acreage	4,724	75,471	86,263
Improved acreage	2,278	33,414	45,846
Unimproved acreage	2,446	42,057	40,417
Mean farm size (acres)	127.7	113.7	134.4
% improved acreage	61.1	44.3	53.1
Value per farm	$2,968.92	$1,819.53	
Value per acre	$23.25	$16.01	
Corn/wheat (bu.)	1.6	5.1	2.7

Source: Manuscript U.S. census of agriculture, Shelby County, Ohio, 1850 and 1860.

hinterland for most of its new residents during the 1850s, and it therefore cast only a very faint "urban shadow" over the surrounding countryside.[23]

Sidney's impact on its hinterland was, in fact, largely indirect. Sidney served as a stimulus to agricultural improvement and as an important transportation link. The area's resulting commercialization of agriculture, in its own turn, supported net immigration. As the county's largest market, Sidney was a focus for agricultural development. Because of their proximity to Sidney, farms in Clinton Township led the transition to commercial agriculture (Table 2.5). A handful of the area's largest commercial farms surrounded the city of Sidney. In 1849, for example, farms were larger in Clinton Township than in the adjacent rural townships. They also boasted more improved acreage and were more valuable. And the corn/wheat ratio in Clinton Township was quite low, suggesting that by 1849 Clinton's farmers were already participating in the region's swelling wheat trade. Farms in the adjacent rural townships were farther from Sidney, their most lucrative marketplace, and from regional transportation routes, the Miami Canal and the Miami River. Those farms were therefore both less intensively worked and less valuable.[24]

But more intensive, commercial agriculture spread quickly to the adjacent townships. Agricultural consolidation proceeded rapidly in the rural townships during the 1850s. In spite of population increases, the number of farms in the inner ring of rural townships fell and farm size rose sharply. The larger farms were being worked more intensively in 1859, and the proportion of improved acreage rose by one-fifth. The corn/wheat ratio fell dramatically, suggesting that Sidney's rural hinterland was now caught up in the regional grain trade that was drawing wheat northward to cities along Lake Erie. Sidney's spectacular growth, in short, was grounded in its own hinterland's integration into an expanding railroad network. The Cleveland, Columbus and Cincinnati Railroad, which arrived in Sidney in 1851, made the city an important link within a new system of transportation. City growth and rural agricultural development were therefore perfectly complementary and, in fact, interdependent. Sidney provided transport, processing, and services for an agricultural hinterland that brought capital and new settlers into the area. Both city and hinterland attracted long-distance migrants and grew simultaneously.[25]

Despite such general economic harmony between city growth and rural development, however, Sidney did cast a distinct "shadow" over urban development within its hinterland. Net population loss within Salem Township, which was the sole exception to growth within the inner ring, actually reflected the decline of the town of Port Jefferson, Sidney's nearest urban rival. Predictably, Port Jefferson's sudden decline reflected its situation on regional transportation routes. Port Jefferson was the eastern terminus of the county's feeder canal that carried produce to the Miami Canal. Before completion of Sidney's railroad link in 1851, Port Jefferson was the primary canal landing and market town to the east of Sidney. With the arrival of the railroad, however, Port Jefferson lost its major locational advantage and much of its economic livelihood to Sidney, a pattern that was repeated time and again throughout Ohio. Salem Township's population plummeted 18 percent during the 1850s, and during a decade of general urban growth Port Jefferson lost 12 percent of its population.[26]

Fully 61 percent of Salem Township's eligible voters emigrated between 1851 and 1855, the highest proportion in the county. Predictably, most of those migratory voters (89 percent) left the study area entirely. But population loss did not signify an end of migration. It resulted instead from an unfavorable balance between immigration and emigration. Despite its population loss, Salem still attracted a good number of immigrants, 114 long-distance migrants between 1851 and 1855. The township lost 159 eligible voters during the same period, however, and so its population fell. Still, 273 voters moved into or out of the township over the four-year period, a gross migration rate of over 100 percent.

The destinations of Port Jefferson's emigrants show the various options that were available to the victims of a town that languished on an outmoded transportation route. Between 1851 and 1855, quite predictably, Salem Township's rate of persistence was lowest among the six townships in the inner ring. Sixty-one percent of Salem Township's eligible voters moved out between 1851 and 1855. Exactly one-half of the township's voters left the area entirely, while 11 percent migrated locally. Of those local migrants, almost all of them (96 percent) moved to an adjacent township, which was the highest proportion in the study area. The high rate of movement to adjacent townships suggests that many local migrants from Salem were responding to local push factors rather than more general pull factors, and they therefore sought out the nearest opportunity to settle down again.

One common strategy of those "pushed" out of Port Jefferson was, therefore, to move to a neighboring township. Forty percent of Salem Township's local migrants were living in Sidney in 1855, but one-half chose Perry Township, just across the river from Port Jefferson. But there was an alternative to emigration from the township. Salem Township alone violated the pattern of agricultural consolidation evident in the area during the 1850s. The number of farms in Salem Township actually increased by one-fifth during the decade, while mean farm size fell 7 percent. Apparently, another common strategy of Port Jefferson's emigrants was to buy farms within the township itself when their town fell into eclipse. A change of livelihood permitted both persistence in the township and access to Sidney's new railroad.[27]

Sidney's role in emigration from Port Jefferson was, once again, indirect. Sidney drew relatively few actual migrants from Port Jefferson while precipitating the town's decline. Salem simply attracted the fewest immigrants of all the townships and so lost population. Sidney's new dominance produced a sudden imbalance of immigration and emigration within Salem Township. Clinton Township did not actually drain off Port Jefferson's population: Most of the emigrants left the area entirely. They simply were not replaced by enough immigrants to sustain the township's growth.

This analysis of migrants to, from, and within a local electorate supports several general conclusions. Both rural and urban electorates in the study area experienced high rates of migration – both immigration and emigration. Different rates of growth and decline concealed broadly similar levels of emigration, which were determined by regional or even national pull factors. But the study area experienced wide variations in immigration. Immigration reflected the operation of local pull factors. Immigration was therefore much more important than emigration in producing population growth and decline. Even areas of population stability and loss could experience high levels of migration, however. Population stability reflected an equal balance between immigrants and emigrants, while population loss reflected an unfavorable balance. Population growth, loss, or stability could all conceal high levels of immigration and emigration among voters.

Long-distance migrants were clearly more important in shaping overall patterns of migration than were local migrants. Increases in the population of both urban and rural townships were supported by long-distance migrants, and actual rates of growth largely reflected the net balance between immigration and emigration over long distances. Even cities growing impressively therefore exerted relatively little influence over patterns of migration and growth within their hinterlands, and most new voters in a community arrived from long rather than short distances.

The minority of population movements that occurred at the local level reveal some important differences between urban and rural migrants. Urban voters were no more likely to migrate than were rural residents, but both immigrants to the city and emigrants from it were more likely to move longer distances. Local migrants preferred adjacent townships, especially the single urban township. At the same time that rural townships attracted fewer long-distance migrants they also kept them longer than did the urban township. Mrs. Bateham was right about one thing: Urban dwellers moved more frequently than did country people.

Finally, the broadest explanation of rates of migration and persistence, growth and decline lay not within the local hinterland but in regional patterns of migration – the more general westward and cityward movements. General patterns of movement were grounded in long-distance migration and were therefore regional. Patterns of local migration were only minor disturbances within deep channels of long-distance movement. Rapid economic changes, grounded in a broad westward advance of settlement and shifting transportation routes, governed the rate and timing of migration, bringing sudden booms to the most advantageously situated cities and sending many others into disappointing decline. Few towns were as successful as Sidney at attracting successive transportation links. But many other cities, towns, and rural townships shared in the frequent and widespread migration that characterized antebellum Ohio. Most eligible voters in the study area moved at least once in the decade before the Civil War, and they moved long distances. The sometimes startling mobility of antebellum voters kept this and many other local electorates in constant motion.

3 From meeting to election: migration and suffrage

The hundreds of thousands of migrants who settled in Ohio before the Civil War depended wholly on their adopted state to grant them rights of citizenship and suffrage. Today, the federal government protects the rights of interstate migrants. Americans are free to move from one state to another unimpeded and to enjoy the full benefits of state citizenship soon after their arrival. Recent Supreme Court decisions have reaffirmed the right of Americans "to travel throughout the length and breadth of our land uninhibited by statutes, rules, or regulations which unreasonably burden or restrict this movement." In particular, the Supreme Court has struck down state laws that prevent or impede interstate migration and those that discriminate against newcomers for extended periods after their arrival. States can no longer, for example, ban paupers from crossing their borders, as California did during the Great Depression. And they can no longer impose lengthy residence requirements for the exercise of rights such as voting or the receipt of welfare payments, two of the most important rights the Supreme Court has guaranteed to migrants in recent years. Today, the 50 states impose on voters an average residence requirement of just 24 days, and in fact migrants to three states – Wisconsin, Kansas, and Oregon – can exercise full political rights the day after their arrival.[1]

Before the Civil War, however, interstate migrants suffered many more legal disabilities and couldn't depend on much protection from the federal government. The modern rights guaranteed to interstate migrants are founded, for the most part, on the due process and equal protection clauses of the Fourteenth Amendment, which was not ratified until 1868. As a result, antebellum migrants had many fewer rights, and those rights varied considerably from state to state and even from year to year. With no federal guarantees, their rights depended on the edicts of state legislatures, the provisions of state constitutions, or the decisions of state courts. Overall, rights of citizenship came much more slowly to interstate migrants, and black migrants, for the most part, enjoyed almost no rights at all. On the rare occasions that interstate migrants did defend their rights in federal courts, quite frequently the Supreme Court simply

48

reaffirmed the power of the states to define their own citizenship. In particular, the Constitution gave the states the exclusive authority to regulate suffrage. Every state therefore imposed its own rules of suffrage and residence on its voters. Migrants who suffered discrimination could only rarely appeal their cases to the federal courts. In Ohio, for example, not a single case involving the rights of migrants reached the U.S. Supreme Court before the Civil War.[2]

Like all states, Ohio enjoyed tremendous authority and latitude over the citizenship and residence of its immigrants. Ohio never denied entrance or citizenship to white migrants. The state did require foreign immigrants to become U.S. citizens before achieving state citizenship. And Ohio, like several other midwestern states, did restrict the immigration of blacks and mulattoes, requiring them to provide evidence of their freedom and to post a $500 bond to guarantee their good behavior. But white migrants were always free to enter Ohio with no restrictions.[3]

But even these white migrants suffered legal disabilities. Ohio discriminated against recent migrants by imposing lengthy residence requirements, often a year or more, for the exercise of some basic rights. Further, Ohio's constitution and early laws amplified this discrimination against recent migrants by delegating authority over two basic rights – suffrage and poor relief – to its local administrative units, townships. Membership in the early Ohio township carried with it far fewer privileges and responsibilities than did membership in the more autonomous New England town, on which it was modeled. The Ohio township was, indeed, largely an administrative unit. But full membership in the Ohio township guaranteed to the individual two important rights. Legal residence in a particular township conferred, on white adult males, the right of suffrage and, on all Ohioans, the right of poor relief. Within a tradition of local control and administrative decentralization, suffrage and poor relief were conferred, entirely and exclusively, by townships.

This dependence on townships for the right of suffrage and for poor relief had several important implications for migrants. First, their legal status in the state of Ohio depended entirely on their status within their local communities. Migrants had to gain legal residence within a township to achieve legal residence in Ohio. Townships were therefore very powerful. They alone conferred legal residence in Ohio and the rights that came with it – in particular, the right of suffrage and the right to poor relief. Second, migrants who were unfairly disfranchised or denied poor relief could not, in the ordinary scheme of things, appeal their treatment to a higher authority. They had to accept discrimination at the hands of the township or take the township to court. Finally, by making the township the locus of legal residence in the state, Ohio put local migrants at an additional disadvantage. Ohio residents who moved within the state retained their state citizenship but had to reestablish legal residence all over again in their new townships before voting or receiving poor relief. Local migrants risked their right of suffrage and their right to poor relief by moving across township boundaries. Suffrage and relief arose only from legal residence within a specific township, an obvious disability for both interstate and local migrants.[4]

Ohio lawmakers intended their townships to serve as basic units of political and social life. Beginning with statehood and throughout the nineteenth century, therefore, the legislature paid close attention to the drawing of township boundaries. The townships represented, for all legal and political purposes, the individuals and communities they contained, and for that reason their physical borders had to be functional and could not be entirely arbitrary. In 1790, for example, an early territorial statute instructed justices of the peace to define townships with "such limits and bounds, natural or imaginary as shall appear to be most proper, having due regard to the extent of the country, and number of inhabitants." A township should not be too large, too populous, or even inconvenient to all its residents. The justices had the authority to subdivide their townships at will "from time to time," to suit the "interest and convenience of the inhabitants." After statehood, the legislature gave the county commissioners the right to draw and adjust township boundaries and permitted 22-square-mile townships where possible, in contrast to the 36-square-mile congressional townships. Throughout the nineteenth century, county commissioners repeatedly divided the most populous townships, often in response to popular petitions, into wards and precincts that better addressed the needs of their residents.[5]

Just as its representatives maintained the right to define and to alter the physical boundaries of a township, so had they the right to define its political and legal boundaries as well. Reflecting a tradition of tenacious town autonomy in colonial New England, legal residence in the Ohio township was "consensual," resting on explicit or implicit acceptance by all the other residents. The consensual nature of the town in colonial New England permitted a careful examination of prospective inhabitants, who could attain full legal membership in the town only with the approval of the town's meeting or its representatives, the selectmen. Newcomers to New England towns achieved legal membership through a careful "personal sifting process" designed to protect both the social homogeneity of the community and the financial resources of the town government. Impersonal criteria, such as ownership of property or a specific length of residence, were necessary at times to assure full acceptance into the New England town. But such impersonal criteria were never sufficient to assure legal residence. New Englanders were careful to distinguish mere physical presence in the town from full legal belonging. Newcomers, as Michael Zuckerman has recently noted, "applied for admission" into the New England town, proving their good character and their financial independence.[6]

Early Ohio laws called for a township that was similar, in this sense, to the New England town. Ohioans combined the township system of New England with the county system of the South and so consciously modeled their townships after the New England town. The state's first election law, passed at statehood in 1803, provided a detailed blueprint for a partial reconstruction of the New England town meeting. Legal residence for voting purposes was to be consensual. Each township was a separate voting unit, and election day, as outlined in this initial statute, brought all voters together in the physical or social center of the township. There was only one polling place for the entire township, a "certain house in each township, as nearly central to the inhabitants as circumstances and conveniences will admit." It was here that voters were, in the language of the statute, to "meet" to cast their ballots.[7]

Suffrage was consensual, because new voters had to win acceptance by all the other voters in the township before casting their ballots. Ohio's first constitution, written in 1802, granted the franchise to white adult male "inhabitants" who had "resided" in the state for one year before voting. The constitution did not, however, define "residence" or even stipulate a particular length of residence in townships, where voting actually took place. In addition to disfranchising interstate migrants for one year after their arrival, therefore, Ohio's constitution left extremely broad discretion to the voters of a township in interpreting both "inhabitancy" and "residence." The constitution did not even require U.S. citizenship of voters, an oversight not corrected until 1809. Newcomers, in short, cast ballots in a township subject only to the approval of all the other voters present. Many early elections actually took place in private homes where fewer than 20 voters literally "met" on election day. Election judges called the name of each voter submitting a ballot. If they heard no objection from the other voters, they simply put the ballot into the box. The judges could question under oath any voter whose qualifications were challenged before deciding whether to accept his ballot or reject it. The voters, in effect, defined their own township's electorate by accepting or challenging other voters. This image of the election as a literal meeting persisted formally and informally throughout the antebellum period. As late as 1831, an Ohio law still referred to the election as a "meeting." And as late as the 1850s, Ohioans sometimes referred more casually to the "spring meeting" or "fall meeting."[8]

Early Ohio laws, however, were much more explicit about qualifications for receiving poor relief, another benefit of legal residence, because here money was at stake. A territorial poor law, borrowing from Pennsylvania's experience, required six qualifications for "settlement" or eligibility for public support. Any one of the qualifications conferred a legal settlement on a newcomer. To gain a legal settlement in a township, a newcomer might hold a public office for one year; pay taxes for two consecutive years; take a lease for $25 a year and live on the premises for one year; have a freehold and live on it for one year; act as a servant for one year, if unmarried; or act as an indentured servant for one year. A fixed term of residence, either one or two years, was an essential ingredient in each of the six qualifications, but, significantly, residence alone was not sufficient to confer a settlement in a township under territorial law. The newcomer must perform a public duty or demonstrate an economic interest in the township to establish residence for poor relief. Physical presence alone, for any length of time, could not produce a settlement.[9]

Such stringent qualifications for poor relief were, of course, designed largely to save the township the expense of supporting nonresident paupers. Ohio borrowed heavily from the experiences of the older states to achieve just this result. The overseers of the poor actually reserved the right to "remove" physically any new inhabitants who seemed "likely to become chargeable," returning them to their townships of origin. Under territorial law, therefore, consensual residence allowed the officials of a township to exclude, physically, immigrants who threatened to become financial burdens. At the same time, a "certificate system," like that of New England, permitted newcomers to move into a new township while actually maintaining legal settlement in their townships of origin. According to statute, the children of such recent migrants, "though born in the township," were legal residents of their parents' original township. Once again, mere physical presence could not confer a settlement. The territorial poor law imposed such a sharp distinction between physical presence and legal belonging that children were not necessarily "residents" of the townships in which they were born. Physical presence alone could not confer legal residence for newcomers, and this disability descended to their children, even those born within the township.[10]

With statehood, township officials gained even more discretion to grant or to deny legal settlement to newcomers. In the new state's first poor law, passed in 1805, the careful qualifications of the territorial statute, combining length of residence with propertyholding or public service, gave way to simpler – and more vague – criteria for settlement. With the introduction of "warning out," another New England tradition, the admission of newcomers to legal residence became explicitly consensual. A warning now permitted the overseers of the poor to "remove" unwanted newcomers symbolically rather than physically. After receiving a warning to depart, migrants could remain in the township, but not as legal residents. Once warned out, they could never gain a settlement through their continuing physical presence. The warning-out provisions of the 1805 poor law permitted Ohio townships to limit their financial responsibilities to a select group of "settled residents" who enjoyed the right to poor relief but whose representatives could deny it to newcomers. Legal residence was now explicitly consensual, conferred on newcomers at the pleasure of the township. The recently arrived poor had to depend on private charity.[11]

In 1816 a new poor law reaffirmed the consensual nature of legal residence in Ohio's townships. The new statute actually extended the warning period from five months to one year, giving the township's overseers more time to take notice of unwanted newcomers. Apparently that task was becoming more demanding. The end of the War of 1812 brought a new wave of westward migrants. Like earlier settlement laws, the law of 1816 simply conferred settlement on newcomers "residing" in the township for one year without warning. But like Ohio's early election laws, none of the state's early poor laws actually defined "residence." Residence for purposes of poor relief was ill-defined, and township officials, not the state legislature, defined their own conception of legal residence, admitting new residents at their own discretion.[12]

The vagueness of these early statutes lent broad discretion to Ohio's communities in the selection of new residents for full legal membership. Under early election laws, newcomers could achieve legal residence, and thus the vote, only upon acceptance by the members of their new communities. Early poor laws similarly protected the township at the expense of the individual migrant. But during the next few decades, consensual membership, resting only on a migrant's acceptance by his new community, gradually grew inadequate to cope with Ohioans' increasing mobility. In the wake of widespread migration, Ohio jurists and legislators conducted a gradual but searching review of the nature of legal residence in their state. Migrants began challenging consensual residence in the courts, and these legal challenges, which grew more frequent, gradually won new rights for migrants. Townships increasingly surrendered their traditional authority to define their own membership. Individual migrants, by contrast, gained more discretion in choosing their own townships of residence. Before the Civil War ended, Ohioans at last had to acknowledge a new, more flexible theory of suffrage that focused not on the community but on the individual. With the challenge of migration, both society and politics took on new rules of belonging.

Rules of legal residence in Ohio responded only gradually to swelling rates of migration. Rules of suffrage and settlement changed dramatically before the outbreak of the Civil War, however, and especially during the 1830s and 1840s, the decades of peak immigration into the state. The recurrent arrival of newcomers and transients in Ohio's townships prompted a thoughtful redefinition of the suffrage that placed increasing emphasis on the political rights of individuals and less on the stability of communities. That gradual redefinition of the suffrage in nineteenth-century Ohio was part of a broader reevaluation of community membership that found support in national legal trends. A movement for suffrage extension, for example, led most northern states, through legislation or constitutional reform, to revoke property qualifications before the Civil War. At the same time, as part of an emerging tradition of judicial activism, antebellum jurists began favoring the rights of individuals at the legal and political expense of communities. The weight of legal claims, in short, was shifting gradually from communities to individuals during this period throughout America. The continual arrival of newcomers and their greater numbers both accelerated and helped to shape that trend toward political and legal individualism.[13]

In 1827, for example, the vagueness of Ohio's poor law prompted a decision by the Ohio Supreme Court about the legal residence of a minor pauper. The dispute arose originally from the rootlessness of the boy's family. In September 1823, the parents of Edmund Jackson had a legal residence in Lebanon Township, Meigs County, on the Ohio River. After her husband's death, Edmund's mother remarried and took all of her children, except Edmund, to live with her new husband in Virginia. In April 1824, the boy, now 17, became a local migrant. He moved to Letart Township, "working for his support," and stayed there until October 1825. But then Jackson left Letart Township and apparently wandered for over a year until he arrived in Jefferson Township, Adams County, 100 miles to the west. There, he fell sick and became a township charge, in December 1826. Jefferson Township refused to accept Jackson as a legal resident and grant him relief. Jefferson Township sued Letart Township, where Jackson had last worked for a living, for the boy's support.[14]

The concept of consensual residence had combined with the westward movement to permit two townships, 100 miles apart, to deny relief to the young migrant. Because the state's poor law was so vague, the Supreme Court had to refer to common law to award the boy a legal settlement in his original home, Lebanon Township, which was not even a party to the suit. As Edmund Jackson learned firsthand, consensual residence was proving a flimsy guarantee of legal rights for migrants in the face of increasing mobility. Obliquely chiding the legislature for its insistence on consensual residence in the township, the Supreme Court noted in passing that "It is perhaps a misfortune that the statute is not more explicit." The more vague the statute, the more consensual the residence, because ambiguity permitted townships to confer settlement on immigrants of their own choosing. Clearly, consensual membership in the township granted too much discretion to the township and too little protection to increasingly mobile individuals.[15]

Beginning in 1827, however, Ohio jurists and legislators began a gradual redefinition of "settlement" that eventually shifted the locus of full legal belonging from the township to the individual. In that year, the Ohio Supreme Court reviewed the case of two townships that were squabbling over the legal residence of a woman who had lived in both. Significantly, the majority decision noted at the outset the increasing need for explicit definitions of residence in Ohio's townships. Up to then, the court pointed out, Ohio had been so prosperous that the court was "rarely called upon to give a construction" to the poor laws of the state. In Ohio, poor relief was traditionally the last resort of only the sick, the idiotic, or the orphaned. As a result, according to the majority of the court, "None but the unfortunate need claim the support of public charity." But the justices foresaw a broader role for Ohio's poor law, one that would require more careful delineation. Despite the state's present prosperity, they reasoned, "The time, however, must and will arrive, when questions of great importance to the community, growing out of the poor laws must be settled, and it is desirable that they should be settled correctly." The boundaries of membership in the township needed more explicit definition to prevent the unjust exclusion of anyone. Ohio jurists now began to listen more closely to newcomers' claims to full legal residence.[16]

The case before the court centered on the one-year warning period established by the poor law of 1816 and demonstrates the palpable injustice of consensual membership in a community. The pauper, Mary Endsly, moved with her father from Wayne Township, Jefferson County, to Stock Township, Harrison County, in 1821. Using the poor law to avoid financial responsibility for the impoverished migrant, Stock Township's overseers warned Mary Endsly out of their township. She refused to leave, and the overseers repeated their warning three more times during the next two years. Finally, in 1825, they removed her back to Wayne Township, where she had her last legal settlement. Wayne Township's trustees, however, simply sent her back to Stock Township. And once again Stock Township sent her back to Wayne. The overseers of Wayne Township relented and finally relieved Endsly, but they still denied her a legal settlement and sued Stock Township for her support.[17]

Endsly herself claimed legal residence and therefore the right to poor relief in Stock Township, where she clearly wanted to live. Although Stock Township's overseers had warned her to leave on four separate occasions, they had let more than one year pass without warning her, permitting Endsly to claim legal settlement. The township's overseers, however, argued that their legal responsibility to Mary Endsly ended forever when she failed to heed their first warning. No length of residence after warning, they argued, would be enough to confer legal settlement on a migrant who had once been warned to leave. The overseers argued that, once they had warned her out, Mary Endsly could never achieve a residence for poor relief in their township. Residence was entirely consensual, to be awarded by the township and not to be claimed by any newcomer.[18]

A majority of the Supreme Court disagreed, however, and they now shifted much of the responsibility for defining legal residence in Ohio from the township to the individual migrant. The majority opinion interpreted the 1816 poor law quite liberally, attempting to turn it into an instrument of social policy that might encourage rather than discourage migration into the new state. Any other construction, as they viewed it, would only damage the interests of Ohio for the sake of its constituent townships' treasuries, punishing migrants for settling in the state. "Ohio is a new state," they reasoned, "and policy dictates that in her different acts of legislation, she should go great lengths to encourage emigration. This can not be done effectually," they continued, "unless the terms upon which a legal settlement may be gained, are made easy." The poor law of 1816 – and the conception of consensual residence which it embodied – were therefore detrimental to Ohio. They protected townships at the expense both of the state's development and of prospective migrants. Common sense, according to the court, clearly demanded that legal settlement in a new region should not be too exclusive, for the sake of the state as well as the individual. Settlement should be as accessible as possible. The court therefore interpreted the law of 1816 quite liberally: A township did not have the right to withhold full membership from a newcomer forever.[19]

After ruling that Mary Endsly was a full legal resident of Stock Township, the court went on to grant individual migrants complete discretion in choosing membership in a new community. Consensual residence, conferred by the township, was not only unwise but also unjust. An individual should have the right to choose full legal membership in a township through physical presence alone. The court stated flatly that "it is residence, and residence alone, by which a person acquires a legal settlement." After a full year's residence, implicit acceptance or explicit rejection by the other residents in a township was irrelevant. An individual could choose membership in a township simply by demonstrating, through residence, a permanent commitment to the community. The majority issued an impassioned defense of the full legal membership that a demonstrated commitment to the community must automatically confer on a newcomer. Once warned, a newcomer "might accumulate any amount of property, might hold any office, might be separately taxed, and contribute largely for the support of the poor, still it would make no difference." Subsequent impoverishment might leave him dependent on his community, but

> Whence is he to derive this aid? Not from the township where he has spent most of his days, where he has accumulated and expended his property, whose poor he has assisted to support, where are his friends and acquaintances. From this township

some forty or fifty years before, he was warned to depart, and there he has no legal settlement. He must be removed to the place he was last settled, there to linger out the small remains of life among strangers.

An individual, the justices declared, must have the right to choose his or her own legal residence.[20]

In a dissenting opinion, however, a conservative minority of the court rejected this new conception of legal residence and still clung to the familiar tradition of consensual belonging. The minority opinion argued that, once warned to leave, a newcomer could never attain legal settlement in a township. In the view of the minority, the length of Mary Endsly's residence had "nothing to do with the case. On being once legally warned, it was proper for her to return to the place of her last settlement." She could remain in the township, of course, but not as a legal resident. "Her subsequent residence in the township, though permitted, was at her peril, and instead of securing to her privileges under the law, subjected her to the penalty of being removed by force." Having once been warned to depart, Mary Endsly must forever remain an "intruder." The minority interpreted the law of 1816 quite narrowly, leaving a migrant dependent for poor relief and full legal belonging on the good will of his new community.[21]

The dissenting opinion noted in passing that the law of 1816 was "carelessly drawn," and it did indeed cry out for judicial reinterpretation. The Ohio legislature, however, was slower in shifting the definition of legal residence from the township to the individual. Legislators responded to the new liberal judicial view of settlement by tightening up the poor law, actually lengthening the legal warning period. Beginning in 1829, it took not one but three years of residence in a township without receiving a warning to confer a legal settlement. Instead of defining the meaning of "residence" more clearly, the legislature lent even more discretion to township officials by giving them more time to warn out newcomers. At the same time, the new poor law excluded blacks and mulattoes from legal settlement entirely. Blacks and mulattoes could no longer secure settlement by posting a $500 bond, as they once could. As part of their broader campaign to restrict the migration of free blacks into their state, Ohio legislators turned to the poor law to exclude them from full legal membership and the accompanying eligibility for poor relief. In short, the innovative judicial retreat from consensual membership in the township simply provoked a stricter legislative defense against migrants, white and black. Legislators placed a more stringent hurdle on the path to full legal residence for whites and denied it altogether to black migrants.[22]

But this retreat to an older conception of consensual residence could be only temporary, because Ohio was on the threshold of its decade of greatest immigration. The continuing judicial challenge to consensual membership after 1830 reflected and reinforced the emergence throughout the United States of a "volitional" conception of legal residence. Under volitional residence, a township itself could no longer choose its own legal residents simply by accepting or rejecting newcomers. Instead, under volitional membership, migrants themselves could choose legal residence in a township through their own free will, through their continuing physical presence alone.[23]

A new poor law, passed in 1831, marked an important turning point in the legislative conception of legal residence in Ohio. That law represented a rather grudging compromise between consensual and volitional residence among Ohio's legislators. The new law conferred legal settlement on whites automatically after one year's residence in a township. At the same time, however, any newcomer warned to leave within a year of arriving could achieve a legal settlement only after staying three more years without another warning. Most newcomers, in other words, might achieve settlement within a year, simply through residence. Their settlement was volitional, achieved through residence alone. But the settlement gained, if any, by newcomers who were warned would be explicitly consensual, achieved through a longer period of residence without additional warnings. Those newcomers who received a warning during their first year in a township attained settlement over a longer period and only in the absence of additional warnings. The overseers of the poor could single out specific newcomers for several additional years of scrutiny. Settlement was to be volitional for some migrants but consensual for others.[24]

At the same time that the legislature was just beginning to write volitional residence into its statutory law, the courts were already invalidating the right of a township to define its own legal membership. They were granting increased freedom to migrants in the choice of a legal residence. In 1831, for example, the Supreme Court ordered Cincinnati Township, Hamilton County, to pay for the maintenance of Martha Good, who was not legally settled in the township. Good was a recent migrant to Cincinnati who contracted smallpox and eventually died. During her illness, the township's trustees argued that only legal settlement could confer the right of poor relief on a pauper, and they gave Martha Good only one dollar, as a "gratuity." The Supreme Court objected, however, and ordered Cincinnati Township to pay for Good's maintenance. They broke new ground by ruling that under Ohio law "any inhabitant" was eligible for poor relief, not just legally settled residents. "Every person residing in a township is an inhabitant," according to the court, "although such person may not have gained a legal settlement." Physical presence in a township alone, regardless of length of residence, entitled a migrant to poor relief. Township officials could no longer draw a line between settled residents and mere "inhabitants" but had a legal responsibility to help all paupers within their township. "Here is no restriction, no limitation," the court concluded. Physical presence alone, regardless of length of residence, must confer the right to poor relief in Ohio.[25]

The way was now clear for white migrants to move freely throughout Ohio without suffering any legal impediments or discrimination. Beyond its theoretical importance, this new-found freedom to move affected, of course, only indigent migrants, because those of substance had always been welcome to settle wherever they pleased. The more liberal interpretation of the poor laws may have directly benefited fewer than 1 percent of all migrants in Ohio before the Civil War.[26] But the new volitional conception of legal residence that was embodied in Ohio's poor law cases eventually had more profound implications that reached far beyond eligibility for poor relief. Beginning in the 1830s and 1840s, the idea of volitional residence spilled over into the political arena and provoked a minor revolution in rules of suffrage that took almost half a century to run its course. Consensual residence, in which suffrage was conferred on a newcomer by his township, gradually gave way to volitional residence, in which a voter could declare his own township of legal residence and then vote there. During this gradual transition from consensual suffrage to volitional suffrage, migrants gained important new political rights.

Just as Ohio's poor law changed gradually to provide migrants with a greater voice in defining their own legal residences, Ohio's election law was following a similar path from consensus to volition. As late as 1840 the right of suffrage in Ohio was still entirely consensual, depending on the acceptance of a newcomer by the other voters in his township. Ohio's first comprehensive election law, passed in 1831 to reduce election fraud, included no qualifications beyond those set forth in the constitution and a few early election laws. Beyond requiring one year's residence in the state, the only

requirement expected of eligible voters was "residence" in a particular township. But the "residence" of a voter still remained un-
defined, depending only on the consensus of the township in which
he offered to cast his ballot. The new law did regularize procedures
for reaching that consensus, probably in response to the growing
numbers and mobility of Ohio voters. Instead of relying on the body
of voters meeting together to accept or reject every ballot, the new
law assigned that task to a "board of election judges." Three election
judges in every township, who were generally the township's trustees, were empowered to review the qualifications of every voter at
the polling place. Suffrage was not yet volitional. The township's
representatives, not the voter himself, had the right to define legal
"residence," and the definition might vary from township to township, from year to year, and even from voter to voter.[27]

In 1841, however, a new election law, designed to "preserve the
purity of elections," defined quite explicitly, and for the first time,
the meaning of a voter's "residence." Under the new law, the election judges of each township applied nine specific rules in determining the residence of potential voters. The new qualifications were
explicitly volitional: The right to vote in a township rested entirely in
qualities of the voter instead of acceptance or rejection by the township. The increasing number of newcomers to Ohio had prompted
the legislature to adopt more impersonal, and therefore more equitable, criteria of belonging.[28]

The nine criteria of residence fell into four categories. One rule
stipulated that, in general, a married man found his residence in the
home of his family. A second required a man to vote in his place of
residence and not his place of business, if the two were distinct.
According to a third criterion, a voter would lose his residence in
Ohio if he voted in another state. The remaining six rules of residence, however, focused on the intentions of the prospective voter.
The first of these stated simply:

> That place shall be considered and held to be the residence of a
> person in which his habitation is fixed, without any present in-
> tention of removing therefrom and to which, whenever he is
> absent, he has the intention of returning.

Residence for voting, in other words, required not only a physical
home but also the intention to remain in that home. Succeeding
rules linked, in a variety of ways, physical presence or absence with
the intention to remain. A temporary absence, if accompanied by
the intention of returning, could not compromise the residence of a
voter. A temporary presence, on the other hand, if not accompanied

by the intention of remaining, could not establish a residence for voting. Absence in another state, with the intention to remain there, invalidated a voter's residence in Ohio. And absence in another state with no firm intention of returning to Ohio did the same.[29]

The final rule summed up the new conception of volitional suffrage, which stemmed from the individual and not from his community: "The mere intention to acquire a new residence without the fact of removal [moving in], shall avail nothing; neither shall the fact of removal without the intention." After 1841, then, the choice of legal residence rested with the voter: His residence depended on his intention to be a resident. A voter could achieve full political and legal residence simply by displaying a continuing physical presence while affirming his intention to maintain that presence. Under the act of 1841, every challenged voter underwent a public interrogation to establish his qualifications to cast a ballot. If the challenge was not withdrawn, the voter could swear to an oath, affirming his legal residence in the voting unit, and then go on to vote. An avowed commitment to his new community, in short, granted the migrant full legal residence within it. The voter, not the township, now determined his own place of legal residence.[30]

The election law of 1841, which combined volitional suffrage with interrogation by a board of election judges, governed Ohio elections until the Civil War. Its considerable impact on the role of migrants within antebellum Ohio's political system is the subject of subsequent chapters. By establishing new and, for migrants, more lenient rules of suffrage, however, the election law reflected the same legal and social climate that was liberalizing eligibility for poor relief during the same period. In fact, the growing volitional foundation of residence reflected a much broader and far-reaching national trend, the development of the legal doctrine of domicile. The doctrine of domicile or legal residence received its first judicial expression as early as 1813 but was not fully enunciated by the U.S. Supreme Court until 1852. By the early 1840s, however, domicile or full legal belonging had come to rest not only on continuous residence in a community but also on the clear expression of an intention to remain there. Domicile represented the judicial manifestation of volitional residence – legal residence achieved wholly through physical presence and the intention to remain. As Justice Joseph Story, one of the doctrine's leading architects, defined it, "that place is properly the domicil of a person in which his habitation is fixed, without any present intention of removing." Domicile, in short, considered an individual's physical presence and his intention when assigning legal residence.[31]

The Ohio Supreme Court issued its first clear definition of domicile in 1839. The court faced the task of determining the legal residence of Samuel B. Wilgus, a pauper who was removed from one township to another and was denied a legal settlement in both. Wilgus was a seaman who spent half the year "upon the lake" and the other half boarding in various Ohio townships. Applying the new principle of domicile, the court determined Wilgus's legal residence by inferring his present intentions from his past actions. Where did Wilgus *intend* to reside permanently, based on his previous behavior? Physical presence, of course, was one basic ingredient in establishing a legal residence. But in response to Wilgus's seasonal migration, the court ruled that, as a commitment to community, physical presence must be continuous:

> It will not suffice that a person shall have been in a township four months in one year, four months in another, and four months in a third. The residence must have been continued for one entire year from the time of its commencement.

But even more important than a clear physical presence was the intention to maintain that presence indefinitely. In determining legal residence, the intention to remain must surely overrule a temporary absence from the township. The individual remained a resident even if "occasionally absent," provided that his intention to return remained "open and manifest." Domicile reflected both the fact of physical residence and the intention to remain: "The residence must not only be *continuous*, it must also be *open and notorious*." Like the act of voting, domicile, in effect, was a personal declaration of belonging.[32]

The doctrine of domicile, in short, combined an individual's intention to remain with his actual physical presence in determining legal residence. In the two decades preceding the Civil War, however, Ohio law shifted dramatically the balance between the two ingredients of legal belonging. Intention gained more importance, and physical presence lost its significance. By 1859 the transition from consensual to volitional belonging was complete: Intention now meant everything, and physical presence had virtually no meaning at all. The individual belonged simply because he *wanted* to belong.

By the early 1850s, for example, Ohio required more than a mere occasional absence to violate legal residence in one of its townships.

In 1853, the Ohio Supreme Court heard the case of a migratory family claiming residence in one of the many townships they had visited. The court stated flatly that the intention to return outweighed absence in determining legal residence. "A person who has gained a legal residence in a place," according to the court, "is never in any instance held to have lost his residence by being absent, when his absence has been accompanied with the intention of returning to such place of abode." Further, an intent to reside was good enough in maintaining legal residence, and settlement no longer required an especially obvious or "notorious" presence in the community. In 1859 the courts reaffirmed the importance of intention by permitting even an indefinite absence without damage to legal residence. A man absent from his home "for years" who claimed no other residence might "claim his former residence, as if it had never been interrupted by his absence." By 1859, therefore, absence meant nothing and intention meant everything in deciding the legal residence of an individual. Belonging was entirely volitional, arising from an individual's intentions alone.[33]

Before the Civil War, migrants had gradually acquired broad rights to establish their legal residences wherever they chose, depending on the developing doctrine of domicile to focus more on their intentions than on their physical presence in a community. Domicile gave migrants the right to establish legal residence in a new township immediately after their arrival and to maintain, if they chose, their legal residence in their townships of origin even while they were absent. Domicile, in short, made widespread migration not only legally possible but convenient. Domicile was a sweeping and powerful doctrine. It did not merely help establish legal settlement but informed the conception of "residence" in nearly every area of law, governing the residence of parties to contracts, legal suits, property disputes, bankruptcies, divorces, and so on. Domicile is indispensable to the functioning of a modern, mobile society. Developed before the Civil War, the doctrine flowered during the late nineteenth century and remains central to the American conception of legal residence.[34]

The political implications of domicile were just as sweeping. By 1860, legal residence in Ohio was entirely volitional. Residence depended wholly on the intentions of the individual and was only incidentally supported by his physical presence in a community. Moreover, acceptance by the community no longer made any impact on the legal residence of a migrant. Migrants legally had the option of selecting residence, immediately, in their new townships or of maintaining, indefinitely, residence in their old ones. If extended to the suffrage, domicile would permit migrants to vote wherever they pleased, simply by claiming legal residence, with no reference at all to their actual physical presence in a township. Indeed, the election law of 1841 grounded the right to vote in the intentions of the voter, once he had met the minimum requirement of one year's residence in the state. "Residence" in the township, according to the doctrine of domicile, rested entirely with the individual. Could a migrant now wander at will, exercising freely the suffrage in any township of his choosing?[35]

In 1863, a landmark court decision forced Ohioans to answer that question. During the Civil War, Ohio permitted, by statute, political participation by soldiers stationed away from home. The statute authorized a polling place for every company of Ohio soldiers, even those stationed in other states, so they could vote in the election of 1863. "Voting in the field" allowed soldiers to cast ballots in their townships of legal residence and represented, in a sense, the first absentee voting in Ohio. The resulting "soldier vote" was heavily Republican and was large enough to decide many elections, not only at the local level but at the state level as well. Quite predictably, the act of 1863 that created the soldier vote faced immediate legal challenges. Most notoriously, John K. McBride, a Democrat who lost the election for probate judge in Wayne County, sued his opponent, Henry Lehman, the apparent winner of the election and a Republican. McBride challenged the constitutionality of soldier voting and asked the county's court of common pleas to reject the ballots of the absent soldiers. After the county court complied, Lehman appealed, and in the resulting decision – *Lehman v. McBride* (1863) – the Ohio Supreme Court set out to define the sources of suffrage in Ohio townships.[36]

The case of *Lehman v. McBride* had clear partisan roots: Union soldiers voted overwhelmingly Republican, and Democrats had a strong political motive for challenging absentee voting. But its implications were more than partisan. The case provoked the first judicial review of the new theory of volitional suffrage. The Supreme Court had its first opportunity to apply the doctrine of domicile explicitly to suffrage. The question before the court was deceptively simple: What entitled a man to vote in a particular township? The answer, however, was difficult. It involved two competing conceptions of the right of suffrage and, more broadly, the rights of migrants to legal residence. The Union soldiers were called away for a specific purpose, but any rights awarded to them would fall naturally to all of Ohio's migrants.

Counsel for McBride, challenging the validity of the soldier vote, drew a traditional portrait of the American election. Suffrage was consensual. The township was, in this sense, much like the New England town, and the election resembled a meeting. The election called together the residents of a township, not to defend their own interests as individuals, but to make a collective decision about the best interests of the whole community. Counsel for Lehman, by contrast, defended the soldier vote. Through volitional belonging, actual physical presence at an election was irrelevant. A man participated in politics to defend his own interests. When casting a ballot, the political individual was acting for himself alone and not for his community. The right of suffrage therefore belonged entirely to the individual himself and did not arise from the voter's membership in any particular community. As a result, voters had the right to travel freely, and migrants had the right to vote wherever they pleased.

McBride's attorneys, who opposed absentee voting, told the court that the purpose of an election was to "gather a true and fair expression of the popular will." As a result, the extension of suffrage must proceed quite cautiously, and a township must guard its own ballot box with care. Only through actual physical observation could the residents of a township "guard the elective franchise." By separating the voter from his community, however, absentee voting promoted "the unavoidable corruption and abuse of the elective franchise." The township alone could protect the purity of its own elections because the township alone conferred the right of suffrage.[37]

Because legal residence was consensual, the right of suffrage not only rested on actual physical presence but was utterly inseparable from it. The traditional conception of an election demanded personal attendance there. "The constitution requires," McBride's attorneys continued, "that all elections shall be by ballot. Let it be borne in mind," they reasoned, "that voting by ballot requires the *personal attendance* of the electors at the polls." Attendance alone gave an election its validity. The legislature, in fact, had no authority "to make the exercise of the elective franchise a mere *transitory* or *migratory* thing, to be exercised *not* at any stated or prescribed election precincts or districts, but anywhere, and in any part of the world where an elector may happen to be on the day of the election." The franchise could not be "migratory," and neither, therefore, could the voter.[38]

The opposing argument, by contrast, viewed physical presence as a mere legal formality, not at all essential to the right of suffrage. The fact that soldiers were absent on the day of the election, according to Lehman's counsel, did not detract in any way from their qualifications to vote in their townships of legal residence. The act of 1863 was meant, quite simply, "to authorize and allow them to exercise the elective franchise in the same manner as if in their townships and wards on the day of election." Physical absence meant nothing in defining the right of suffrage.[39]

Suffrage was "personal," independent of the community. Lehman's attorneys, in their defense of soldier voting, went on to wrench the right of suffrage away from the community and deliver it intact into the hands of the individual. Suffrage actually "followed" the individual when he left the township. "The act under consideration," they argued, "is a *personal* statute, operating upon the *person*, and giving *personal* rights – the elective franchise – and is intended to protect and guard this right wherever the *person* may be at the time to exercise the right." Protection of the franchise was entirely the responsibility of the individual. He alone defended his own right to vote simply by offering to cast a ballot. If he cast that ballot from outside the township, he still defended and retained his right of suffrage there: "Being a citizen and resident of the state, this law follows each soldier, and allows him the *personal* right guaranteed to him by the constitution." Physical presence or absence was irrelevant on election day.[40]

Lehman's attorneys summed up their conception of volitional suffrage by defining the voter as a political individual. The voter cast a ballot to defend his own personal interests in society and not those of the larger community. It seemed obvious that any individual could defend his own interests in spite of physical absence. "He may," for example, "make a deed or a will to convey land in this state, wherever he is." Voting was quite similar. Why should he not "vote for officers to take care of his interests at home" as well? If the individual was merely defending his own personal interests through voting, absence from his community made no impact on suffrage.[41]

The case of *Lehman v. McBride* therefore presented the court with two distinct and conflicting interpretations of the sources of suffrage. If the right of suffrage was consensual, stemming from acceptance by the community, then absence from the township on election day must disfranchise the individual. Similarly, presence in the township was not enough to secure suffrage. If, by contrast, political belonging was volitional, arising entirely from the intention of the individual to remain a resident, then physical presence or absence meant nothing. And neither did acceptance or rejection by the community. In short, the court had to decide whether an individual voted for his community or for himself alone.

A majority of the court, all Republicans, upheld the constitutionality of the soldier vote and therefore embraced the notion of volitional suffrage. The majority stated flatly that actual residence was necessary to confer the right of suffrage but absence alone was never enough to revoke it. "To qualify a person for voting for township officers, residence in the township is clearly necessary," the majority asserted. "But it does not follow, as a logical consequence, that the right to vote can be exercised only within the township." The franchise defined a relationship between a representative and his constituents. Representation was direct, linking voters and not places with their representatives. Suffrage made no "reference to the places where elections may be held." Individuals, not places, elected representatives.[42]

In upholding absentee voting, the majority of the court were clearly looking to the future. In a rapidly changing society, Ohio's electoral practices could not be too rigid. They must be flexible enough to accommodate unforeseen circumstances. They must, in fact, be "modified, from time to time, as the ever-varying circumstances of the unknown future might seem to require." The act of 1863, for example, was a reasonable response to civil war because it protected the rights of voters. The idea of volitional suffrage, arising more from intentions than from physical residence, had permitted the legislature to alter the letter of the law in order to preserve its spirit. But the court made it clear that any such modifications in the franchise must favor the rights of individuals. Volitional suffrage provided a new, more practical flexibility that protected the rights of individual voters. Voters could move freely without suffering disfranchisement.[43]

But instead of looking to the future, a dissenting minority of the court remained committed to the past. Clinging to tradition, Justice Rufus P. Ranney, the lone dissenter and the court's only Democrat, persisted in depicting the election as a meeting. Political tradition, Ranney insisted, demanded "a public meeting of the electors, within a prescribed election district." The election, as he viewed it, must bring all the voters together in a single place at a single time. Ranney clung, quite clearly, to a consensual definition of the American election. It was, he argued, "a time and place, and meeting of the electors, residing within defined limits, for the *joint* performance of a high public duty." The franchise belonged explicitly to the community, not to the individual, and voting was a public rather than personal act. Residence requirements, therefore, were designed to protect not only voters but also "the community whose franchise they exercise." Election laws, in effect, protected the members of the community "against their own frauds." They defended the community against individuals.[44]

If suffrage was consensual, as Ranney asserted, then the township itself must defend its own electorate. "There is no weight in the argument," he concluded, "that the right to vote is a *mere* personal privilege, carried by the elector wherever he may go, and properly exercised wherever he may be." Instead, it was a *"public franchise,* belonging to the whole community." When he cast his ballot, the voter must consider "the common benefit of the whole." Ranney rejected the idea of volitional suffrage, resting wholly in the intentions and interests of the individual voter.[45]

But the gradual transition from meeting to election, inherent in the shift from consensual to volitional residence, was now complete. Over half a century, Ohio law had gradually withdrawn more and more discretion from the township and granted more and more to individuals in the choice of legal residence. The decision in *Lehman v. McBride*, upholding absentee voting, was a clear expression of a new principle of volitional suffrage. Full political membership in a community was consensual no longer; it was volitional, achieved at the discretion of the individual. Representation was no longer virtual; it was direct, linking representatives with voters instead of with places. Ohio jurists had rejected, at last, the lingering conception of the election as an opportunity for deliberation by the community. A new political individualism made the election an expression of individual rather than communal interests. The meeting had become an election. When suffrage was volitional, residence alone enfranchised the voter, and no subsequent period of absence, however lengthy, could disfranchise him again.

The decision in *Lehman v. McBride* confirmed the validity of soldier voting without explicitly guaranteeing a completely volitional suffrage to all migrants. Indeed, true absentee voting did not appear in Ohio for another half-century.[46] But the injection of domicile into the evolving notion of volitional suffrage ensured that, eventually, voters would win the right to move freely within Ohio without suffering disfranchisement. Suffrage was now explicitly tied to domicile in Ohio law, and domicile heavily favored the legal rights of migrants.

Within a year of *Lehman v. McBride*, for example, the U.S. Circuit

Court for southern Ohio linked suffrage and domicile so closely that they became, for some purposes, indistinguishable. The case involved an Ohio man who moved west to Illinois in 1856 and voted there. The migrant had a grievance against his former employer in Ohio and eventually brought suit in the federal court, claiming that, because he had voted there, he was now a legal resident of Illinois. The court agreed, ruling that the act of voting by itself was conclusive evidence of a migrant's legal residence. The act of voting was a public declaration of residence and was sufficient to establish a new domicile. The court upheld the principle that "An exercise of the right of suffrage is conclusive." The volitional foundation of suffrage in Ohio was now complete: The right to vote in a new home did not derive from legal residence there but established it. Ohio migrants could vote where they pleased, and their very act of voting made them legal residents.[47]

During the next decade, Ohio courts embraced the full implications of volitional suffrage. In 1878, hearing the case of *Esker v. McCoy*, the Ross County Court of Common Pleas applied the doctrine of domicile explicitly to migratory voters. "To be entitled to exercise the right of franchise in a certain precinct," the court concluded, "requires the concurrence of two things – the act of residing in connection with the intention to do so." This was a restatement of the now familiar doctrine of domicile. The court went on to rule that the intention to reside could never be "constructive," inferred from behavior; it must be a "mental fact" alone.[48]

By 1878, therefore, the "mental fact" of belonging was enough to enfranchise any migrant on election day. The example of seven canal boatmen, whose residence was in question, provided a crucial link with a legal principle of long standing. Ohio's migrants, it seemed obvious, were very much like seamen. In the face of migration, the traditional law of the sea might logically govern the emerging law of belonging on land. It was obvious from experience that seamen might possess "a permanent abode at the home port" and yet "retain their domicile of origin though absent for long periods, voyaging to different parts of the earth." The search for a precedent had led quite naturally to the sea. If a voyager on the ocean could remain a settled resident so, reasoned the court, could a voyager on the land. On land, as at sea, the mere fact of mobility must shift important rights to the individual. The individual had a right to belong to his community simply because he wanted to, and suffrage must therefore be "carried by the elector wherever he may go."[49]

4 The defended community: migration and elections

On October 10, 1848, Riley F. Warner came to Liverpool, Ohio, to vote in the gubernatorial election. While he was at the polling place, another voter challenged his eligibility to vote there. Warner himself believed that he was a legal resident of Liverpool Township, but he had trouble convincing the election judges. As Warner put it, "I considered Liverpool my home as much as any where," and, after all, he had been born in Liverpool. "My father's people lived there, and I returned to Liverpool as often as once in two weeks." The board of election judges asked him a few questions, but when asked if he was indeed a resident, Warner had to admit that he wasn't quite certain: "I did not understand what constituted a resident sufficiently to answer." The judges asked Warner a few more questions, haggled over his ballot, and then rejected it. "One of the board stated that the answers were satisfactory to him," Warner recalled later, but "the two others decided that I was not a voter, and rejected it." Warner rode out to two other townships to vote, but the judges rejected his ballot there as well. Riley Warner, in fact, was not certain just where he resided legally and so could not vote anywhere that day.[1]

Riley Warner's half-hearted confrontation with Liverpool's election judges and his frustrated attempts to vote in three different townships in one day demonstrate the dilemma that many migrants faced in exercising their political rights before the Civil War. The emerging concept of volitional residence increasingly freed individuals, in theory, to choose their own communities of legal residence. By 1878, migrants could claim full legal and political membership in any community simply through their own declarations of belonging. This is precisely what Riley Warner tried to do when he offered his ballot in Liverpool Township. In practice, however, the new notion of volitional residence posed obvious political problems for communities, because there were so many migrants moving through them. Ohio legislators were therefore much less sensitive than were jurists to the political rights of migrants. As the notion of volitional suffrage gradually evolved, lawmakers had a difficult time devising electoral practices that could fairly represent the interests of both migrants and the long-time residents of communities. Until the Civil War, the Ohio legislature continued to defend the community against migratory voters. Antebellum election laws granted the ultimate authority over legal residence not to the voter himself but to election judges, who acted as representatives of the community. As a result, volitional suffrage was translated into electoral practice only imperfectly, leaving many migrants, like Warner, uncertain of their own legal residences.

The political status of migrants proved so troublesome for both voters and policymakers because prevailing democratic theory was rife with contradictions. On one hand, equal access to the ballot box was considered essential to political freedom. If Americans were political equals, within the bounds of a limited suffrage, then they demonstrated that equality most forthrightly at the polling place. Americans could argue, as two leading Ohio lawyers did, that "At the ballot box all persons having the qualifications of electors are equals." Echoing a popular faith in the profound leveling influence of the ballot box, they went on to assert that "If there be political equality in regard to anything, under our institutions, it is in regard to the right of suffrage." They and many other Americans, including the political philosopher George Sidney Camp, actually equated a broad franchise with freedom itself. "Each citizen being allowed his equal vote," Camp reasoned, "he thus enjoys the utmost possible amount of human freedom, and all that man ever could or did desire." Similarly, Governor Salmon P. Chase told his constituents that "The right of suffrage is sacred. It is the right to vote which makes the citizen a sovereign." Suffrage, in fact, was a key ingredient in defining citizenship itself. Samuel Jones, a Massachusetts political theorist, argued in 1842, for example, that "A citizen, then, is a person entitled to vote in the elections; he is one of those in whom the sovereign power of the State resides." Many Americans believed that political equality rested on equality at the ballot box. An "equal vote," which was an antebellum catchword, brought equal representation and was an essential foundation of American democracy.[2]

In practice, however, migration lent an inherent inequality to electoral participation. In spite of a growing volitional conception of community membership in American law and politics, it still seemed like common sense to many political theorists that only recognized residents of a voting unit ought to vote for its representatives. Representation in America is, after all, direct rather than virtual. Officeholders represent actual people rather than vague interests or places. Democracy itself therefore demanded proof of residence in a voting unit, and the most widely feared form of electoral fraud during the nineteenth century was voting by nonresidents. Many Ohioans deemed nonresidents to be not only fraudulent voters but also uninformed voters and hence a double danger to democracy. "A person that has but come into the state, is not supposed to be well enough acquainted with the government to take part in it," stated the author of a textbook on Ohio government. "Nor would he be likely, being a stranger, to know what persons to vote for." A newcomer needed time to make the acquaintance of both the institutions and individuals in his new home. As an Ohio governor put it, "The people should know their representatives well, and they, their constituents."[3]

A practical result of such political distrust of newcomers was a constant call for their temporary disfranchisement. Samuel Jones, a conservative advocate of residence requirements who also clung tenaciously to property qualifications, stated flatly that "A person who is not a member of the community, can have no right to interfere, or take any agency in the management of its affairs. If he does so," Jones continued, "he invades the rights of the members and becomes an intruder." A newcomer should bide his time, gradually acquaint himself with his new community, and gain the confidence of its members. He should wait "for his character and qualifications to become generally known; and to identify his interests with those of the community where he lives." Jones went on to propose a standard residence requirement of one year for enfranchising a newcomer and called for the outright disfranchisement of habitual migrants. "A mere transient person," as Jones put it, "has no right to vote any where." Democracy demanded, in short, a period of disfranchisement for newcomers. Communities ought to extend the franchise only to "known voters."[4]

Length of residence was therefore an important political qualification, and throughout the Midwest voters and officeholders faced demanding residence requirements that increased substantially with each level of responsibility. Ohio required one year's residence in the state of all voters, one year's residence in a county for state representatives, two years' residence in a county for state senators, and four years' residence in the state for the governor. Every accretion of political power required a lengthier residence. In fact, Ohio lawmakers sometimes evoked the image of "probation" when discussing residence requirements. A delegate to the Ohio Constitutional Convention of 1850–51, for example, declared that "persons

removing from other States into our own, should undergo a probation of one year, to acquire a knowledge of our laws and institutions." When translating rules of suffrage into actual electoral practices, Ohio legislators had to balance their notions of political
equality against such claims of the community to protection against
intruders.[5]

These two interests became increasingly difficult to reconcile.
Ohio's first constitution, adopted in 1802, granted the franchise to
all white adult males who had resided in the state for at least one
year. The framers of the Constitution of 1802 required actual residence only in counties and not in townships, and they imposed a
taxpaying qualification that could be, as it often was, satisfied by
two days' labor on the public roads. An early election law, written in
1809, required voters to be United States citizens. Those initial, simple rules of suffrage, as Chapter 3 pointed out, served the state well
until 1831, with frequent but only minor changes. Because suffrage
was consensual during these early decades, election rules could be
simple. Only voters known and accepted by the rest of the electorate
were permitted to cast ballots.[6]

As the number of newcomers to Ohio swelled, however, residence requirements acquired new importance. During the 1830s and
1840s, increasing rates of migration brought many more newcomers
to the polls every year, and a growing volitional conception of suffrage gave more discretion to individuals in choosing legal residences. The Ohio legislature responded to these developments by
codifying election rules. In 1831 a new election law required an
actual residence in townships and empowered a local election board
of three judges to review the qualifications of all potential voters.
Now voters needed to demonstrate an actual residence in the voting
unit itself, not just the county, and three representatives of the
community were charged with the task of sorting out legitimate
from fraudulent voters.[7]

Still, the law of 1831 required residence in voting units without
attempting to punish or even to define nonresident voting. In the
wake of Ohio's most rapid population growth, however, the legislature substantially revised these rules of residence just ten years
later. The election law of 1841, which put new emphasis on the
residence of potential voters, governed Ohio elections until well
beyond the Civil War. The law defined, for the first time, the meaning of "residence" as a suffrage requirement. Mirroring the growing
volitional conception of community belonging, the new law gave
preponderant weight to a voter's intentions in its definition of resi-

dence. Immigrants, of course, must be naturalized citizens, and the legislature never altered that suffrage requirement. Interstate migrants must have lived in Ohio for at least one year, a requirement imposed by the state's constitution. But within those limits, residence for voting depended almost entirely on a voter's own intentions. In general, a voter resided and could therefore cast a ballot wherever he wanted to reside. It was this volitional aspect of Ohio's election law that emboldened Riley Warner to claim residence in Liverpool Township simply because he "considered" it his home.[8]

The new law of 1841 established explicit rules of residence to determine whether recent migrants were eligible to vote and therefore provided objective standards that voters could meet simply by staying put. But the law also empowered a local "election board" to interpret these new rules of residence. It was this imperfect leap from theory to practice that put many migrants at a political disadvantage. The legislature wrote objective criteria of residence but still permitted representatives of the community to interpret and apply them. A board of three election judges and two election clerks supervised the balloting in each voting unit, and they had the right to question every voter. The three judges, or any voter at all, could challenge the qualifications of a potential voter. Once challenged, the voter took an oath and underwent a public interrogation administered by the judges.[9]

As a safeguard against fraud, the election law gave the judges a precise series of questions to ask the challenged voter. Almost all of the questions centered on residence. To determine the citizenship of a potential voter, for example, the judges asked him two questions:

> 1st. Are you a citizen of the United States?
>
> 2nd. Are you a native or naturalized citizen?

They could then demand proof of naturalization, if necessary. But most of the questions dealt with internal migration. To test a voter's residence in Ohio, the judges asked him a series of five questions:

> 1st. Have you resided in this state for one year immediately preceding this election?
>
> 2nd. Have you been absent from this state within the year immediately preceding this election? If yes, then
>
> 3rd. When you left, did you leave for a temporary purpose, with the design of returning, or for the purpose of remaining away?
>
> 4th. Did you, while absent, look upon and regard this state as your home?
>
> 5th. Did you, while absent, vote in any other state?

Such interrogations focused on both the actions of the potential voter and his intentions – his "designs," as the law put it – which were at that time the two ingredients of legal residence. The judges might go on to ask a similar series of questions to determine residence in the voting unit itself. Any voter who refused to answer any question automatically forfeited his right to vote in that township.[10]

While listening to the voter's answers during the interrogation, which was conducted publicly, a challenger might withdraw his challenge and permit the voter to cast his ballot. But if the challenger was still not satisfied, the voter could press his claim of residence by taking an additional oath from one of the election judges and then voting. Fragmentary evidence suggests that such "swearing" at the ballot box found frequent application. In Clinton Township, Shelby County, for example, 9 percent of all voters swore an oath of eligibility during the 1840s. About one in 11 new voters, in other words, made a sworn affirmation of their qualifications in response to a public challenge. The volitional conception of membership in the community permitted such "sworn" voters to gain legal settlement simply by swearing that they were or intended to become legal residents.[11]

Even after administering the election oath to a challenged voter, however, the judges could still reject a tendered ballot. This clause represented a lingering violation of volitional suffrage and preserved a vestige of consensual suffrage in Ohio elections. Under the theory of volitional membership, of which swearing was one expression, voters derived their residence in a township entirely from their own intentions, by meeting objective qualifications of residence and affirming their intentions. In practice, however, the election law of 1841 defended the community by leaving many voters dependent on the election judges. The election judges alone accepted or rejected any voter's ballot, acting as representatives of their communities. It was this provision of the law of 1841, of course, that gave judges their authority and made the other provisions of the act enforceable. But, in general, the election judges were also the township's trustees. They were the incumbent executives of the township and therefore the leaders of the local party in power. Newcomers needed, in practice, the permission of the party in power to gain a residence for voting. This was in fact Riley Warner's chief impediment to voting in 1848: He was a Whig trying to vote in a heavily Democratic township. Under the law of 1841, therefore, residence requirements took on distinctly partisan implications.[12]

The new law, which was designed to protect the "purity of elections," also provided strict penalties for voting by nonresidents. Interestingly, the severity of the punishment was not uniform for all offenses but increased with the distance traveled by the nonresident voter. Voting in the wrong township within a county, for example, brought six months' imprisonment. Voting in the wrong county, however, was punishable by up to three years at hard labor. Crossing a state line to vote illegally brought the most severe sentence, up to five years in the state penitentiary. Presumably, intrastate migrants were less dangerous to democracy – and to the community – than interstate migrants, and local migrants even less so. The less strange the stranger, the less severe his punishment.[13]

This procedure of challenge, oath, interrogation, and a second oath substituted for some form of voter registration, an idea still in its infancy. In the absence of voter registration, a legitimate voter needed to have friends in the township who would stand up for him on election day. As one theorist put it, "every person, having the requisite term of residence, and having the other qualifications, will have many acquaintances, by whom the truth can be proved." The public interrogation was designed to sort out legitimate residents from fraudulent voters at the polling place itself.[14]

In general, Democrats defended the enfranchisement of migrants and opposed the most stringent features of the new election law, such as the power of the election judges to reject the ballot of any sworn voter. Whigs favored the law but recognized the various problems of enforcing it, especially in heavily Democratic areas, such as Cincinnati. As a result, Ohio Whigs guided a rudimentary voter registration law through the legislature in an attempt to enforce prevailing rules of residence and suffrage. The Registry Law of 1845 required voters in Ohio's urban townships – townships that contained more than one election district – to register with a Board of Registry at least one month before a general election. Registration would therefore ensure that all voters had indeed resided in the district for at least one month before an election. Township assessors in Ohio's largest cities and towns were to compose an alphabetical list of eligible voters before September 10 of each year, and election judges could consult those lists at the polling place to determine eligibility. Challenges were now to be issued and defended well before election day before boards of registry, and the most recent newcomers to Ohio's urban townships therefore faced almost automatic disfranchisement. Legal voters, on the other hand, could now feel secure in their suffrage.[15]

Interestingly, the Whig authors of the new Registry Law did not restrict registration to cities and towns but extended it to several entire counties. They singled out Cuyahoga, Pickaway, Montgomery, Summit, and Portage counties for registration, because they lay astride Ohio's canal system, a focus for frequent, short-term migration. Ohio's "canal counties" were renowned for their restless migration. They gained population much faster than did the state's other 48 counties, especially during the peak settlement years of the 1840s, and they attracted the most migrants. In 1850, for example, 43 percent of the residents of the canal counties were migrants to Ohio as compared to only 35 percent in all the other counties. In both 1850 and 1860, the canal counties contained almost three times the proportion of foreign immigrants as did the rest of the state. Many of the canal counties were Democratic strongholds. Between 1840 and 1860, Democrats outpolled Whigs and Republicans 48 percent to 46 percent in the canal counties. Whigs and Republicans, by contrast, outpolled Democrats 49 percent to 46 percent in all the others. The disparity between Democrats and Whigs in the canal counties increased throughout the 1840s and 1850s and actually reached 10 percent in 1853, when the Whigs were at their weakest. By 1845, migration was a partisan issue, and Ohio Whigs were determined to bar the state's most transient voters from the ballot box. The new Registry Law kept migrants away from the polling place entirely.[16]

Whigs generally defended the Registry Law of 1845, but Democrats were almost unanimous in their opposition to it. One Whig editor supported the new law as an important safeguard against fraudulent voting. "Let us have a Registry Law," he argued while the bill was still pending. "No honest voter will be deprived of any right thereby, and all the scoundrels will be completely 'barred out.'" Like many Whigs, he viewed transient voters automatically as fraudulent voters. In his eyes, they were by definition dishonest, and migrants at the ballot box were therefore "scoundrels."[17]

Democrats, by contrast, worked against the law both in the legislature and at the polling place. Almost two years after its passage, Samuel Medary of the Columbus *Ohio Statesman* was still complaining that "It has been of no earthly use, except to saddle the people with an unnecessary expense." Medary's assertion that the Registry Law was of no use, however, proved more than simply rhetorical. It was a self-fulfilling prophecy, because Democrats violated the law at every opportunity. Hearing an election contest in 1848, for example, the Democratic Committee on Privileges and Elections in the Ohio House labeled the law "utterly unconstitutional." The members of the committee actually supported the Medina Township assessor who disobeyed the law. "The committee," they wrote, "attaches no importance to the fact that it was (as it should have been) disregarded." Under oath, the marshal of the town of Medina actually flaunted his contempt for the Registry Law. "I made no register of the names of electors in said election district at any time during my present term of office as marshal," he testified, "and no such was made and posted up to my knowledge." An interrogator asked the marshal, "Why did you not make such a register?" "Because I thought the law requiring it was repealed," he answered, "and the locofocos always said it was unconstitutional, and I was sworn to support the constitution." Like the election law of 1841 itself, the Registry Law depended on local enforcement.[18]

Against this backdrop of partisan bickering over residence requirements, a convention met in Columbus during the summer of 1850 to write a new state constitution. By 1850, residence laws had become a political issue, and the delegates to the constitutional convention drew heavily on personal experiences to guide them as they argued about rules of residence, the foundations of suffrage, and the proper political role of migrants. Democrats dominated the convention and the Committee on the Elective Franchise. Quite predictably, the committee's report provoked a heated debate on the floor of the convention, prompting one delegate to complain that "There is so much difficulty in being heard over the echoes and reverberations of this Hall." Democrats in the convention tended to plead the cause of migrants, while Whigs defended the right of communities to select their own legal residents. The "reverberations" therefore arose, in part, from partisan differences. Whigs believed that migrants, and especially foreign immigrants, voted overwhelmingly Democratic, and Democrats depended on partisan strongholds in Ohio's canal cities and counties. Whigs therefore supported election rules that disfranchised newcomers, while Democrats proposed rules that favored recent migrants.[19]

True to their principles, Whigs elected delegates to the constitutional convention who had been in Ohio longer than their Democratic counterparts. State-level political leaders could generally claim long residence in their state and districts. Members of the 1845–46 Ohio legislature, for example, had resided in Ohio an average of 26 years, unusually long by antebellum standards, and there was no difference between Whigs and Democrats or between the Senate and the House. The typical delegate to the Constitutional Convention of 1850–51, by contrast, had lived in the state even longer, for 31 years. Further, Whig delegates claimed, on average, 35 years residence in Ohio, over five years more than the typical Democratic delegate. In theory, unusual persistence rather than partisan connections gave all the delegates their political authority to rewrite Ohio's constitution. Their journal, in fact, listed the delegates' length of residence in Ohio but not their partisan affiliations. But apparently Whig leaders and voters valued exaggerated persistence even more than did Democrats.[20]

The convention's Committee on the Elective Franchise, which was dominated by Democrats, reported an article that reflected their experiences with transient voters. Just as under the Constitution of 1802, the franchise would belong to all white adult males who were U.S. citizens and had lived in Ohio for one year before an election. These provisions had stood unchanged and unchallenged for over 40 years. Significantly, however, the proposed article required an actual residence in the voting unit itself, an innovation. This was a lesson of widespread migration and perhaps a concession to Whigs. But the Democratic proposal went on to grant the legislature broad authority to define the meaning of "residence" in a voting unit, as that body had been doing since 1841. The Democratic proposal therefore required residence in rural townships and urban precincts but also kept residence requirements firmly under legislative control.[21]

Several Democrats actually found their party's suffrage provisions too conservative and tried to amend them from the convention floor. H. S. Manon of Licking County, for example, an Ohioan for only 13 years, attempted to reduce the required residence in the state to a mere six months. Only 20 of 111 delegates voted for his amendment. Joseph Thompson of Stark County, a longtime Ohioan, wanted to extend the franchise to noncitizens. Charles Reemelin of Hamilton County, a German immigrant and relative newcomer, heartily agreed. Reemelin urged the delegates to define the boundaries of the state's electorate for themselves, without reference to U.S. citizenship. He argued that Ohio should reserve the right to decide who was a citizen and a voter in the state, instead of "surrendering to the United States an attribute of sovereignty." Reemelin was shrewdly clothing a liberal suffrage reform within the conservative shroud of state sovereignty. He observed in passing that "He did not suppose that at this moment the minds of members are ready to take hold and discuss this subject." He was right, and the amendment fell to defeat.[22]

Whigs, by contrast, considered the new suffrage rules far too lenient. G. J. Smith of Warren County, a lawyer and a 50-year-old

Ohio native, suggested that the constitution stipulate one year's residence in the state during the year immediately preceding an election, presumably to bar return-migrants from the polls for a full year. This was already common practice, and the amendment passed without debate. Joseph Barnet of Preble County, for 46 years an Ohioan, attempted to retain Ohio's traditional taxpaying qualification, which the Democratic proposal abolished. Barnet, as a typical Whig, argued that "no person who contributed nothing in support of the government, should be allowed to partake in its powers." William Sawyer of Auglaize, another Ohio native but a Democrat, challenged that amendment, objecting to property qualifications of any kind. Sawyer, a blacksmith, quoted the Democratic dictum that it should be "the man, and not the property, that gives the right – the man and not the ass." Other Democrats argued more practically that, although propertyless, a migrant might still deserve the franchise. Older men, for example, "coming late in life, to reside with their children perhaps," were still worthy citizens. After listening to such Democratic objections, Barnet quietly withdrew his amendment.[23]

But by far the most heated exchanges surrounded the meaning of residence in a voting unit and involved the majority Democrats in an intraparty struggle. Rufus P. Ranney was a Democratic delegate from Trumbull County who later won election to the Ohio Supreme Court and was the lone dissenter in the landmark decision *Lehman v. McBride*. Already in 1850, Ranney was a vehement opponent of volitional suffrage for migrants. True to his principles, Ranney provoked a heated debate during the constitutional convention by suggesting that the new constitution leave "residence" without a definition, as did the old one. Ranney preferred the traditional, consensual interpretation of "residence." Residence, in his words, must be "*bona fide*" only, not measured by rigid temporal standards. If it was to be consensual, residence must be achieved only through acceptance by the other voters in a township.[24]

In particular, Ranney opposed giving the legislature new authority to stipulate a standard length of residence in a voting unit. He could "see no reason why the elective franchise should be so placed as to be varied to suit the caprices and changes of opinion of the General Assembly." A legal residence, Ranney argued, ought to be conferred by the community. He agreed wholeheartedly that "persons removing from other States into our own, should undergo a probation of one year, to acquire a knowledge of our laws and institutions." But local migrants should not be judged by uniform temporal standards. It was obvious to all that "A man, through poverty or otherwise may be so circumstanced as to be obliged to remove from one township to another in the county, every year." And now the convention was giving the legislature the authority to "deprive him of his vote for a long series of years, and one may entirely lose a previously acquired franchise." Although Ranney professed a concern for the rights of local migrants, he was really defending the community. As he later argued in his minority opinion in *Lehman v. McBride*, Ranney felt that suffrage should remain consensual. A migrant should earn the franchise only through acceptance by the members of his new community and not at the discretion of the state legislature.[25]

Moderate Democrats, however, defended the right of migrants to an impartial, objective suffrage. They challenged Ranney's commitment to consensual residence in favor of various forms of volitional suffrage, earned by satisfying some uniform criterion of residence. William Hawkins of Morgan County, for example, looked to a rigid period of residence to prevent electoral fraud. Time alone was the best criterion of legal residence in a voting unit and of commitment to a community. "Different constructions have been given to the law, in different places," Hawkins pointed out. "In one, the place of a man's residence has been decided to be, the place where his washing was done; in another, where he takes his food; in a third, the place where his wife resides." Consensual residence was not only unfair to migrants but also encouraged fraud. Transient laborers, for example, might congregate en masse during a harvest. "Such men, may, with a loose rule," Hawkins argued, "be considered citizens of the county in which they vote." Hawkins therefore welcomed "a little discretion" on the part of the legislature to bring uniformity to criteria of residence.[26]

A Democrat from Licking County agreed that the new suffrage rules must balance the rights of migrants with a defense against fraud. He hailed from one of Ohio's canal counties where, "Every year, the mere transient, homeless, hands of canal boats were allowed by the trustees to come to the polls and vote on the day of election." In the canal counties, in fact, it had "become the practice to accumulate a large number of boats to come in for the purpose of allowing the hands to control the election." The Democrat from Licking considered it "evident that the crew of a canal boat, who have no home, and who are perfectly transient, ought not to have the right to go from place to place and decide who shall be the local officers of the State." A partially volitional residence, achieved by

satisfying some objective criterion, would permit genuine newcomers to vote while preventing electoral fraud. Consensual suffrage only fostered electoral corruption while disfranchising many
legitimate voters. John Larwill, a Wayne County Democrat, offered
Ranney a similar compromise. He wanted some length of residence
fixed in the new constitution, a partially volitional criterion, but one
that was independent of the legislature. Still another Democrat defended Ohio's most transient voters. "A man may find it necessary
to move every year," Thomas J. Larsh of Preble County reminded
the delegates. Larsh could not understand "why the existence of an
occasional fraud should be made the pretext for the perpetration of a
constant fraud [disfranchisement] upon a large number of citizens."
The community could not be trusted to dispense suffrage without
legislative supervision.[27]

But the most forceful defender of Ohio's transient voters actually
proposed a completely volitional definition of residence. G. Volney
Dorsey, a Democrat from Miami County, demanded actual residence in a voting unit, to be sure, but he opposed the application of
any consensual or even temporal definition of the word. In fact,
Dorsey considered any criterion of residence at all unjust. "We have
a large population on the canals of our State," Dorsey argued, "who
reside only upon boats; and which would be the greater wrong – to
allow them to vote where they are, or to disfranchise them altogether?" Two Democrats, Ranney and Dorsey, now stood at opposite
extremes on the question of suffrage. Ranney clung to a completely
consensual conception of residence, while Dorsey proposed a completely volitional suffrage. "In what county would you allow such a
citizen to vote?" Ranney asked Dorsey. "In the county where he is
on the day of election," was Dorsey's reply. "This would not do in a
close township or county," Ranney retorted, and then he asked
Dorsey, "Would the gentleman permit him, under such circumstances, to vote where he might choose to be?" This, of course, was
a succinct definition of volitional suffrage. "I am aware of the
abuse," Dorsey answered, "but to deprive men of their rights is a
greater abuse." In his defense of the migrant, Dorsey concluded
with an observation that would not find judicial expression in Ohio
for another generation, until *Esker v. McCoy* in 1878: "He must have
a residence somewhere; and where it is, he should have the right to
vote." Dorsey was advocating a completely volitional definition of
legal residence. Ranney's amendment, which represented a return
to consensual electoral practices, lost by a vote of 50 to 22.[28]

The final suffrage provisions of the new constitution therefore represented a compromise between Dorsey's defense of the migrant and Ranney's commitment to the community. In advocating a return to a traditional, consensual suffrage, Ranney emphasized the integrity of the community. Legal residence could never be automatic. It must be earned by the newcomer in some way and conferred by the community, even at the expense of disfranchising migrants and permitting electoral fraud. The new constitution ought to protect the community against migrants, and a consensual suffrage empowered the community to defend itself. Dorsey, by contrast, defended not the community but the individual. Pleading the cause of migrants, Dorsey supported a completely volitional residence, a sort of "suffrage on demand" that followed the individual wherever he traveled.

Moderate Democrats, who proved to be the majority, proposed a more flexible, legislative definition of residence as the best guarantee against fraud. Suffrage was not entirely volitional, because the legislature could impose a lengthy residence requirement on voters. Suffrage was not wholly consensual either, because newcomers could achieve legal residence by meeting a uniform temporal standard. The constitutional compromise therefore reflected a pragmatic conception of migrants, a realistic portrait drawn from experience by moderate Democrats. Migrants were an occasional threat to the community, to be sure, but they were by no means universally dangerous. Probation rather than exile was enough to ensure their good behavior. Neither the community nor the migrant but the legislature defined legal residence. This was a practical compromise that balanced the integrity of communities against the political rights of migrants.

Under the new constitution, therefore, voters must be U.S. citizens and residents of the state for at least one year. The constitution required actual residence in the voting unit itself but empowered the legislature to define such "residence." The legislature in fact did not exercise its authority until 1857, in an amendment to the law of 1841, which remained in force. Beginning in 1857, every legal voter must have lived in the state for one year, in the county for 30 days, and in the township for 20 days. In effect, intrastate migrants, moving between counties, were disfranchised for a month, while local migrants, moving between townships, were disfranchised for 20 days. On the other hand, such migrants had an unquestioned right to vote after meeting these uniform suffrage requirements. By the end of the 1850s, suffrage was partially volitional, obtained by meeting an objective standard of residence.[29]

These basic rules of suffrage remained unaltered well into the twentieth century. After relaxing rules of residence for migrants, however, Ohio policymakers turned to a new device to regulate the political participation of newcomers. With residence declining as an important political qualification during the late nineteenth century, Ohio followed the example of other states by gradually adopting registration requirements. Early registration laws, passed in 1877 and 1885, targeted recent migrants and urban areas for the most intense scrutiny. In effect, the early registration laws substituted severe registration requirements for the previously stringent residence requirements of an earlier age. By 1921, in fact, no one could obtain a legal residence in a voting unit for political purposes without first registering to vote. Under volitional suffrage, voters had the right to choose their own legal residences, but under the new system of registration they also had to take pains to exercise that right well before an election. Modern registration laws appeared, and in fact became necessary, only when the strict residence rules of the antebellum period were giving way to a completely volitional suffrage.[30]

As they gradually altered their state's electoral practices, Ohio's jurists and legislators often worked at cross purposes. Jurists responded to a wave of judicial activism after 1815 by extending new rights to migrants in selecting their own legal residence. Between 1802 and 1878, Americans' increasing mobility contributed heavily to a new theory of suffrage that emphasized the needs and intentions of individual voters rather than the political integrity of communities. The rising concept of volitional membership in the community gradually permitted transient voters to achieve suffrage more easily, within townships of their own choosing. Volitional suffrage made no reference to acceptance or rejection by the other residents of a voting unit. By 1878, any newcomer could obtain legal residence, and therefore the franchise, simply by claiming it. Volitional suffrage gave migrants new freedom to move without losing political rights. Migration, in short, helped to produce a judicial redefinition of suffrage that placed primary emphasis on the intentions of the individual.

At the same time, however, Ohio's legislators moved only cautiously toward volitional suffrage. In both 1831 and 1841, they wrote laws that tied suffrage to actual residence in townships rather than counties. Additionally, the new election laws, like those of other midwestern states, empowered a local board of election judges to review the qualifications of all potential voters before permitting them to vote. Those local election judges received broad authority at the expense of migrants. The legislature recognized volitional suffrage but also took on the task of defining "residence" for purposes of voting, a right that they retained under the Constitution of 1851. Significantly, however, local election judges had the final authority to interpret that new definition, and they gradually became official judges of residence within their townships. The judges' new authority to define "residence" for voting had important political implications. The judges were, in general, the township's own trustees, and the winners of one election now stood as judges of every voter's eligibility to vote at the next election.

Perpetuating a long tradition of neighborliness and voluntarism, Americans like to picture their communities as natural rather than artificial institutions. As part of his portrait of the New England town, for example, de Tocqueville argued that "The village or township is the only association which is so perfectly natural that, wherever a number of men are collected, it seems to constitute itself." Some historians have drawn on that tradition to portray the nineteenth-century community as wholly natural and spontaneous, growing up wherever people settled down. The Turnerian emphasis on equality and opportunity led many frontier historians, especially, to focus on spontaneity and informal cooperation in the building of new communities. Shared values and common goals bound strangers together from necessity and drew newcomers naturally into the fold. One historian, for example, celebrated the "togetherness" that was achieved in nineteenth-century towns "without numerous, formal social organizations." Newcomers won membership in such a natural community "simply by living within its boundaries."[31]

Political membership in the antebellum community, however, was more difficult to achieve and was neither natural nor automatic. Antebellum election laws, designed to disfranchise those whom their authors perceived as fraudulent voters, gave broad discretion to settled residents in accepting or rejecting newcomers as legal voters. Politically, nineteenth-century communities were not natural but were "defended communities." Historians have noted the role of voluntary associations in promoting and perpetuating a sense of community in the midst of social and political turmoil. But they have slighted the role of formal political institutions, such as parties and elections, in similarly blunting the most disruptive effects of migration in the midst of economic development and population growth. Formal and frequently complex rules of residence governed legal and political admission into the antebellum community. Acting as election judges, township officials could scrutinize newcomers and migrants at the polling place. Accepting most voters, challenging a minority, and rejecting still others, election judges could defend their communities and temper the political disruption occasioned by heavy migration.[32]

Election judges could and frequently did interrogate newcomers at the polling place before ruling on their eligibility to vote. The election judges might accept a ballot without question, as Arza Pearson, a judge in York Township, Medina County, recalled doing in 1848. "John Hewitt came to the polls and voted, by giving me the ballot," Pearson remembered. "I put it in the ballot box, and proclaimed his name."[33]

The judges might also challenge a voter's residence before letting him vote, as George C. Baker discovered in Canaan Township. Baker came to vote in the presidential election of 1848, but someone challenged his ballot on grounds of his residence. The judges "swore" Baker, and after he testified that he had lived in the township for four or five weeks and "in consideration of . . . his intention of residing there," the judges accepted his ballot.[34]

Finally, the judges could administer the election oath, interrogate a voter, and still reject his ballot, as the judges of Liverpool Township did to Riley Warner. Another voter, George C. Miller, recalled a similar experience in Guilford Township. "I offered to vote on the 10th of October last, at the State election," he remembered, "and my vote was not received." When asked why the judges had refused his ballot, Miller explained that "They thought I had lost my residence. There was some disagreement about it. I understand that two of the judges so decided." And so Miller lost his right to vote in Guilford Township. As a migrant, in fact, he had no legal right to vote anywhere.[35] Widespread migration, the new volitional theory of suffrage, and the statutory authority of election judges to screen newcomers all combined to complicate the casting of ballots in antebellum elections. This imperfectly volitional suffrage put migrants at a political disadvantage and permitted township trustees to defend their communities' franchise.

5 "A movable column": migration and voting

A contemporary observer of migration, Ohio's commissioner of statistics, wrote during the 1850s that in any city or county "the existent people are not a uniform body whose natural increase we can calculate, but a movable column, of which one part is just coming in, and another going out."[1] This image of a human column moving ceaselessly through a community is very familiar to historians of nineteenth-century society. Social historians long ago faced the fact that within any ten-year period during the nineteenth century most Americans moved. They have devoted a tremendous amount of thought, energy, and argument to the precise measurement of that constant movement through nineteenth-century communities and to its implications for nineteenth-century society. Political historians, by contrast, have been slower to recognize the mobility of nineteenth-century voters and to assess its impact on political organization and behavior.

In Ohio, the westward movement, the rise of cities, innovations in transportation, and foreign immigration all combined to draw millions of migrants through the state during the antebellum decades. Most migrants traveled long distances instead of moving just locally. Further, communities in all stages of development – growth, stability, and decline – could equally experience high levels of immigration and emigration. That "tide" of long-distance movement had political implications, because during these years Ohio gradually relaxed its rules of suffrage for migrants. Both the courts and the legislature slowly granted migrants greater rights in choosing their own legal residences. Increasingly, migrants were free to move within the state without losing their right to vote, because their intention to reside in a community became the basis of their suffrage. There were no uniform rules of residence, and local election judges had broad authority to enfranchise or disqualify newcomers. But often even the most recent migrants could vote simply by taking an oath and declaring legal residence on election day.

As a result, nineteenth-century voters were, like Americans in general, a "movable column," with one part "just coming in, and another going out," filing endlessly through every community. The

88

local electorate, as the discussion of Shelby County's experience suggests, was tremendously unsettled, with a great many voters moving into, out of, and through the area. In fact, historians can count on the typical voting unit they study to lose most of its voters every few years or so and to accept just as continuously a stream of new voters in their place. A typical community, even a growing city or town, might retain only a small minority, perhaps only 5 to 10 percent, of its voters over a single decade. The majority of voters were members of a "movable column" of migrants who might vote only once or twice in a community and then move on.

The manuscript U.S. census reveals general patterns of migration into and out of a community at ten-year intervals. Quadrennial enumerations are somewhat more precise, disclosing the movement of only eligible voters at four-year intervals. A third kind of record, poll books, is even more precise in disclosing the movement of voters through towns and townships. Poll books record the names of only actual voters, eligible voters who actually cast ballots on election day. And poll books are annual or even semi-annual records, because they were taken down at every election. Poll books are therefore a crucial resource for a thorough examination of the impact of migration on local political behavior. They permit a much closer look at the column of voters as it moved through a town or township, a dynamic rather than static portrait of the local electorate that reflects the constant migration of voters through the community.

Poll books, which are nominal records of electoral participation, list the names of all individuals participating in an election. Under *viva voce* voting, poll books also provide a record of their actual votes. Ohio, however, never used *viva voce* voting, and so the state's poll books do not reveal partisanship. Ohio's poll books are therefore simply lists of voters' names. This chapter uses poll books to examine the impact of high levels of migration on actual electoral participation at the local level. Much like survey data on modern political behavior, poll books permit examination of a broad range of demographic, social, and economic influences on patterns of individual-level participation. Dissatisfied with aggregate analysis of electoral behavior, many political scientists have turned to individual-level survey data to scrutinize various sources of popular participation in our own day. One of their most important contributions has been to sort out numerous nonpolitical influences on patterns of participation. Demographic, socioeconomic, and cultural variables can interact unpredictably at the level of the individual to play a primary role in determining who participates in politics and who does not. By shifting attention away from aggregate rates of voter turnout to patterns of participation among individuals, poll books can recast the historical debate over nineteenth-century electoral participation in much the same way.[2]

Students of nineteenth-century participation, who lack complete and reliable survey data, must obviously depend much more heavily on aggregate voting returns to measure and explain levels of political involvement. They therefore tend to focus on national or state-level political events and institutions, rather than on the behavior of individual voters, when explaining variations in voter turnout. By recording the political behavior of voters by name, however, poll books reveal with precision *who* voted in a particular election. They therefore reveal not only the size of the active electorate but also subtle economic, social, and demographic variations in its composition from year to year and from place to place.

The number of American poll-book studies is fast increasing, and a basic poll-book methodology is beginning to emerge. Standing alone, poll books permit the precise reconstruction of the voting histories of specific individuals. More important, when combined with other individual-level records, such as a manuscript census, tax roll, county history, or plat map, they disclose relationships between the demographic, social, and economic characteristics of individual voters and their political behavior. By making such links for all the voters in an election, historians can construct, in effect, a collective biography of an entire electorate. Further, poll books free students of political history from dependence on artificial political units, such as counties, townships, and wards. Once identified and linked to additional sources, the voters in a political unit can be readily reaggregated into a wide variety of socioeconomic groupings based, for example, on age, nativity, occupation, or wealth. Selection of additional variables for study is limited only by the availability of the necessary nominal records.[3]

Because of their obvious flexibility, individual-level voting data therefore encourage new approaches to the historical analysis of voting. They allow, often for the first time, the introduction of political variables into recent models of social behavior that are grounded in analysis of individual-level records, such as the U.S. census. Most important for this study, the records of individual-level voting contained in poll books permit us to link rates of electoral participation directly with patterns of migration. An electorate that appears stable or even stagnant on its surface can often, on closer inspection, come alive with the motion of voters constantly on the move. Poll books permit a microscopic examination of an electorate in motion and suggest that migration, in combination with newly relaxed rules of suffrage for migrants, dominated patterns of political participation in antebellum communities.

Ohio's poll books were compiled on election day as the voters cast their ballots at the polling place. As each voter cast his ballot, one of the three election judges called out his name, and two election clerks each copied his name into a poll book. After the election, the clerks could compare the two poll books to make any necessary corrections and ensure accuracy. Originally, Ohio's poll books contained the names of all voters participating in every election throughout the state, but today the poll books are rare, surviving for only a handful of townships.[4]

Party competition ensured the precision and completeness of Ohio's poll books, even during an age of semiliteracy. Not only party leaders but any voter at an election could challenge any other voter. Once challenged, a voter had to defend publicly his right to cast a ballot. As a public act, voting was therefore subject to intense partisan scrutiny. Further, election clerks were local party leaders, and they therefore made it their business to ensure the accuracy of their poll books, if only to enforce party discipline. Election clerks therefore went out of their way to identify voters and avoid confusion. Clerks sometimes listed the occupations, residences, nationalities, or other personal characteristics of voters who shared common names. One clerk, for example, distinguished between "Philip Smith, Brewer" and "P. Smith (wood sawyer)." Other poll books included "William Cooper (blacksmith)," "John Wilson, Farmer," and "Wm Johnston (Bsmith)." When two John Wilsons voted in 1860, Clinton Township's clerk listed "John Wilson (Town)" and "John Wilson (Hardin Road)." Other voters appeared as "John Duncan (Irishman)," "John Garrard, Dutchman," and "A. J. Green (Blind man)" to ensure proper identification.[5]

Election clerks also made prolific use of middle initials to identify voters, as well as suffixes such as "sr." and "jr." to signify fathers and sons. One clerk, for example, entered John Shaw, 1st, John Shaw, 2d, and John Shaw, 3d, into his poll book. That practice suggests not only an insistence on accuracy but also a general familiarity with voters in the neighborhood. Another clerk ensured accuracy by listing simply "John Murphy (dad)." As a result of such precision, even the most exhaustive investigations of contested elections found little evidence of fraud and few discrepancies in poll books. Under oath, election clerks time and again showed a remarkable command over the names in their poll books. One intensive inquiry that heard over 100 witnesses and produced almost 300 pages of testimony turned up discrepancies in the poll books of only one or two votes per township. At the very least, the number of names in each poll book and the number of ballots cast had to match at the end of election day. The precision of Ohio's poll books prompts confidence in their accuracy as records of voting and, secondarily, facilitates linkage with other records, such as the U.S. census.[6]

This chapter analyzes the behavior of 6,000 voters listed in over 100 poll books from eight Ohio townships. The most logical place to begin a community-level analysis of the impact of migration on voting is Clinton Township, at the center of the Shelby County study area. Clinton is one of the few townships for which the manuscript U.S. census, quadrennial enumerations, and poll books all survive. Further, it is important to trace patterns of voting through a long run of poll books, at least ten years, and Clinton Township meets this requirement. Clinton Township's poll books survive for an entire decade, 1850–60, with the exception of the election of 1859. Ohio held its presidential elections in November, like all the other states, but held elections for state, county, and local officials in October. Clinton Township's poll books record the names of all voters participating in these October elections. The highest offices contested were U.S. representative, in even-numbered years, and governor, in odd years. A close analysis of the township's poll books reveals a complex process of frequent population turnover and confirms the geographical instability of the local electorate.

Clinton Township provides a good illustration of the impact of migration on local political participation. The published U.S. census shows that Clinton Township's population blossomed with the arrival of the railroads during the 1850s, increasing by 50 percent during the decade. As a myriad of migration studies have shown, however, overall population growth is a poor measure of the stability or movement of a community's population. This was certainly true of Clinton Township. Despite the township's impressive growth, most white adult males who lived there in 1850 moved out of the township by 1860. To be more precise, a comparison of the manuscript censuses of 1850 and 1860 shows that only 27 percent of Clinton Township's 1850 residents persisted until 1860. Death, rather than emigration, claimed a number of these men, of course. But after correcting for mortality, persistence in Clinton Township during the 1850s was still only 29 percent. Of the 384 eligible voters living in the township in 1850, only 105 persisted through the decade. Fully 82 percent of the eligible voters living there in 1860 were newcomers. Aggregate census figures are obviously of little help in assessing the stability or instability of a community's population. The manuscript census shows more accurately that while Clinton Township's population was booming, in fact seven out of ten eligible voters were moving away. Each of those emigrants was replaced, in turn, by two new voters.[7]

But because this "column" of arriving and departing voters was continuous, it kept moving through the township between censuses as well. For this reason, the political historian cannot trust even the manuscript census to reveal the entirety of the column's movement. Quadrennial enumerations have already shown that only 43 percent of Clinton Township's eligible voters persisted over four years, with 53 percent leaving the county and only 4 percent moving locally. But a full assessment of the impact of migration on the local electorate depends on poll books, an annual record of actual political participation. Poll books, in fact, reveal the full mobility of Clinton Township's voters. Individual-level voting records confirm at the outset that U.S. census figures, both aggregate and manuscript, do not do justice to the impact of migration on the township's electorate. Previous migration studies suggest that annual turnover in nineteenth-century communities was often much higher than ten-year rates would suggest, and this was true in antebellum Ohio. In fact, three-fifths of Clinton Township's voters appeared in neither the 1850 nor 1860 censuses. The majority of voters, in other words, were migrants who arrived in the township after 1850 and left it again before the end of the decade. The decennial census could not capture such "intercensal" movement. Persistent voters, those appearing in both censuses, were heavily outnumbered by more transient voters moving into and out of the township constantly year after year.[8]

The U.S. census recorded the addition of only 200 new voters to Clinton Township's electorate between 1850 and 1860. But in fact over 800 new voters arrived and departed during the same decade. During a typical year, in fact, 110 voters moved out of Clinton Township, and they were replaced by 130 new voters who moved into the township every year. Yet the U.S. census, capturing only the beginning and the end of this long column of voters, recorded a net increase of just 20 voters per year. So many migrants moved through the township that the 105 eligible voters who resisted the tide of migration and stayed put from 1850 to 1860 represented a mere 7 percent of all of the township's voters.

Table 5.1. *Ten-year rates of turnout in Clinton Township, 1850-60*

Times voting	Number of voters	% of voters
1	667	46.9
2	215	15.2
3	128	9.1
4	80	5.7
5	83	5.9
6	54	3.8
7	48	3.4
8	35	2.4
9	58	4.1
10	45	3.2
	1,413	99.7

Source: Poll books, Shelby County, Ohio, 1850-60.

Most voters did not linger long in Clinton Township, and poll books therefore disclose a continual reshuffling of the local electorate from one election to the next. Only 3.2 percent of Clinton Township's voters turned out in all ten elections between 1850 and 1860. Only one-sixth participated in more than five of the elections, and almost one-half of the township's voters, or 47 percent, cast only one ballot during the decade (Table 5.1). Poll books reveal that the great majority of voters were only short-term participants in the township's elections. As a summary figure, mean turnout represents the average number of elections in which individual voters went to the polls. With Clinton Township's 1,413 voters casting a total of 4,128 ballots in the ten elections, the individual mean turnout was 2.9 elections. The average voter, therefore, participated in only 29 percent of the township's elections during the 1850s. The typical voter, in other words, cast only three ballots in the township before moving on again.[9]

Further analysis, however, lends some detail, and order, to this broad overview of movement through the township. Almost one-half of all voters cast only one ballot in Clinton Township, so they must have played a vital political role in the typical election. The restriction of this analysis to a ten-year period exaggerates the number of one-time voters in the first and last elections in the series of ten, 1850 and 1860. But after correcting for this overcounting, Table 5.2 shows that, on average, one-time voters actually outnumbered ten-time voters in the eight elections from 1851 to 1858. The average election was decided by more one-time than ten-time voters. Less

Table 5.2. *One-time, ten-time, and first-time voters in Clinton Township, 1850-60*

	% one-time	% ten-time	% first-time
1850	(16.3)	13.6	----
1851	11.5	12.0	(40.6)
1852	10.0	12.2	(33.5)
1853	9.9	13.4	20.3
1854	9.7	11.8	25.6
1855	14.5	10.7	28.6
1856	15.8	9.8	29.3
1857	17.6	10.6	31.3
1858	16.2	9.0	23.4
1860	(33.6)	8.7	33.6
Mean, 1851-58	13.2	11.2	
Mean, 1853-60			27.4

Source: Poll books, Shelby County, Ohio, 1850-60.

consistent or transient voters who actually voted only once during the decade represented a substantial proportion of the township's active electorate. Moreover, as the township's population grew, the proportion of one-time voters increased. The number of ten-time voters, of course, remained constant at each of the ten elections, and their proportions therefore dwindled as Clinton Township's electorate grew. Ten-time voters, in short, were increasingly outnumbered by one-time voters with each passing year.

As a result of the constant movement of migrants through the area, first-time voters also played a vital role in deciding elections in Clinton Township. Those voting for the first time in Clinton Township represented more than one-fourth of the participants in the average election. Once again, the restriction of this analysis to ten years inflates the number of first-time voters, this time in the initial election in the series of ten, 1850, as well as in the elections of 1851 and 1852. After 1852, however, the proportion of first-time voters fell below the decade's mean, suggesting that estimates of first-time voting for the following years reflect little, if any, bias. After 1852, an average of 27 percent of voters at each election were voting in the township for the first time (Table 5.2). Many of these first-time voters, of course, never voted in the township again. In fact, fewer than one-half of all first-time voters (47 percent) remained in the active electorate for at least another year. A majority of first-time voters, in other words, became one-time voters in the township.

Only about one in 31 of Clinton Township's voters cast ballots in all ten of the elections during the 1850s. Eighty percent of all voters participated in only five or fewer of the elections. The typical voter cast only three ballots in the township. But the local electorate did display important elements of continuity. One indication of short-term continuity is the fairly high proportion of voters in an election turning out to vote in the following year. In fact, the average electoral persistence of individuals across a pair of elections was 62 percent. Almost two-thirds of all voters in one election voted again the following year. And, as a rule, those who voted in more than one election in the township tended to vote in consecutive years. Long-term discontinuity over an entire decade did conceal a moderate level of continuity over the short run, from year to year. But even this short-term continuity was largely restricted to consecutive elections. Typically, only about one-third of all voters in an election could be found casting ballots even two years hence. As a result, any search for continuity in types of elections, such as congressional or gubernatorial elections (even and odd years), yields even less stability than does a look at consecutive elections.

Of course, the most promising place to look for continuity in the local electorate is not among two- or three-time voters at all but among nine- and ten-time voters. Although they were a small minority, the most persistent voters, by voting more often, lent the most important dimension of stability to the local electorate. Ten-time voters cast ten times as many ballots as one-time voters, nine-time voters nine times as many, and so forth. Focusing on the total number of ballots cast by voters reveals a more uniform distribution of electoral participation when voting consistency is taken into account (Table 5.3). Ten-time voters, for example, represented only 3.2 percent of all voters in Clinton Township but actually cast 10.9 percent of all ballots. One-time voters, on the other hand, representing almost half of the total electorate, cast only one-sixth of all ballots. The inconsistent participation of the majority of voters masked this moderate degree of long-term continuity provided by more persistent voters. Simply by voting in a township more often, persistent voters cast more ballots during the decade. While one- and two-time voters played an exaggerated role in the local electorate over the short run and in single elections, nine- and ten-time voters were more important over the long run and certainly over an entire decade.

Initial analysis of rates of participation by individual Ohio voters during the 1850s presents a clear picture of long-term electoral turnover at the local level. That turnover, however, was tempered by

Table 5.3. *Percent of votes cast by rate of participation in Clinton Township, 1850-60*

Times voting	Number of voters	Number of votes	% of total votes
1	667	667	16.2
2	215	430	10.4
3	128	384	9.3
4	80	320	7.8
5	83	415	10.1
6	54	324	7.8
7	48	336	8.1
8	35	280	6.8
9	58	522	12.6
10	45	450	10.9
	1,413	4,128	100.0

Source: Poll books, Shelby County, Ohio, 1850-60.

moderate continuity in the short run and among a minority of more persistent voters. The vast majority of voters, however, participated in fewer than one-half of all elections, and almost one-half of them voted only once. The typical election found one-time and first-time voters casting a quarter of all ballots. Among the majority of voters, continuity appeared only in the short run, with less frequent voters tending to participate in consecutive elections. A minority of voters also lent stability to the local electorate by participating more consistently over the long run. Still, the majority of voters were migrants who remained politically peripheral. Viewed from this perspective, the local electorate contained a constantly shifting assortment of short-term political participants. The great majority of Clinton Township's voters were only short-term participants in local politics, moving into the township, voting once or twice, and then moving on again. Most voters never developed deep political roots within the community.

Generalization of these patterns of participation from Clinton Township to the rest of Ohio requires poll-book analysis of additional study areas. A second study area is Paint Township, Highland County. Unlike Clinton Township, whose population grew by 50 percent during the 1850s, Paint Township lost population during the decade. Paint Township lay in southern Ohio, a region of generally sluggish economic and population growth. Before the Civil War, Highland County as a whole was still growing but only slowly, by less than 1 percent a year. The county sits squarely in the old Virginia Military District, a region dominated by southern settlers early in Ohio's history. The county was erected two years after statehood, in 1805, and was settled primarily by southerners. As late as 1850, southerners still outnumbered northerners in Paint Township by three to one. As its name implies, Highland County is nestled in the rolling hill country of southern Ohio, on the divide that separates the Miami and Scioto river valleys. As a result of its terrain, which yielded little good farmland, and its situation at the periphery of both valleys, Highland County was slow to attract important routes of transportation. Canals and even turnpikes bypassed the county. Eventually, railroads broke this economic isolation during the 1850s, but population growth still remained sedate.[10]

Paint Township illustrates the hazards of using net population change to estimate rates of migration through a community. Paint Township, which had no towns, was left out of Highland County's new railroad network. Unlike Clinton Township, which was urban and still growing during the 1850s, Paint Township was rural and economically isolated. Its population appeared stable, even stagnant, on the surface, falling by 1.2 percent between 1850 and 1860. And yet almost as many migrants passed through Paint Township as through Clinton Township during the decade. The difference is that most of them were emigrants. Paint Township lost more emigrants but gained many fewer newcomers than Clinton Township did. Persistence in Paint Township between 1850 and 1860 was only slightly higher than that in Clinton Township, 32 percent. Despite its apparent stability, Paint Township lost the majority of its eligible voters during the 1850s, and in 1860 the majority of voters were newcomers.

Table 5.4 shows how Paint Township's electorate could remain essentially stable on its surface for ten years and yet conceal impressive currents of migration. Paint Township started with many more eligible voters than Clinton Township did but failed to grow at all during the decade. Emigration just barely outpaced immigration, and so the township's population fell slightly. And yet two-thirds of all eligible voters had disappeared from the township by 1860, only to be nearly replaced by newcomers. Within this apparently stable population, turnover was broadly similar to that occurring within Clinton Township, but it was somewhat slower. Overall, one-time voters outnumbered ten-time voters, but not by such a wide margin as in Clinton Township. Only one-fifth, as compared to over one-fourth, of all voters in the typical election were voting in the township for the first time. And in Paint Township, ten-time voters out-

Table 5.4. *Rates of participation in eight townships*

	Paint	Ravenna	Clinton	All eight
% population change, 1850-60	- 1.2	32.5	50.0	28.8
% emigration, 1850-60	68.5	56.5	72.6	63.8
% immigration, 1850-60	67.6	88.9	122.7	92.7
Eligible voters, 1850	518	542	384	2,035
Total voters during decade	1,321	1,780	1,413	6,033
Number of ballots cast (% of all voters)				
1	36.0	42.9	46.9	41.4
2	17.9	15.9	15.2	16.1
3	11.4	8.7	9.1	9.9
4	8.2	5.7	5.7	7.0
5	5.0	4.4	5.9	5.3
6	4.4	4.6	3.8	4.6
7	3.9	4.6	3.4	4.0
8	3.0	4.0	2.4	3.6
9	4.1	4.9	4.1	4.3
10	6.2	4.2	3.2	3.9
% first-time voters per election	19.9	21.5	27.4	23.3
% one-time voters per election	8.6	10.6	13.2	10.4
% ten-time voters per election	18.2	13.2	11.2	12.7
Mean turnout per voter	3.4	3.2	2.9	3.2

Sources: Poll books, Highland County, Ohio, 1850-60; poll books, Portage County, Ohio, 1856-66; poll books, Shelby County, Ohio, 1850-60; poll books, Auglaize County, Ohio, 1850-60.

numbered one-time voters in the typical election by a wide margin. Finally, mean turnout in Paint Township was 3.4 elections, as compared to only 2.9 elections in Clinton Township.

Emigration occurred in both Clinton and Paint Townships at roughly the same rate. But immigration into Clinton Township far surpassed immigration into Paint Township. This is why Clinton Township grew so impressively and Paint Township's population remained stable. This is also why Clinton Township experienced more rapid electoral turnover during the 1850s. Not more emigrants from the township but many more immigrants to it produced a larger proportion of first-time and one-time voters and smaller pro-

portions of six- through ten-time voters. And yet population stability in Paint Township concealed patterns of electoral turnover
parallel to but somewhat lower than those occurring in Clinton
Township.

Ravenna Township, Portage County, represents a third study
area. Portage County, which lies in eastern Ohio in the Western
Reserve, was erected in 1807 and settled largely by northeasterners.
The 1820s and 1830s were the decades of greatest growth in eastern
Ohio. Like the rest of the Western Reserve, Portage County benefited from the opening of the Erie Canal, shipping wheat and wool
to Buffalo through the Ohio Canal and Lake Erie. Portage County
received an additional economic boost in 1840 with the opening of
the Pennsylvania and Ohio Canal, which ran through the county
and eastward to Pittsburgh. As in much of eastern Ohio, however,
population growth peaked during the 1840s, and during the following decade Portage County lost more residents to the westward
movement than it attracted, in spite of two new railroads.[11]

Ravenna Township contained the village of Ravenna, Portage
County's seat and population center. Eastern Ohio was the first part
of the state to experience sluggish growth and population decline,
but like Ohio towns and cities in general Ravenna village continued
to grow even in the wake of net emigration from the rest of the area.
Here, as elsewhere, the new railroad network stimulated urban
growth. Ravenna Township violated the regional pattern of population decline by growing a hefty 32 percent during the 1850s. As a
result, Ravenna Township, like Clinton Township, was largely urban and still growing, albeit not as rapidly as more westerly cities
and towns.[12]

Table 5.4 shows that, in most respects, Ravenna Township oc-
cupied an intermediate position between Paint Township, which
did not grow at all during the 1850s, and Clinton Township, which
grew spectacularly. Emigration was lowest in Ravenna Township,
and persistence in the township was an impressive 44 percent. But
immigration into Ravenna Township was intermediate between that
into Paint and Clinton townships. Because immigration generally
controlled rates of growth during the nineteenth century, Ravenna
Township's growth was intermediate as well. As a result, electoral
turnover in Ravenna Township was also intermediate. Ravenna
Township stood squarely in between Paint Township and Clinton
Township in every category of electoral turnover: one-time voters,
ten-time voters, first-time voters per election, one-time voters per
election, ten-time voters per election, and mean turnout per voter.

An interesting feature of Table 5.4 is the apparent relationship between electoral turnover and population increase. None of the townships experienced much electoral stability during the period, but electoral turnover did rise perceptibly with population growth. Clinton Township displayed the greatest population growth as well as the most severe electoral turnover. Ravenna Township's growth was more sedate, and so was turnover within its electorate. Paint Township actually lost population during the 1850s, and its electoral turnover was least of all. Paint Township's experience provides a sort of base rate of electoral turnover, representing levels of turnover within an apparently stable population. High rates of electoral turnover characterized all the sample townships, not only those experiencing rapid population growth. Overall, there was surprisingly little variation in the patterns of electoral participation disclosed by poll books. But electoral turnover and population growth – and, in particular, immigration – were related. Net population growth reflected high levels of immigration, and growth therefore represents a rough index of relative electoral instability. Electorates that grew had more immigrants and so relatively more electoral turnover.

Patterns of voter turnout over a series of ten elections were, in fact, remarkably uniform in the three study areas despite wide differences in population size and in overall population growth and decline. Table 5.4 puts Clinton Township's experience in a broader statewide perspective. Overall, the table suggests that Clinton Township's voters were broadly representative of those elsewhere in Ohio. Movement through all three townships was high during the 1850s, including Paint Township, whose population appeared quite stable on the surface. In all three townships, a majority of eligible voters emigrated or died during the 1850s, and a substantial number of new voters appeared. In each instance, the total number of voters far exceeded the number present at the beginning of the decade, on average by a factor of three. One- and two-time voters represented a majority in each township. Only one in 25 voters participated in all ten elections. At the typical election, first-time voters represented from one-fifth to one-quarter of all voters, and ten-time voters only slightly outnumbered one-time voters. Overall, the average voter participated in just over three elections in the three townships.

High levels of migration, both immigration and emigration, brought a "column" of voters moving through all three study areas. Migration resulted from both immigration into a voting unit and emigration from it, and so even an area whose population seemed stable on the surface could experience the same kinds of turnover found in a rapidly growing region. The final column in Table 5.4 summarizes the movement of voters through eight sample townships – Clinton, Paint, and Ravenna townships and five additional townships. The five additional townships were largely rural and lay in Auglaize County, just north of Shelby County in the Maumee Valley. Intensive analysis of local electorates in four regions of the state suggests that the rates of electoral turnover discussed here were a general phenomenon throughout Ohio during the period.[13]

Overall, immigration into the eight townships outstripped emigration from them, and so, like Ohio as a whole, they grew moderately. As in the individual townships, one- and two-time voters were a majority in the pooled sample. Ten-time voters were a tiny minority, about 4 percent. First-time and one-time voters played an important role in the typical election. Voters cast an average of three ballots in a township during the decade. Finally, the eight townships hosted three times as many voters during the 1850s as simple voting returns might suggest. Figure 5.1 shows graphically the domination of all eight townships by one- and two-time voters.

Poll-book studies of eight townships suggest that Ohio's local electorates were not stable communities of settled voters who turned out consistently year after year. A look beneath aggregate voting returns shows that most voters were migrants and were therefore only short-term participants in their communities' political life. Among individual voters, migration emerges as a dominant influence on patterns of political participation. Further, the relationship between migration and voting holds true across the state, in four of Ohio's five regions – the Miami Valley, the Scioto Valley, the Western Reserve, and the Maumee Valley. The repetition of such a consistent pattern in diverse townships prompts confidence in the projection of this image of electoral turnover throughout Ohio during the 1850s.

But such consistency in these patterns might also suggest that the 1850s were a period of unusual social and economic turmoil. A similar examination of poll books over a longer period might confirm a more traditional picture of electoral stability, one disturbed only by infrequent episodes of disruptive turnover. The following poll-book analysis traces patterns of voter turnout in Clinton Township from 1822 to 1860, and it prompts confidence in the projection of electoral turnover during the 1850s backward over the preceding generation. A more extended poll-book analysis suggests, in other

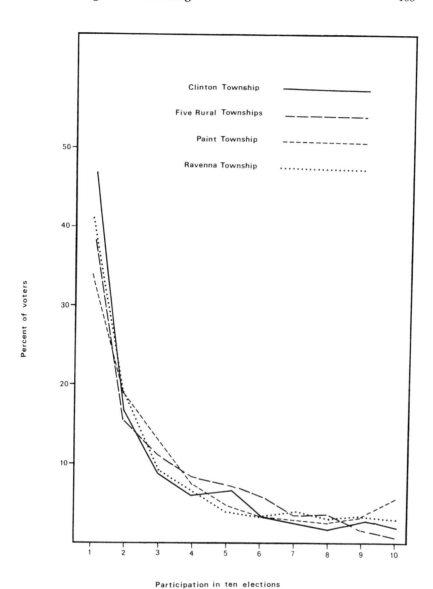

Figure 5.1. Ten-year rates of turnout, all voters in eight townships. *Sources:* Poll books, Shelby County, Ohio, 1850–60; poll books, Auglaize County, Ohio, 1850–60; poll books, Highland County, Ohio, 1850–60; poll books, Portage County, Ohio, 1856–66.

Table 5.5. *Rates of turnout by decade, Clinton Township, 1822-60*

Times voting	1822-31	1830-39	1840-49	1850-60
1	44.0 %	46.8 %	38.6 %	46.9 %
2	14.6	17.0	15.7	15.2
3	11.9	9.9	8.5	9.1
4	9.7	8.9	7.6	5.7
5	4.1	5.7	5.4	5.9
6	3.7	3.1	4.5	3.8
7	3.4	2.4	3.7	3.4
8	4.5	2.1	2.8	2.4
9	2.2	2.8	4.7	4.1
10	1.9	1.3	8.5	3.2
	100.0 %	100.0 %	100.0 %	99.7 %
N	268	707	870	1,413

Source: Poll books, Shelby County, Ohio, 1822-60.

words, that long-term patterns of voter turnout in Clinton Township actually varied little between the township's first election, held in 1822, and the Civil War.[14]

Clinton Township's active electorate expanded from a mere handful of 36 voters, in 1822, to 585 voters in 1860. But long-term patterns of voter turnout in the township stood virtually unchanged during the intervening decades. During the 1850s, almost one-half of the township's voters turned out in only one election, and only 3.2 percent voted in all ten. A similar pattern held true in each of three earlier decades – 1822–31, 1830–39, and 1840–49 (Table 5.5). In each series of ten elections, a large plurality of voters cast only one ballot, and between three-fourths and nine-tenths cast only five or fewer. The levels of electoral turnover disclosed by poll books during the 1850s were in fact typical of Clinton Township from its inception. Turnover in both the active and eligible electorates was the rule and not the exception in Clinton Township throughout the antebellum period. Rapid and frequent turnover within the local electorate characterized not just a single decade but an entire generation. In short, rates of electoral turnover during any given decade appear largely unrelated to the size of the local electorate, stage of development of the township, or party period.

The 1840s did bring a slight trough in electoral turnover in Clinton Township, with one-time voters falling to 39 percent of that decade's electorate and ten-time voters increasing to 8 percent. Analysis of voting in pairs of elections, an important measure of short-term stability, confirms the characterization of the 1840s as a low point in voter turnover. The proportion of voters in one election casting a ballot in the following year climbed steadily from 63 percent during 1822–31 to 65 percent during the 1830s and finally to 72 percent during the 1840s. The index then fell back to 62 percent during the following decade, 1850-60. The high point during the antebellum period came in 1843–44, with four-fifths of all voters of 1843 turning out in 1844. By contrast, the low point occurred in 1854–55, when only one-half of all voters returned to the polls. Examination of one measure of short-term stability therefore points to the mid-1850s as a low point in Clinton Township.[15]

Such a long-term analysis emphasizes the fluidity of the local electorate throughout all stages of a community's history. At no time during its development did Clinton Township enjoy a period of demographic stability in which the majority of voters were long-settled residents. Even during the pioneer period of the township, when all voters could meet within a private home to cast their ballots, most voters were very recent newcomers, and many were through-migrants. During the 1820s, when elections drew an average of only 67 voters, 25 voters would typically leave the electorate before the next election, only to be replaced by 32 new voters every year. Election procedures were more personal within such a small electorate, but migration was nonetheless a political fact of life from the township's very inception.

Table 5.6 translates the decade-by-decade rates of voter turnout displayed in Clinton Township's active electorate into a general pattern of electoral participation over an entire generation. Table 5.6 suggests that we can confidently extrapolate from ten-year rates of turnout to an entire 37-election series, 1822–60. Fully 1,266 of the township's 2,644 antebellum voters, or almost one-half of them, cast only one ballot in the township. Only 15 percent cast two ballots, and over 80 percent participated in only five or fewer of the 37 elections. Overall, the township's 2,644 antebellum voters cast a total of 9,816 ballots for an average rate of participation of only 3.7 elections. Just as one-time voters numerically dominated Clinton Township's electorate over each series of ten elections, so they also dominated the local electorate over an entire generation. The typical voter in Clinton Township participated in fewer than four of the October elections held in the township before the Civil War.

At the other extreme, no one participated in all 37 of the annual elections, but one voter did participate in 34 of them. Still, only .5 percent of voters participated in more than 25 of the elections, and

Table 5.6. *Number of ballots cast, all voters in Clinton Township, 1822-60*

Ballots	N	Voters %	Ballots	N	Voters %
1	1,266	47.9	21	7	
2	406	15.4	22	9	
3	217	8.2	23	9	1.4
4	140	5.3	24	5	
5	114	4.3	25	8	
6	76	2.9	26	6	
7	68	2.6	27	3	
8	41	1.6	28	3	
9	42	1.6	29	0	
10	41	1.6	30	1	
11	32		31	0	0.5
12	25		32	0	
13	24	4.3	33	0	
14	15		34	1	
15	17		35	0	
16	10		36	0	
17	21		37	0	
18	9	2.6			
19	16				
20	12		2,644	100.2%	

Source: Poll books, Shelby County, Ohio, 1822-60.

fewer than 2 percent in more than 20. Throughout the antebellum period, Clinton Township's electorate was dominated by short-term participants, and especially by one- and two-time voters. And those high levels of turnover were remarkably uniform over the 37 elections. They did not reflect sporadic episodes of unusual disorder. They characterized Clinton Township's electorate consistently from its inception in 1822 until the Civil War. Such continuity suggests that temporally and spatially broad demographic processes, such as migration, made a great impact on patterns of participation within Ohio communities.

Who, then, held electoral power in Clinton Township? Viewed over the short run, short-term participants cast the majority of all ballots in individual elections. Throughout the antebellum years, transient voters – through-migrants settled only temporarily in Clinton Township – participated freely in the township's electoral process. One-time voters and first-time voters therefore represented an important proportion of the township's active electorate in any single election. Short-term participants clearly held the balance of local

political power over the short run and did so from the very beginning of the township's political organization.

Over the long run, by contrast, a minority of persistent voters
exercised disproportionate electoral power in the township. Persistent voters were overrepresented at the ballot box even over a
single decade. Certainly over a longer period that overrepresenta-
tion was even more evident, and a small minority of geographical
persisters could provide a core of local political experience and electoral continuity over an entire generation. The .5 percent of Clinton
Township's voters who participated in 26 to 34 elections before the
Civil War, for example, actually cast 3.9 percent of all ballots during
the period. One index of long-term representation – percent of ballots cast divided by percent of voters – therefore stood at 7.8 for
these most persistent and long-lived members of Clinton Township's electorate (3.9% / 0.5%). In other words, a small minority of
self-selecting persisters wielded almost eight times as much electoral
influence over the period as their numbers alone would indicate.

At the other extreme, voters casting five or fewer ballots constituted 81 percent of the township's antebellum electorate but actually cast only 39 percent of all ballots. Their index of representation
therefore stood at only .48 during the period (39% / 81%). The least
persistent participants were underrepresented over the long run by
50 percent. Intermediate rates of electoral persistence produced intermediate levels of long-term representation in the township's elections. The index of representation was 2.1 for voters casting 6 to 10
ballots, 3.4 for those casting 11 to 15, 4.8 for those casting 16 to 20,
and 6.4 for those casting 21 to 25 ballots. Clearly, short-term electoral power belonged to short-term participants, while long-term
electoral influence was one important political reward for geographical persistence. Simply by casting more ballots, the most persistent
voters were overrepresented in the long run. They stood still while a
long "column" of migratory voters filed by.

This movable column contained the majority of voters before the
Civil War and was continuous throughout the antebellum decades.
The most perceptive contemporaries gauged its broadest outlines
and adjusted their political behavior and expectations to minimize
its impact. Undoubtedly, however, most voters simply took the ebb
and flow of the electorate for granted. One wonders, for example,
whether William D. Rodgers and Henry Kenton appreciated their
peculiar political roles in Clinton Township. On October 12, 1858,
Rodgers and Kenton went to the courthouse in Sidney and stood

together at the ballot box to vote. In most respects, Rodgers was a thoroughly typical resident of Sidney. He was 48 years old, a transplanted Pennsylvanian, a merchant of moderate circumstances, and a father of four. Like most long-term residents of Clinton Township, Rodgers held a public office, but only a minor one and for only one term. What set Rodgers apart from the other 500 voters in Clinton Township was his remarkable political longevity. In 1858, Rodgers was voting in his twenty-seventh consecutive election in the township. He cast his first ballot in Clinton Township in 1833 at the age of 21, and he never missed an election for the next three decades. Henry Kenton, by contrast, was a newcomer to Sidney who had never voted in the city before and would never vote there again. Someone challenged Kenton's right to vote, in fact, and so like many newcomers he had to swear to an oath of eligibility before casting his ballot.[16]

Rodgers was a model voter, staying put in one community all of his adult life and never missing an election. Kenton was a migrant, moving through the city between census years and fending off a challenge to cast his only ballot in the township. Yet the two of them stood together at the ballot box: Henry Kenton, the transient, who was a typical voter, and William Rodgers, a model voter and a pillar of the community, who was literally one in a thousand.

6 The core community: migration and leadership

Students of modern political participation have shown clearly that today a host of demographic factors, including education, occupation, income, age, sex, marital status, race, and mobility, play a prominent role in shaping patterns of political involvement.[1] Similarly, patterns of political participation in antebellum communities reflected a wide variety of demographic as well as political processes. The incessant migration of most voters through the community was the most obvious and important demographic influence on participation. But the socioeconomic status, fertility, aging, mortality, and even geography of nineteenth-century electorates also made prominent impressions on rates of participation. Such demographic trends not only affected patterns of voter turnout but also imposed limits on participation at higher levels, such as officeholding.

The Harrod family of Union Township, Auglaize County, provides a good illustration of the political impact of demography on political participation. The Harrods were one of the most politically powerful families in Union Township. Their power arose, however, not from any unusual political skills or partisan connections nor even through their economic position or social status. An important source of the Harrod family's political power was their demographic stability. The population of Union Township, like that of many other Ohio communities, was unsettled. Union Township's electorate grew by 40 percent between 1850 and 1860, but the township still lost one-half of its adult males during the same decade. The township also accepted 167 immigrants as new voters, an immigration rate of 93 percent. Through all this population turnover, however, the Harrod family remained firmly rooted, persisting both in the community and in politics. The 14 Harrods who voted during the 1850s represented just 2 percent of the township's electorate. Yet the Harrods cast fully one-tenth of all ballots over the entire decade. Their assets were in fact almost entirely demographic. The Harrod family was large, most of their men survived the decade, younger Harrods continually came of age in the community, and a majority of them stayed in Union Township. Demographic factors, including fertility, mortality, aging, and especially migration, were enough to concentrate local political power in the hands of this extended family, a tiny minority of the township's voters.[2]

A complete appreciation of the "column" of voters that played such a prominent role within antebellum communities demands a close look at a wide range of demographic as well as political influences on both voting and political leadership. Migration, most prominently, but also fertility, aging, and mortality drove a "column" of voters through the community and awarded exaggerated political influence to the minority of voters who remained settled. Such demographic dimensions of participation joined partisan organization in bringing eligible voters to the ballot box or keeping them away on election day and fitting men for public office. They therefore made a large impact not only on patterns of voting but also on the distribution of local political power. The geographical mobility of most voters constricted the available pool of local leaders and limited the recruitment of officeholders to a select group of long-term persisters. Patterns of migration therefore helped to shape the process of political recruitment as well as strategies of party organization at the local level.

Once again, Clinton Township represents a likely study area in which to examine the impact of demographic factors, such as migration, first on voting and then on officeholding. Rates of population turnover in Clinton Township confirm the general pattern of restless migration that characterized the nineteenth-century United States. To review, aggregate census data reveal that Clinton Township's population increased by 50 percent between 1850 and 1860. But aggregate census data invariably obscure the true extent of geographical mobility among individuals. Examination of the manuscript census confirms that persistence in the township was very low. Only 105 eligible voters persisted through the 1850s, a rate of just 27 percent. Previous migration studies have uncovered ten-year persistence rates ranging widely among various communities during the nineteenth century – anywhere from under 25 percent to over 50 percent. Clinton Township's persistence rate was therefore on the low side but not unusual for the antebellum Midwest.[3]

Although they were indeed low, ten-year rates of persistence in the township hardly begin to explain levels of electoral turnover. Ten-year rates of persistence are the easiest to calculate, which is one reason that they are cited so frequently and are considered a standard measure of persistence and migration. But ten-year rates are also the most deceptive and actually explain little of the population turnover that occurred from year to year within communities. Clinton Township provides a good illustration. The 279 eligible voters who disappeared from Clinton Township's census rolls between 1850 and 1860 help to explain some of the township's electoral drop-off from year to year, but they still account for only 28 voters per year, just one-sixth of all the dropouts. Most dropouts from the local electorate never appeared in the census at all and are therefore not represented in ten-year rates of persistence and migration. The situation is similar among the 471 eligible voters listed for the first time in the 1860 census. They account for some of the first-time voters who were so prominent in Clinton Township's electorate. But they numbered only 47 per year – about one-third of all new voters. Ten-year rates of migration are therefore deceptive, overlooking five-sixths of all dropouts from the electorate and two-thirds of all newcomers.

Previous migration studies demonstrate clearly that annual turnover within any community was usually much higher than ten-year rates would suggest. One of the most important contributions of recent migration studies is their discovery that ten-year rates of population turnover severely underestimate annual rates. In 1970, for example, Stephan Thernstrom and Peter Knights introduced methods for calculating annual rates of persistence and migration from noncensus records. Examining annual records of residence (city directories) in Boston during the 1880s, Thernstrom and Knights uncovered rates of migration approaching 50 percent *every year*. It is now clear that rates of migration calculated from annual records could be up to five times higher than decennial rates alone would suggest. This was certainly true in Clinton Township.[4]

Poll books, as annual records of residence in a voting unit, reflect such higher, and much more accurate, annual rates of population turnover. They reveal, for example, that 60 percent of all voters in Clinton Township came and went without leaving their names in the township's census rolls. Including these intercensal migrants, fewer than 7 percent of the township's adult males persisted from 1850 to 1860. These 846 intercensal migrants actually represented a majority of all the voters in the township. They therefore accounted for most of the turnover within the local electorate from year to year. Keeping in mind these intercensal migrants, voters who did not appear in census records, we can now evaluate the demographic sources of electoral turnover within Clinton Township.[5]

Migration was the most important demographic influence on electoral turnover within Clinton Township, but not the only one. The mortality, fertility, and aging of the local electorate also contributed to electoral turnover. Mortality joined emigration in removing voters from the township. The fertility and aging of the population joined immigration in introducing new voters to the local electorate.

Two demographic processes – emigration and death – continually removed voters from the township's electorate. Overall, four-fifths of all men who voted in Clinton Township sometime during the 1850s left the township or died by 1860. These 1,126 voters disappeared gradually, of course, from one year to the next. Because they were continually replaced by new voters, their departure is not apparent in aggregate voting returns. But in the typical election, well over one-fourth of all voters were casting ballots in Clinton Township for the last time. Because so many of these dropouts never appeared in the township's census rolls, however, it is now impossible to determine precisely who they were and whether emigration or death was the reason for their disappearance. Moreover, because we know nothing about the ages of most of these dropouts, we cannot even form a very good estimate of their expected mortality. By selecting the highest rate of death from available life tables, however, we can draw an upper limit to the incidence of death among these voters. These estimates suggest that no more than 2 percent of all voters at a typical election died within the following year. These deaths could therefore account for no more than 8 percent of all the dropouts, who represented one-quarter of the electorate. Emigration, rather than death, must have drawn away 92 percent of all dropouts from the electorate.[6]

Two additional demographic processes – immigration and political maturation – constantly contributed new voters to the local political system. These 1,317 new voters represented an astounding 93 percent of all participants in the township's elections during the decade. But just as emigrants withdrew from the local electorate gradually and fairly uniformly from year to year, so did these new voters enter it. First-time voters represented over one-fourth of all participants in the typical election. Taken together, then, new voters and imminent dropouts accounted for, on average, about one-half of the voters in every election. They were the primary source of the continual turnover that characterized the local electorate. But because new voters consistently outnumbered dropouts at the polling place, Clinton Township's electorate grew almost every year.

Surprisingly, migrants accounted for almost all of the first-time voters in Clinton Township – 98 percent. Young men coming of age, who represented a second source of new voters, therefore contributed a mere 2 percent of first-time voters. There was a surprisingly small pool of young men in Clinton Township in 1850, only 87 males aged 11 to 20 and due to reach political maturity by 1860. Additionally, persistence among these teenagers was a good deal lower than among the township's adult males – only 17 percent. In fact, just 29 of them ever voted in the township at all, and political maturation therefore made almost no impact on patterns of voter turnout. Political maturation actually brought fewer than three new voters to the polling place during the typical election. Of the 132 new voters who appeared in Clinton Township every year during the 1850s, only three were young persisters who were coming of age. The rest were immigrants.

Quite clearly, patterns of electoral participation in Clinton Township were more the result of external demographic processes – immigration and emigration – than of internal ones. Internal demographic processes, such as the death and aging of settled residents and the fertility of the community, made only a small impression on patterns of participation. Instead, the dramatic growth of the local electorate reflected a healthy surplus of immigrants over emigrants. By the same token, electoral turnover was largely the result of migration, reflecting mostly the passage through the township of transient voters who arrived, voted in one, two, or three elections, and then moved on again. Ninety-two percent of all dropouts were emigrants, and 98 percent of all new voters were immigrants into the township.

In areas experiencing less marked movement, of course, internal demographic factors loomed larger. Paint Township, in Highland County, represents a study area that did not grow at all during the 1850s. Whereas Clinton Township's population grew by 50 percent during the decade, Paint's declined by 1.2 percent, from 518 eligible voters to 512. But the voters of Paint Township displayed a similar mobility, with some minor variations. Apparent population stability concealed the movement of hundreds of voters through Paint Township. In fact, Paint Township's eligible voters behaved much like Clinton Township's. Turnover was only slightly lower. A majority of voters left the township, and a majority were newcomers.

Persistence was a little higher in Paint Township – 32 percent as compared to 27 percent. There were therefore fewer emigrants from Paint Township. About three-fourths of all voters were gone by 1860, as opposed to four-fifths in Clinton Township. Because there were somewhat fewer emigrants from Paint Township, death accounted for a slightly larger proportion of political dropouts, only 8 percent in Clinton but 10 percent in Paint. Still, emigration claimed 90 percent of all dropouts. Overall, therefore, Paint Township's higher rate of persistence meant that the township lost about one-tenth fewer voters during the 1850s.

By far the greatest difference, however, lay in the number of newcomers. Rates of emigration were roughly similar. Paint Township kept only 60 more persisters than Clinton Township did. But rates of immigration diverged sharply, and Paint attracted 500 fewer newcomers than did Clinton Township. This difference in levels of immigration, in fact, accounts for Paint Township's failure to grow. New voters only barely managed to replace political dropouts, and the township's electorate grew very little during the decade. The lower immigration and emigration combined to slow somewhat the passage of migrants through Paint Township. As a result, only 35 percent of all voters were through-migrants, as compared to 60 percent in Clinton Township.

As one consequence of this lower immigration, there were about one-fifth fewer first-time voters in Paint Township. And more of those new voters – about seven times more – were settled residents reaching political maturity. At the beginning of the 1850s, Paint Township had a much more mature population than Clinton Township. The voters of Paint Township were not older but they had more children, and so the township had many more young men aged 11 to 20. Following the pattern of their elders, these young men were also slightly more persistent than the voters of Clinton Township, and so more of them voted during the decade. Overall, immigrants accounted for only about 85 percent of all new voters in Paint Township, as compared to 98 percent in Clinton Township. Young men coming of age represented about 15 percent of all new voters.

Because Paint Township was more isolated than many growing urban areas, such as Clinton and Ravenna townships, which lay on important routes of transportation, through-migration was also comparatively low. Paint lost fewer newcomers than Clinton Township did, and lost a smaller proportion through emigration. Similarly, Paint gained fewer new voters and acquired a smaller proportion of them through immigration. As a result, turnover within the local electorate was much lower during the entire decade and from one election to the next.

Figure 6.1 summarizes this difference in the rate of electoral turnover in the two townships. The figure shows the proportion of all voters in 1855 participating in each of the other elections from 1850

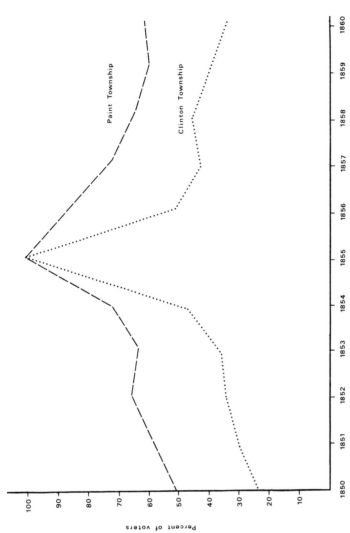

Figure 6.1. Percent of all 1855 voters participating in each election, 1850–60. *Sources*: Poll books, Shelby County, Ohio, 1850–60; poll books, Highland County, Ohio, 1850–60.

to 1860. In Clinton Township, a typical election – in this instance 1855 – attracted many more new voters than did the same election in Paint Township. In fact, a large majority were newcomers. In Paint Township, however, fewer than 30 percent of the 1855 voters were newcomers. Similarly, in Clinton Township a majority of the 1855 voters never voted in the township again. The comparable figure was, again, only about 30 percent in Paint Township. Because of the township's isolation and sedate growth, electoral turnover in Paint Township, although high, was less dramatic.

Figure 6.1 suggests that both townships contained a base population of active voters who remained settled and turned out fairly consistently from year to year. This base population of more persistent voters represented about 50 to 60 percent of the electorate in Paint Township and 30 to 40 percent in Clinton. Each individual election, however, brought out a surge of one-time voters, recent migrants to the township who came to the polls for only one election and were likely never to vote in the township again. These were the one-time and first-time voters who played such an important role in the typical election. The inconsistent participation of the majority of voters in Clinton Township and of a substantial minority of voters in Paint Township therefore concealed a moderate degree of continuity provided by a core of more persistent voters.

Those persistent voters played the most important role in bringing stability to the local electorate. Most voters were short-term residents who moved into the area and out again between censuses, and only a small minority stayed put for at least a decade. A description of this persistent minority is crucial to understanding their political role and to distinguishing them from the majority of migratory voters. Social historians have thoroughly analyzed patterns of migration during the nineteenth century, examining differences between persisters and migrants. The same conclusions that they have drawn from their work can therefore come to the aid of political historians.

Previous migration studies indicate clearly that patterns of migration in the past were seldom random. Most social historians agree about the kinds of people who were most likely to move. During the nineteenth century, geographical persistence was a privilege that few could afford. Those highest on the socioeconomic ladder could put down roots wherever they chose. But the less fortunate – and they were the majority – seized economic security wherever they could find it. Many Americans never found economic security and simply kept moving. Nineteenth-century migration therefore mir-

rored, for the most part, an often endless search for economic opportunity. Here, social historians have found a pattern within the
apparent disorder of migration. Among measurable personal characteristics, age, occupation, wealth, and sometimes birthplace distinguished those who stayed from those who moved.[7]

Social historians now routinely analyze rates of migration within
the communities they study and use them as an important interpre-
tive framework in which to arrange more subtle details of nineteenth-century social life. Political historians who have become familiar with those same patterns of migration can call on them to help
analyze nineteenth-century political life as well. At first glance,
Ohio's local electorates might seem a hopeless jumble of footloose
transients, a chaotic and temporary "gathering of strangers."[8] But
historians can rather readily make sense of that electorate and find
hidden patterns within the apparent disorder. Patterns of migration
favored the persistence of the most highly skilled and economically
favored voters. As a result, persisters commanded precisely the
kinds of resources and organization they needed to dominate their
communities' political life. Persisters were an unrepresentative but
economically, socially, and politically favored minority.

Intensive examination of the 1,701 eligible voters who lived in
Clinton Township sometime during the 1850s illustrates the exaggerated political influence of the minority of voters who stayed behind. Table 6.1 focuses on all 384 eligible voters who lived in Clinton
Township in 1850 and separates persisters from nonpersisters. Clinton Township's voters confirm the broadest conclusions of previous
migration studies. Overall, persisters were wealthier and more occupationally skilled than nonpersisters. Among adult men who
owned any real property at all in 1850, persisters were overrepresented and nonpersisters underrepresented in every category of
wealthholding. Overall, 62 percent of persisters owned real property in 1850, but only 38 percent of nonpersisters did so. This difference between persisters and nonpersisters was most dramatic at the
highest level of wealthholding, possession of $3000 or more real
property. Nonpersisters were overrepresented in only one category
of wealthholding, propertylessness. In 1850, persisters held 60 percent more real property, on average, than did nonpersisters. In fact,
only 12 percent of all nonpersisters held as much real wealth as did
the typical persister.

Occupationally, merchants and professionals were most heavily
overrepresented among persisters. The persistence of artisans and
farmers was generally intermediate, and they were represented fair-

Table 6.1. *Social characteristics, 1850, of persisters and nonpersisters in Clinton Township*

	Persisters	Nonpersisters	All adult males
Occupation[a]			
None	5.8 %	20.9 %	17.0 %
Artisan	39.4	35.4	36.4
Merchant/professional	34.6	18.5	22.7
Farmer	16.3	17.5	17.2
Laborer	3.8	7.7	6.7
Wealth[a]			
$0	38.5 %	62.0 %	55.9 %
$1-999	19.2	13.8	15.2
$1000-1999	18.3	10.4	12.5
$2000-2999	6.7	4.0	4.7
$3000+	17.3	9.8	11.7
Mean wealth	$1,612.10	$1,003.20	$1,162.10
Age[a]			
11-20 years	12.6 %	20.5 %	18.5 %
21-29	24.4	24.7	24.6
30-39	26.1	19.6	21.2
40-49	26.1	17.9	20.0
50-59	5.9	12.2	10.6
60+	5.0	5.1	5.1
Mean age (years)	37.3	38.5	38.2
Nativity			
Ohio	35.6 %	35.4 %	35.4 %
Northeast	36.5	33.3	34.2
South	11.5	16.5	15.2
Europe	16.3	14.8	15.2
Residence			
Urban	79.8 %	69.7 %	72.3 %
Rural	20.2	30.3	27.7

[a]Significant difference between persisters and nonpersisters at .05 level.
Source: Manuscript U.S. census of population, Shelby County, Ohio, 1850 and 1860.

ly equally among persisters and nonpersisters. Laborers and the unemployed, by contrast, were heavily underrepresented. Persisters therefore tended to enjoy status as a merchant or a professional and ownership of valuable property. Nonpersisters, who were more often laborers or unemployed, held property of less value.

Age also distinguished persisters from nonpersisters. Table 6.1 suggests that persisters were, on average, slightly younger than those who moved on. Breaking eligible voters down into age cohorts and correcting for mortality, however, tells another story. Age and persistence were strongly related. Men between 30 and 49, the most numerous age cohort, were overrepresented among persisters. Men 40 to 49 at the beginning of the decade persisted most often, at the rate of 43 percent. Men 30 to 39 persisted at a lower rate, only 29 percent. But younger men persisted even less often. Men who were 21 to 29 at the beginning of the decade stayed in Clinton Township at the rate of only 18 percent. Similarly, young men between 11 and 20 in 1850, who might be expected to come of age in the township and represent new voters, persisted at the lowest rate of all. Only 15 of them, or 17 percent, persisted through the decade. Older men also persisted less often than men in their middle years. Eligible voters 50 and older, like men in their twenties, persisted at the rate of only 18 percent. Age joined occupation and wealth in helping to distinguish migrants from nonmigrants. Among all five socioeconomic characteristics – occupation, wealth, residence, age, and nativity – age, occupation and wealth showed significant differences between persisters and nonpersisters. Residence and nativity, by contrast, were not significantly related to geographical persistence.[9]

Among measurable personal characteristics, only occupation, wealth, and age show a direct, statistically significant relationship with persistence. The bivariate relationships presented in Table 6.1, however, cannot reveal indirect relationships between persistence and the other variables, residence and nativity. Nor can such a bivariate analysis show hidden interactions among the various socioeconomic characteristics that might have influenced the decision to stay in Clinton Township or leave. Residence and nativity, in other words, might prove to have affected persistence by acting indirectly through occupation, wealth, or age. Similarly, the apparent relationship of persistence with occupation, wealth, and age might actually reflect the dominance of only one of the variables, with the other two acting through it only indirectly.[10]

A multivariate analysis of persistence would reveal both direct relationships between personal characteristics and persistence as well as indirect relationships among all six variables. Log-linear contingency table analysis provides such a multivariate test of direct and indirect relationships among categorical variables. Log-linear analysis, in effect, tests the independence of variables arranged in all possible combinations. Such an analysis would reveal the indirect influence of residence and nativity on persistence, if any, as well as the influence of the remaining three variables – occupation, wealth, and age – upon one another.[11]

An initial log-linear analysis of the sources of persistence and migration in Clinton Township shows, not surprisingly, that all six variables – persistence, occupation, wealth, age, residence, and nativity – were very closely related, both directly and indirectly. Persistence was, most basically, the result of all the other variables acting together in one degree or another. But of all the measurable personal characteristics of Clinton Township's electorate, occupation alone shows a direct relationship with persistence. Wealth and age therefore lose prominence in a multivariate analysis and represent only indirect influences on persistence, acting through occupation. Residence and nativity, however, gain explanatory power as indirect sources of persistence and migration, because they also acted indirectly through occupation, wealth, and age. But occupation exerted the only direct influence on the decision to leave Clinton Township or to stay. Wealth and age acted indirectly through occupation, and residence and nativity made an even less direct impact on persistence. Log-linear analysis reinforces the earlier portrait of persisters as a generally exclusive minority of voters whose economic standing, and especially their occupational skills, set them apart from the majority of voters, who were migrants.[12]

Simply by persisting, this rather atypical minority of older, wealthier, and more occupationally skilled voters wielded unusual political power. Most obviously, because they lived in the township longer than the nonpersisters, they were overrepresented at the ballot box. Although persisters represented only 7 percent of all voters during the 1850s, they actually cast one-fifth of all ballots. Only two of the persisters failed to vote in at least one of the elections, and only one-tenth of them voted in fewer than five. At the other extreme, almost one-third of the persisters voted in all ten years, with about 60 percent casting at least nine ballots during the decade. The pattern of participation among geographical persisters was just the opposite of that of the electorate as a whole. Persisters were overrepresented at the ballot box and therefore enjoyed an exaggerated voice in local affairs.

Persisters were also overrepresented at a higher level of political involvement, in the holding of public office. In fact, their influence was even more exaggerated in public office than at the ballot box. The idea of a small "core" of economic elites controlling political life as well as economic affairs is traditional in the analysis of nineteenth-century communities. Beginning with the earliest quantitative community studies, collective biography has invariably disclosed a small elite of economic leaders dominating political office in nineteenth-century cities and towns. Historians continue to disagree heatedly over the precise composition of the ruling elite, over the sources of their power, and over the proper methodology for measuring their influence. But all of them acknowledge the concentration of community power in the hands of a small minority, usually representatives of the economic interests prevailing in a particular time and place. Community power in the nineteenth century, as in the twentieth, lay in the hands of a small core of active civic leaders.[13] Historians have only recently begun, however, to attribute the exaggerated power of such "core leaders" to their unusual persistence, drawing on the insights of modern migration studies to view persistence itself as a rare and valuable political resource.[14]

Population turnover within antebellum communities imposed severe demographic limits on opportunities for political leadership and partisan recruitment. Historians have traditionally recognized a number of demographic limits on political advancement during the nineteenth century, including age, occupation, wealth, ethnicity, and religious background. Such demographic dimensions of participation joined partisan considerations in fitting some men for public office and positions of party leadership and excluding others. It is now clear that an additional demographic constraint, the dynamics of population turnover, also limited the local pool of available political leaders. An examination of community leaders that places their experiences within a broader demographic context, one that considers the geographical mobility of the nineteenth-century electorate, helps to illuminate additional demographic foundations of political organization. Persisters acted not only as a social and economic elite but as a political elite as well. Persistence afforded the most wealthy and occupationally skilled voters an exaggerated voice at the ballot box, and political office was just as assuredly the preserve of persisters.[15]

Again, Clinton Township's experience confirms the general pattern. There were three levels of local government in Shelby County – county, township, and (in Sidney) city government. There were nine offices at the county level, ranging from county commissioner and sheriff to surveyor and probate judge. Quite predictably, Clinton Township, as the county's seat of government and largest settlement, was overrepresented in county office. Although it was only one of 14 townships, Clinton provided Shelby County with over one-half of its officeholders during the 1850s. Government at the township level consisted of five offices – a justice of the peace, three trustees, a clerk, a treasurer, and an assessor. The city of Sidney was also overrepresented in township government, providing Clinton Township with almost all of its officials. City government consisted of four officials – mayor, clerk, treasurer, and marshal – and a five-member city council.[16]

Just as there was a rapid turnover of both residents and voters in Clinton Township during the 1850s, so was there a frequent turnover among officeholders. Ninety-five men held local office during the decade, filling the available seats for a mean of just less than two years each. All local offices were contested annually, but rotation in office was most frequent at the lower levels. City officials served, on average, only 1.6 years each during the decade. Mean tenure in township offices was slightly higher – 2.1 years – and the average county official served even longer, 2.5 years. Mean tenure increased with each level of local government, but even the average county office was filled by four men during the decade.

Because they belonged to a small core of economically powerful persisters, however, officeholders were not very representative of the electorate. Table 6.2 considers all the men who persisted in Clinton Township from 1850 to 1860 and distinguishes between officeholders and nonofficeholders. Just as merchants and professionals persisted in the township at a higher rate than average, so were they heavily overrepresented in political office as well. In fact, 62 percent of all officeholders were merchants and professionals. Only these occupational groups were overrepresented in political office. In particular, farmers, laborers, and the unemployed were most heavily underrepresented. Not a single laborer, in fact, held public office during the 1850s.

Wealth also distinguished officeholders from nonofficeholders. Among all persisters who held any property at all, officeholders were overrepresented in every category of wealthholding. Nonofficeholders were overrepresented only among the propertyless. Further, officeholders came most frequently from the highest levels of wealthholding in the township, and almost one-third of them owned real property valued at $3000 or more. In fact, officeholders held almost twice as much real property, on average, as did nonofficeholders. Economically, persisters were not very representative of all voters in the township, and officeholders were not very representative of all persisters. They were an elite within an elite, holding 38 percent more wealth than even the typical persister.

Table 6.2. *Social characteristics, 1850, of persisters and officeholders in Clinton Township*

	Officeholders	Nonofficeholders	All persisters
Occupation[a]			
None	3.4 %	6.7 %	5.8 %
Artisan	31.0	42.7	39.4
Merchant/professional	62.1	24.0	34.6
Farmer	3.4	21.3	16.3
Laborer	0	5.3	3.8
Wealth[a]			
$0	17.2 %	46.7 %	38.5 %
$1-999	20.7	18.7	19.2
$1000-1999	20.7	17.3	18.3
$2000-2999	10.3	5.3	6.7
$3000+	31.0	12.0	17.3
Mean wealth	$2,216.84	$1,162.62	$1,612.10
Residence[a]			
Urban	96.6 %	73.3 %	79.8 %
Rural	3.4	26.7	20.2
Age			
21-29 years	20.7 %	30.7 %	27.9 %
30-39	34.5	28.0	29.8
40-49	44.8	24.0	29.8
50-59	0	9.3	6.7
60+	0	8.0	38.2
Mean age (years)	42.0	37.3	38.2
Nativity			
Ohio	31.0 %	37.3 %	35.6 %
Northeast	44.8	33.3	36.5
South	13.8	10.7	11.5
Europe	10.3	18.7	16.3

[a]Significant difference between officeholders and nonofficeholders at .05 level.
Sources: Manuscript U.S. census of population, Shelby County, Ohio, 1850 and 1860; *Combination Atlas Map of Shelby County, Ohio,* 12; *History of Shelby County, Ohio,* 346, 349.

One other measurable personal characteristic – residence – distinguished officeholders from nonofficeholders. Urban or rural residence did not affect persistence within the electorate as a whole, but residence did affect access to political office among persisters. Four-fifths of all persisters lived in the city of Sidney during the 1850s, but almost all officeholders hailed from the city. Only four of the persistent officeholders, in fact, lived in rural Clinton Township. The county seat dominated the highest levels of political participation and leadership in the township. Among the five socioeconomic characteristics of persisters – occupation, wealth, residence, age, and nativity – only occupation, wealth, and residence showed significant differences between officeholders and nonofficeholders.[17]

Among persisters, officeholding was unrelated to age and nativity. Not surprisingly, men between 30 and 49 years of age dominated public office, and especially men in their forties. The typical officeholder, in fact, was 42 years old. Men younger than 30 or older than 49 were slightly underrepresented in office, and in fact no one 50 or older managed to win elective office. These older men, however, belonged to the least numerous age cohort to begin with. Northeasterners and southerners were also slightly overrepresented in office, while Ohio natives and European immigrants were underrepresented. These differences of age and nativity, however, were not statistically significant. By themselves, youth and foreign birth did not preclude election to political office in Clinton Township.

A log-linear analysis confirms the relationship of officeholding with occupation and residence. Controlling for all the other variables, only occupation and urban versus rural residence show a direct relationship with officeholding. Wealth recedes as a source of election to public office, exerting an influence on officeholding only indirectly through occupation. Similarly, age and nativity show only indirect relationships with officeholding, also acting through occupation. Occupation and residence exerted the most important influence on election to office. Officeholding, occupation, and residence, in fact, were all directly interrelated. Wealth, age, and nativity affected officeholding only indirectly, through occupation. Among persisters, officeholders were distinguished primarily by their status as merchants and professionals and their residence in Sidney. They were distinguished only secondarily by their wealth, age, and nativity, and these personal characteristics were all reflected indirectly in officeholders' occupations. Clinton Township's leaders represented an economic, and especially occupational, elite that was firmly entrenched within the county seat.[18]

There were many local political offices open to residents of Clinton Township, about one for every 20 adult males in 1850. Turnover in office was high, giving the township's voters an even greater opportunity to participate in politics at a higher level. But political office belonged, in general, to the very wealthy and especially to those wealthy merchants and professionals who were persisters. Ninety-five men held elective office in Clinton Township, at the city, township, county, or state levels, during the 1850s. The 105 eligible voters who persisted from 1850 to 1860 represented just 7 percent of the township's voters during the decade, but they supplied more than two-fifths of all officeholders. Surprisingly, three out of every ten persisters held an elective office during the 1850s. Nonpersisters, men who were present in 1850 but not in 1860, were also overrepresented in office. They made up about one-sixth of the electorate but accounted for one-third of all officeholders. Together, men who were residents of Clinton Township at the beginning of the decade represented fewer than one-fourth of all voters but held three-fourths of all political offices during the 1850s.

At the other extreme, newcomers to the township's electorate were underrepresented in office. Newcomers represented about three-fourths of all voters during the 1850s but held only one-fourth of all offices. Through-migrants, voters who came and went sometime during the decade, suffered the most severe political disabilities. Through-migrants represented over one-half of the eligible electorate but held only one-seventh of all offices. Only ten of the through-migrants, in fact, out of a pool of 1,300, held an elective office while living in Clinton Township. Persistence was, in practice, an important qualification for public office. About one-third of all persisters held office during the 1850s, but only one-tenth of nonpersisters did so. Despite their numbers, just over 1 percent of new voters held office. Finally, a negligible proportion of through-migrants managed to do so. They were effectively barred from leadership roles by their transience, which not only put them at a legal disadvantage but also denied them the political experience and expertise, the familiarity with their community, the partisan contacts, the reputation, and the social and economic position demanded of successful political leaders.

Despite their numbers, the 1,300 newcomers who voted in Clinton Township after 1850 made little impression on the local structure of power. For the most part, power remained the preserve of persisters, who were heavily overrepresented in political office. In the face of widespread migration and impressive growth, the township's persisters maintained stability by ensuring that, as long-term residents, political leaders would typically come from the most stable and secure economic and social circles. Further, the few new voters who did manage to attain office during the 1850s were even more economically successful than even the typical persister. The eight officeholders who appeared in the 1860 census for the first time possessed more than twice as much real wealth as the typical persister and even 75 percent more than the typical officeholder. They were, to a man, either substantial farmers or wealthy merchants and professionals. Newcomers to Clinton Township had to win overwhelming social and economic acceptance in their new community before attaining public office. Real political power belonged to the small minority of voters who enjoyed both economic success and persistence. Persistence and officeholding were both socially and economically exclusive. But political office, unlike voting, did not come automatically with persistence. Political leadership required even more stringent personal qualifications.[19]

Newcomers have always faced such political disadvantages, of course, and the liabilities of late arrival are a political fact of life. But social historians' recent revelation that migrants were quite often a majority in nineteenth-century communities puts that political fact of life in new perspective. Political recruitment focused on a surprisingly small pool of potential leaders. When newcomers voted in Clinton Township, they cast most of their ballots from necessity for old residents and not for one another. In practice, long residence went hand in hand with public preferment and political experience in qualifying men for office. In the midst of so many migrants, persistence was an important, because rare, political asset. Persistence fitted only a relative handful of men for leadership roles within their communities.

Patterns of officeholding join the variations in voter turnout disclosed by poll books to suggest a core model of local political participation. Routine geographical mobility lent fluidity to the local electorate, limiting frequent migrants to only short-term political participation as both voters and officeholders. Patterns of migration favored the persistence of selected social groups. In general, the more wealthy and the occupationally skilled persisted longer. They therefore participated more frequently in elections and dominated political office. A select minority of voters, a "core community," was consistently overrepresented both in office and at the ballot box. The core community was a small, relatively stable group of economically successful persisters who were active in politics. Table 6.3 presents the outlines of Clinton Township's core community. The members of the core community were more geographically persistent than peripheral voters, and they stood higher on their township's socioeconomic ladder. The members of the core community were also distinguished by their consistent participation in elections, and hence these "core voters" were overrepresented at the polls. Table 6.3 reveals also that within the core of persistent voters there was an

Table 6.3. *Clinton Township's core community: Mean rate of turnout by social groups, 1850-60, percent*

Officeholders	89.0
Persisters	
Age 35-44	87.4
$5,000+	86.5
Merchants, artisans, and professionals	84.7
All persisters	78.7
Other age groups	77.0
$0-4999	76.0
Farmers and laborers	71.7
Nonpersisters	65.7
Mean, all voters	70.0

Sources: Poll books, Shelby County, Ohio, 1850-60; manuscript U.S. census of population, Shelby County, Ohio, 1850 and 1860.

additional hierarchy of electoral participation. At the center of the core were officeholders, who turned out for elections at the greatest rate of any identifiable social group, 89 percent. Geographical persisters turned out at an overall rate of 79 percent, and among the persisters men in their middle years, the more wealthy, and the merchants, professionals, and artisans turned out most frequently. Outside of the core were the majority of voters, participating in elections at an average rate of only 66 percent.

I have identified such stable cores of persistent and politically active voters in nine additional communities in three midwestern states. Simply because of the dynamics of migration that drew away the majority of voters over any given decade and continually replaced them with new voters, every midwestern community I have examined contained such a stable and unrepresentative core community. The core community consisted of the "permanent residents" of a city or town, long-time residents who were also long-term participants in local politics. Through their very persistence, the members of the core community were consistently overrepresented at the ballot box. Through their domination of political office, the core community could, to a large degree, control political decision making within their communities. As "town fathers," old families, "county barons," substantial merchants, or a "courthouse clique," the core community could even control the local political process itself. Overall, their continuing presence in the community in the midst of so many migrants enhanced their own political power, and it simultaneously tempered the impact of migration on local politics. With a core community of wealthy, occupationally skilled, middle-aged, politically active persisters controlling local affairs, newcomers – whatever their numbers – could make little impact on local political life. Such a core community fostered political continuity, provided crucial political leadership, and represented one important foundation of order in a community routinely experiencing migration.[20]

Within a mobile electorate, equal suffrage, even for white adult males, was an ideal that rarely found full expression. Divergent patterns of migration, grounded in age, wealth, and occupation, produced unequal opportunities for participation in antebellum Ohio. In the midst of both local and long-distance migration, a small core of persisters was consistently overrepresented at the ballot box. Patterns of migration favored the persistence of merchants, artisans, and professionals. Persistence, material success, and long-term participation in local politics were, in general, synonymous. Migration put newcomers and transients, already at an economic disadvantage, at a political disadvantage as well. Frequent migration afforded, in the long run, a self-selecting minority of voters a disproportionate voice in the conduct of local political affairs. Historians who study the leaders of midwestern communities have always understood that they were frequently unrepresentative – politically, economically, and socially – of the cities and towns that they governed. Only recently have historians focused on persistence as one of the sources of these local leaders' success and of their influence.

The social historian Thomas Bender summed up the conclusions of two decades of persistence studies by observing that nineteenth-century communities contained "two populations," a core of powerful persisters and a periphery of largely powerless transients. "There were apparently two populations in nineteenth-century towns," Bender observed, "an economically successful permanent group who shaped the values and direction of social life in the town, and a floating, largely unsuccessful group." What was true of local society was true of local political life as well. In a strikingly similar observation, an Ohio Supreme Court justice noted the same phenomenon during the 1850s. Frederick Grimké, brother of the famous Grimké sisters of South Carolina, was an associate justice of the Ohio Supreme Court for thirteen years. Grimké drew on his familiarity with politics in both northern and southern towns to paint a remarkably astute portrait of a stable core at the heart of the antebellum community:

> Anyone who has lived in any town in the United States long enough to make an accurate observation of the structure of society and the dispositions of the people who inhabit it must have noticed that there is a constant tendency towards what may be called the supremacy or precedence of certain individuals or families. These will, perhaps, be composed of old residents, of the merchants, of professional men, etc.

This was, and is, a commonly held view of nineteenth-century society and politics. What contemporaries did not realize, or at least articulate, is that, in addition to political and economic factors, demographic trends – the fertility, aging, mortality, and especially the migration of voters – went far in determining the size and composition of this powerful core community.[21]

According to any strict definition of "community," the migrants who participated only temporarily in their townships' political affairs were indeed members of their new communities. But surely they did not experience the same richness and intensity of social, cultural, economic, and emotional ties enjoyed by the members of the core community.[22] Demographic characteristics – most obviously their mobility but also their age, occupation, and economic standing – kept them from participating fully in their community's political life. Formal and informal political qualifications that were broadly demographic put many potential voters and officeholders at a political disadvantage and restricted both the formal and informal boundaries of the active electorate. Demographic constraints became political constraints as well, acting formally through suffrage and officeholding qualifications and informally through the give and take of politics.

Some demographic qualifications, although wholly unintended, could yet be profound. Geographical distance from the polling place is an example of one such demographic hurdle to participation. Ohio's law requiring townships to establish only one polling place when practicable, "as nearly central to the inhabitants as circumstances and conveniences will admit," was well intended. It was designed to bring all the voters of a township together on election day and to make the election, in the words of the minority in *Lehman v. McBride*, a "meeting of the electors, residing within defined limits, for the *joint* performance of a high public duty." This venerable holdover from the New England town, however, inadvertently

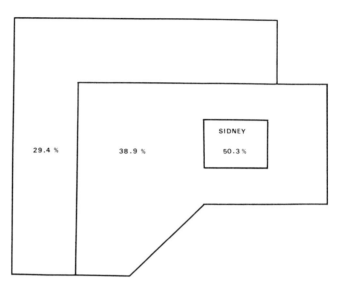

Figure 6.2. Rates of turnout in two elections, 1858 and 1860, by distance from the polling place, Clinton Township. *Sources:* Poll books, Shelby County, Ohio, 1858 and 1860; plat book, Shelby County, Ohio, 1859.

transformed the distance of voters' homes from the polling place into one more demographic barrier to equal participation.[23]

Reliance on one polling place put residents of a township's borders at a distinct political disadvantage. In Clinton Township, for example, voters in Sidney turned out in a pair of elections, 1858 and 1860, at the rate of 50 percent (Figure 6.2). But participation in those two elections faded with distance from Sidney. Eligible voters in a surrounding ring one to two miles from the polling place turned out at a much lower rate, only 39 percent. The residents of a still more distant area of the township, two to three miles from Sidney, turned out at the lowest rate of all, only 29 percent. These differences in rates of turnout were not related to the social or economic status of rural voters and did not reflect a political difference between farmers and nonfarmers. They reflected only geographical distance from the polling place. In fact, this same "distance decay," as geographers term this phenomenon, could also occur in an entirely rural township. Voters living in the center of Rootstown Township, Portage County, turned out in the same pair of elections, 1858 and 1860, at the rate of 56 percent. Just as in Clinton Township, however, participation faded with distance from the polling place (Figure 6.3).

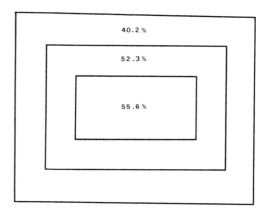

Figure 6.3. Rates of turnout in two elections, 1858 and 1860, by distance from the polling place, Rootstown Township. *Sources:* Poll books, Portage County, Ohio, 1858 and 1860; plat book, Portage County, Ohio, 1859.

Voters could literally get lost on their way to the ballot box. In 1846, for example, Hiram Peppard of Wayne County recalled that on election day he and a friend left work at noon to go to vote, but they "got lost and went out of the way, I suppose, a mile."[24]

Geography therefore joined age, fertility, mortality, and migration as a demographic influence on local political participation. Demographic constraints on voting and officeholding, including migration, joined legal qualifications and political considerations in drawing the boundaries of local political life. Acting both formally and informally, they helped to concentrate power within the hands of a core of geographically persistent local leaders.

7   Migration and local politics: an antebellum election

On October 13, 1846, the voters of Wayne Senatorial District elected a state senator by just one vote, 2,441 to 2,440. The incumbent and loser, a Whig, immediately questioned the validity of the election returns. His apparent defeat gave the minority Democrats a tie in the Ohio Senate and thus a veto over changes in Ohio's banking policy, the issue that had divided parties and dominated the state's politics for a decade. Given the narrow margin of defeat and the stakes involved in the election, the contest was almost inevitable. The Whig challenge to the Democratic victory began, in fact, the moment the county clerk finished tabulating the official returns. Election challenges were frequent during this period, and the Whig organization was quite prepared to launch a contest. But the Whig candidate, Levi Cox, was initially reluctant to challenge the election returns. An impromptu Whig meeting coalesced at Howard's Tavern in the United States Hall in Wooster, the Wayne County seat, and throughout the night local Whigs wandered in off the city's streets to debate their course of action.[1]

During the meeting, as many as 20 of Cox's supporters pressed him to contest the election. His supporters were mostly Whigs, but there was also a sprinkling of "soft" Democrats, who sided with Whigs on the banking issue and favored the legalization of banknotes or "soft" money. Cox had already received several letters from Columbus and elsewhere urging him to break the tie in the Senate by winning back his seat. Yet Cox was quite hesitant, torn between party loyalty and a sense of personal honor. Cox confided later that he did not want to keep his seat unless he had a "clear and decided majority of all the votes given." In the end, Cox gave in to the demands of party and issued a challenge to the winner of the election, Joseph Willford, a hard Democrat.[2]

Cox's challenge provoked one of the most heated election contests in Ohio history. The Wayne County dispute took a full year to run its course, and in a rare move the Ohio Senate ordered the complete record of the contest to be read into their published journal. The result is a 272-page verbatim transcript of the sworn testimony of 115 participants in the Wayne County election of October 13, 1846.

132

During six weeks in November and December 1846, two justices of the peace presided over an inquiry into the conduct of the senatorial election. Meeting in Wooster, the contestor and the contestee, along with their attorneys, heard the depositions of the 115 witnesses and then questioned them at length. The transcript, which is complete, stands as a remarkable record of political and social life within a single Ohio county during the late 1840s. The transcript records over 1,500 questions and answers that focus on the election but also touch on a wide variety of political and social activities, including the migration histories of many of the voters in Wayne County. The Wayne County testimony permits a detailed reconstruction of the way elections were conducted in antebellum Ohio, the way election laws that focused on residence permitted election judges to interrogate migratory voters before accepting their ballots, and the ways in which parties used election laws that dealt with migration as a crucial part of their political strategies. Cox's carefully prepared election challenge, as a detailed portrait of local political organization, necessarily laid bare a wide range of subtle interrelationships between migration and electoral politics.[3]

Historians have long recognized the various ideological, ethnic, and economic dimensions of antebellum politics that emerged in the form of issues and organizations to help decide elections. Those same ideological, ethnic, and economic dimensions of politics went very far to decide elections in Wayne County, Ohio, just as they did elsewhere. But the interaction between migrants and persisters represented still another dimension of antebellum political life. Events in Wayne County highlight hidden subtleties of political organization in the midst of incessant migration. The mobility of nineteenth-century voters continually posed problems for both migrants and persisters. Migrants and persisters alike tried to use election laws to their own best advantage. On election day, migrants sought enfranchisement, full political acceptance into their new communities. Persisters, as members of the powerful core community, faced continual challenges to their political authority in the wake of a stream of newcomers and transients. As election judges and settled voters, persisters had the legal authority and the political incentive to court and, by the same token, to challenge newcomers to their voting units. Indeed, the results of an election in any Ohio township largely reflected the success of such a local core community, whether Whig or Democratic, at managing such challenges and screening new voters for political acceptability.

In 1846, Wayne County was a likely location for such a bitterly

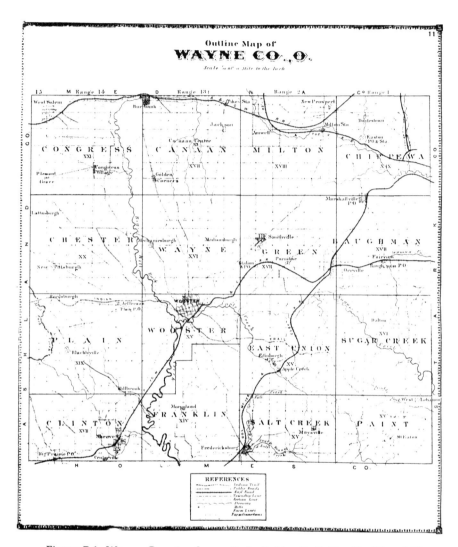

Figure 7.1. Wayne County. *Source:* J. A. Caldwell, *Caldwell's Atlas of Wayne County*, 11.

contested election, because it was a traditional focus of the banking issue that had dominated Ohio politics for a decade. Further, the county shared in many of the economic and social changes that were transforming the region. Wayne County is located in northeastern Ohio, just south of the Western Reserve in a tier of four counties –

Table 7.1. *Agriculture in Wayne County and Ohio in 1849*

	Wayne County	Ohio
Population density, 1850	58.5/sq. mi.	48.0/sq. mi.
Mean farm size (acres)	115.4	179.1
Mean improved acreage (%)	60.9	54.7
Mean value per acre	$28.18	$19.93
Mean implements value per farm	$99.58	$71.00
Wheat, bu. (per 100 acres)	170.6	80.5
Corn, bu. "	187.3	328.3
Oats, bu. "	127.6	74.9
Rye, bu. "	3.8	2.4
Horses "	3.1	2.6
Cows "	3.3	3.0
Swine "	10.7	10.9
Sheep "	27.7	21.9
Wool, lbs. "	76.3	56.7

Sources: DeBow, *Seventh Census*, 862-8; DeBow, *Statistical View*, 290-3.

Ashland, Wayne, Stark, and Columbiana – that were settled before 1820 mostly by Pennsylvanians and by a minority of Germans. Like other agricultural areas in eastern Ohio, the county underwent an economic transition with the opening of the Ohio Canal in 1832. The farmers of Wayne now found flourishing markets for their wheat, wool, butter, and pork at Massillon and Fulton on the canal, at landings that they reached by wagon roads. Like most of the counties that lined the Ohio Canal, Wayne County flourished during the 1830s and 1840s. Wayne was part of Ohio's Backbone Region, the important wheat counties that had their commercial focus at Massillon. The local economy reached a peak in 1850, when the county boasted a population density 20 percent higher than that of the state as a whole. In the same year, one-third of Wayne County's residents were interstate migrants to Ohio, and almost one-tenth were foreign-born.[4]

The county's early introduction to the regional grain trade provoked rapid agricultural development. By 1850, the county stood far ahead of the Ohio average on every measure of agricultural improvement (Table 7.1). Farms tended to be smaller than in the rest of the state, boasting more improved acreage and a higher value per acre. Wayne County's farmers had invested heavily in intensive, commercial agriculture, putting a good deal of their money into farm machinery and taking up 93 percent of their county's acreage as farmland. The shift from corn to wheat culture, which was an important sign of the commercialization of agriculture, was far advanced. At the same time, Wayne's farmers exceeded the state average in most categories of livestock, another indication of commercial production.[5]

Population growth accompanied agricultural development. During the 1840s, the county experienced an increase of 14 percent, and 14 of the 16 townships saw their population grow. As in most regions, however, population growth was uneven, ranging from a decline of 3.6 percent to an increase of almost 50 percent. Within the trend toward population growth, local increases depended on local conditions and, in this instance, on transportation routes. The most spectacular growth in Wayne County, as elsewhere, was urban. During the 1840s, the city of Wooster grew by almost one-half, claiming 4,122 residents in 1850. Wooster attracted more than its share of both long-distance and local migrants. The remainder of Wooster Township, which was rural, showed only moderate growth, less than 10 percent.[6]

Economic growth crested during the 1840s, however, and Wayne County matched the pattern set throughout eastern Ohio by losing population after 1850. The decline was slight, only 1.5 percent, but it ended the bounding growth of the previous decade. Wayne County's sudden stagnation reflected the general decline of the Ohio Canal and its replacement by the Miami Canal as an artery of trade and migration. Still another blow to the local economy was the area's failure early on to attract a railroad. City boosters chastised their rural neighbors for their neglect of reliable and economical transportation links. One of them predicted bitterly that they would "nap" until reduced to "triumphantly wending their way to Mansfield in their ox wagons, in search of a market." Another booster lamented that the county was about to be "left high and dry" without a railroad. By 1850, the "tide of emigration" had shifted westward, and Wayne County lost more migrants than it welcomed. Wooster proved the only exception, gaining population throughout the 1850s. In fact, Wooster cast a "shadow" over the surrounding countryside. Rural Wooster Township lost the most residents of all the townships, reflecting a net population shift from country to town.[7]

Wooster's politicians had become deeply involved in the management of economic growth during the 1830s and 1840s. Wooster was an important Whig and soft Democratic stronghold, not least because of the Bank of Wooster, which fought hard for its very existence after the Panic of 1837 and in the wake of banking reform.

During the Panic of 1837 and for the next decade, the establishment of an adequate currency and a reliable banking system dominated political debate. The bank issue violated traditional party loyalties by pitting hards against softs at every level of government. Ohio's softs, advocates of a controlled paper currency, found an important rallying point in the embattled Bank of Wooster. Debate over the recharter of this Whig stronghold bitterly divided the Ohio Democracy into hard and soft wings.

In the wake of wholesale bank failures and as part of a general revulsion against paper money, Democrats and Whigs joined forces to support "small note" laws during the late 1830s. The small note laws limited the supply of paper currency by prohibiting bank notes worth less than five dollars. But soon a Democratic governor, Wilson Shannon, divided his party by advocating moderate "bank reform" – a system of local banks providing a controlled paper currency. Shannon alienated the hard wing of his party, which remained steadfast in opposition to all banks, by allying his own soft wing with the Whigs. As a result, Thomas Corwin, a Whig and a soft, defeated Shannon in the election of 1840. But the hard Democrats captured both houses of the legislature in the following year and set out to impose stringent reforms on Ohio's archaic banking system.[8]

The result, the Latham Banking Act of 1842, replaced Ohio's traditional special bank charters with a system of general incorporation. But the Latham Law horrified Ohio Whigs. The new law imposed strict restrictions on banks, the most important of which was the "locofoco principle" – individual liability of stockholders and bank officers for losses incurred by noteholders. This personal liability remained a political issue for the next several years and stood as a crucial rallying point for hard Democrats. As part of a compromise between hard and soft Democrats, Shannon won nomination for governor once again in 1842. Reunified and riding a general wave of "locofoco" or hard sentiment, Ohio Democrats went on to recapture the statehouse and to retain both houses of the legislature by wide margins.[9]

In the following year, Democrats amended the Latham Law to permit old banks whose special charters had expired to reorganize under the stringent, general law. But the "locofoco" Latham Law was actually meant to be prohibitive, and in protest against personal liability Ohio bankers refused to reincorporate. On January 1, 1843, the charters of 13 of Ohio's 23 banks expired, leaving the state with only ten banks and a clearly inadequate supply of currency. Severe economic contraction undermined popular support for the hards, and Governor Shannon's well-known sympathies for "softer" reforms prompted Whigs to attempt a modification of the Latham Law.[10]

On January 1, 1844, two more Ohio banks lost their charters, leaving only eight authorized banks operating in the state, including the Bank of Wooster. The politically astute directors of the Wooster Bank, the leading politicians in Wayne County, had cleverly fashioned a coalition between soft Democrats and Whigs, and their influence among softs in both parties stretched far beyond Columbus and all the way to Washington. During 1843 and 1844, softs throughout Ohio busily fashioned a bipartisan "bank party." The resulting division between soft and hard Democrats permitted both a successful attack on the Latham Law and an important Whig victory at the polls.[11]

As an opening salvo against the Latham Law, Ohio softs attempted to amend the act to exempt the Bank of Wooster from its harshest provisions. The bank's directors had Whig and Democratic allies across the state and friends in Washington as well. The defection of Samuel Lahm, the Democratic state senator from neighboring Stark County, represented the first challenge to the solid Democratic defense of hard money. Lahm, who had an interest in the Bank of Wooster, persuaded three Democratic colleagues to vote with the Whigs on exempting the bank. As a result, the legislative "bank party" thwarted the Democratic majority and extended the bank's charter for another six years, to 1850. Although the new charter included stringent safeguards, the bitter fight over the Wooster Bank had splintered the Ohio Democracy into two warring factions. For his defense of the Bank of Wooster, Lahm won the support of Wayne County Whigs. During the same session, the legislature extended the charters of four more banks, and the Wooster Bank Bill therefore represented, according to one historian, "the first break in the hitherto solid front of the Democrats on the banking question." In the eyes of Samuel Medary, editor of the Columbus *Ohio Statesman* and a leading hard Democrat, the Bank of Wooster stood "at the bottom of all our troubles in Ohio."[12]

Quite understandably, hard Democrats publicly repudiated their soft brethren and nominated David Tod, a hard, "Van Buren" Democrat, for governor in 1844. Standing united against a divided adversary and bolstered by support from soft Democrats, the Whigs easily carried the election. The softs put one of their own, Mordecai Bartley, into the statehouse and won both houses of the legislature. Popular demand for a sound but adequate currency had combined with the political machinations of Ohio bankers to sweep the bank party, Whigs and soft Democrats, into power. The Wooster Bank Bill was the entering wedge that forced Democrats to move toward a more flexible philosophy on banking.[13]

In 1845 the Whigs used their new majority to enact a banking law that abolished individual liability, the "locofoco principle." The Kelley Bank Act repealed the Latham Law and established limited collective liability for Ohio banks. The Kelley Law created a three-tiered banking system that stood unaltered for the rest of the decade. Joining the traditional individually chartered banks were a system of state banks and independent banks regulated by a Board of Bank Commissioners. The Kelley Law proved popular with voters, and Ohio Whigs gained an even stronger hold on both houses of the legislature in the fall of 1845.[14]

During the dramatic campaign of 1846, which resulted in a tie in the Ohio Senate, hard Democrats were determined to recapture both their own party and the state. In February, Democrats reported a bill to repeal the Kelley Bank Law in an attempt to flush out soft Democrats for disciplinary action. Only two soft Democrats voted with the Whig majority, and the hards restored some unity to their party. During the summer, in fact, the hard wing gained control of the state Democratic convention. Unified over resistance to the Kelley Law, the Democrats once again nominated David Tod for governor as a very hard or "Pot Metal" candidate. Soft or "Cass" Democrats threatened to meet in a separate convention. Soft Democrats in Wayne County, a probank stronghold, actually held a convention in January to repudiate the nomination of Tod and to call for a new state convention. With party lines shattered by the banking issue, both Democrats and Whigs viewed the election of 1846 as a "referendum on the bank question." In October the Whig nominee for governor, William Bebb, narrowly defeated the Pot Metal candidate with a plurality of 48.3 percent.[15]

Although the Whigs captured the governorship and the Ohio House by a comfortable margin, they could manage only a tie in the Senate. The surprising defeat of the Whig incumbent from Wayne County, Levi Cox, denied Ohio Whigs a complete victory. Control of the Senate fell to a minority of soft Democrats, who elected one of their own to the speakership. With a tie in the Senate and a Democratic speaker, Democrats could veto any and all Whig legislation. It was in the midst of this continuing struggle between Whigs and Democrats, softs and hards, that Cox challenged the right of his opponent, Joseph Willford, a hard Democrat, to represent Wayne

County. The Wayne County election contest was the Whigs' only hope of breaking the legislative stalemate.[16]

Like Whigs and Democrats across Ohio, Wayne County voters fought the election of 1846 on the banking issue. Wayne County was a soft stronghold, and after the Panic of 1837 Whigs had constructed an elaborate political organization in Wooster that stretched across Ohio, all the way to Washington, and even involved the White House. Traditionally the county's majority party, local Democrats were still divided in 1846. Soft Democrats pledged to vote for local Whig candidates, and so the county's voters were showered with a multiplicity of party labels. Available tickets varied across the county's 16 townships, depending on each party's strengths and weaknesses. Voters could cast a pure Whig ballot or a "Mixed" ticket composed of Whigs and soft Democrats. The county's soft Democrats also fielded a separate slate in some townships, adopting the label "Independent Democrats." But in demonstration of the bank party's unity in Wayne County, every soft ballot, whether Whig, Democratic, or Mixed, carried the name of Levi Cox for state senator. Hard Democrats laid claim to their party's traditional label and stood solidly behind Willford.[17]

As the "bank party," Wayne County Whigs painted themselves as advocates of commerce and progress, lambasting the "hard money, free trade, low wages" principles of local Democrats. Whigs constantly lamented the economic stagnation threatened by the Latham Law's locofoco principle. They charged that "twenty good and solvent banks" were "nearly all voted out of existence by locofoco legislation." Ohioans had to make do, Whigs pointed out, with a dwindling paper currency that "consists of the worst class of the paper of the surrounding states." Democrats retaliated by pointing to the repeated bank failures of the previous decade, reserving their harshest condemnation for the local Bank of Wooster, which they labeled a "corrupt swindling concern." They further charged that the bank was about to go under. Whigs found it difficult to defend their bank against the avalanche of Democratic invective and, flushed with their recent electoral and legislative success, did not really try. "It would be an endless task," one of them moaned, "to undertake the refutation of all the base slanders set afloat by the Hard press in various parts of the State, regarding the Bank of Wooster."[18]

In keeping with their emphasis on encouraging trade, Wayne County's Whigs found an obvious political stronghold in the town of Wooster. The local Whig organization centered on the county seat. Wooster boasted more than its share of Whig leaders, who tended to be merchants, lawyers, and bankers. The local Democratic party had broader roots within Wayne County's rural townships, but Whig campaigns were always orchestrated from Wooster. During the campaign of 1844, for example, Wooster Whigs set up Clay Clubs in several townships as early as April to reach out to rural voters. Such rural Clay Clubs received constant supervision from Wooster Whigs, who included "numerous Clay Club speakers, good and true, who will turn out at a moment's notice and address them, whenever they shall be organized." One such Clay Club, for example, met at the schoolhouse in rural East Union Township to hear a speech by Judge Smith Orr of Wooster, a prominent Whig who later founded the railroad town of Orrville. The meeting of another Clay Club, in Plain Township, was enlivened by the patriotic airs of the Wooster glee club.[19]

In the thick of the campaign, the county's Whig Central Committee set up mass meetings in every township. Wooster Whigs assured their "country friends" that speakers from Wooster, called "stumpers," would address every meeting. Typically, a Whig campaign crested with a county-wide mass meeting. In August 1844, for example, a reported crowd of 8,000 attended a mass meeting that began with a parade and speeches by local Whig notables and ended with a long address by Thomas Corwin, former governor and future senator. In September 1846, as many as 1,500 Whigs gathered to hear gubernatorial candidate William Bebb in a grove just north of Wooster. Bebb, who was not feeling well, spoke for only 20 minutes on banks and currency. Such Whig campaigns mirrored similar activity by local Democrats. Matching the Clay Clubs that were organized from Wooster, Wayne County Democrats established Hickory Clubs to support Van Buren and his antibank policies. Wooster was also the center of Democratic campaigning. Both Whigs and Democrats held their meetings at the county courthouse, sometimes simultaneously. It was to the streets of Wooster, too, that county Democrats thronged to sing, dance, and drink in raucous celebration of their victories.[20]

But the real business of politics was often less visible. The Whig Central Committee gathered at the courthouse in the dead of winter and attracted only a handful of party leaders. A typical Whig meeting was addressed by General Cyrus Spink and Levi Cox and then settled down to elect officers for the coming campaign. A central committee of six included D. N. Sprague, editor of the *Wooster Democrat*, and John P. Coulter, president of the Bank of Wooster. In addition to nominating candidates and running the local campaign, the central committee tallied voting returns from all the townships within their district. This, too, they did in Wooster, sending messengers back and forth to Wayne Senatorial District's 20 townships. Wooster was the hub of Whig organization. Sprague, for example, used the *Wooster Democrat* to ask his "friends in the country" to bring in the result of the election in their respective townships, "as soon as canvassed." That way, he explained, "their messengers will be enabled to take back with them the result in the whole county, thus giving every one the earliest possible information." During every election, Whig leaders or "regulars" called on volunteers, usually younger men, to carry out such routine tasks of party organizing. One Whig noted that "the Regulars, it is true, bore the burthen of the fight; but it should not be forgotten that they received important aid from a gallant army of Volunteers." It was this system of messengers, young Whig functionaries, that permitted Wooster Whigs to mobilize so quickly after Cox's narrow defeat in 1846. The very network of messengers and correspondents that gathered the election returns was well situated to lay the groundwork for Cox's subsequent challenge of their validity.[21]

Length of party service was the distinguishing characteristic of "regulars" and the main criterion in selecting Whig candidates and officers. Long party service required long residence in the county, and Whigs consistently portrayed their candidates as "old residents." Announcing their ticket in 1847, for example, Whigs assured the public that their nominees were "old citizens of the county." In other years, they boasted proudly that "Most of the gentlemen on the ticket are well known to nearly every voter in the county," and they emphasized the length of residence of individual candidates. Samuel Cutter of Wooster, for example, the Whig nominee for sheriff, was "born and raised in Wayne County and has been nearly twenty years a resident of this town." Similarly, John Brown of Chippewa Township, a candidate for state representative, was a "Mechanic and Farmer – one of the 'bone and sinew' of the county. He also," Whigs assured the local electorate, "is an old resident." And Levi Cox had been "well known to the voters of this county for more than twenty years."[22]

And so October 1846 brought a campaign, though not a result, that was typical in most respects. Whigs faced the task of returning the incumbent Wayne County senator to the legislature. That task seemed simple, with local Democrats in disarray, still bitterly divided into hards and softs because of the Wooster Bank debacle. The incumbent was a likely Whig candidate. Levi Cox was remembered

60 years later as "the pioneer of the legal profession and printing press in Wooster," combining the two skills that were most valued by antebellum politicians. Fifty-two years old in 1846, Cox was a native Pennsylvanian who had arrived in early Wayne County at the age of 19. Within two years of his arrival, in 1817, Cox established the county's first newspaper, the *Ohio Spectator*, published at Wooster. As a shrewd attorney, Cox rose to prominence among Wayne County Whigs. He was county prosecutor for 15 years and county auditor for 14 more, and during the 1830s he served as trustee of both Wooster town and township. Cox went to the Ohio Senate in the Whig landslide of 1844 that followed Democratic division over the Wooster Bank Bill. He ended his political career with an appointment as presiding judge of the Wayne County Court of Common Pleas, an office he filled from 1848 to 1852. A bachelor until late in life, Cox died in Wooster ten years later, remembered in a county history as a man who "permanently and continuously lived" in Wooster for 47 years, indeed an unusual feat in antebellum Ohio.[23]

Cox was the archetypical Wooster politician. Officeholders from Wooster were older than the general population, far wealthier, better educated and occupationally skilled, and more apt to be native Americans. The 75 Wooster men who held local or county office within five years before or after 1850 were, on average, 43 years of age in that year. Wooster men in general averaged only 37 years. The officeholders held real wealth averaging $3700, as opposed to $1226 among their constituents. Nearly one-third of them were professionals, mostly lawyers and physicians, and 92 percent of them were American-born. Only 80 percent of all eligible voters were natives. Finally, native Pennsylvanians dominated political office. Nearly two-thirds of the Wooster officeholders were migrants from Pennsylvania, as opposed to only 50 percent of their constituents. These officials represented the kind of core community that could use their persistence, their strategic situation at the center of the county, their wealth, their education, their age, and their political experience to dominate local affairs. And Wooster was overwhelmingly Whig, 63 percent Whig in 1846. Cox, a wealthy, middle-aged lawyer from Wooster who hailed from Pennsylvania, was a typical Whig regular.[24]

Cox's opponent, by contrast, represented rural Wayne County. Compared with Judge Cox, Joseph Willford seemed a relative newcomer to county politics. A Greene Township farmer, he left little impression on his county's historical record. Forty-nine years old in 1846, Willford was, like Cox, a native Pennsylvanian. He arrived in

Ohio in 1818 at the age of 21, but the date of his arrival in Wayne County was never recorded. Willford's only political experience was two years' service as one of Wayne County's two state representatives, from the rural district. Whigs considered him uncouth and inexperienced, and indeed his letters betray his lack of formal schooling. Whigs delighted in comparing Willford's sketchy background with the imposing political reputation of Judge Cox. This striking contrast in personal reputations and political experience, as well as the continuing disarray in Democratic ranks, left Wayne County Whigs wholly unprepared for their stunning defeat at the hands of an upstart by a single vote.[25]

Whigs believed that local Democrats had cheated Cox out of a rightful victory. Already on election night rumors were circulating that many Democrats had cast ballots illegally and that Whig voters with a perfect right to vote had been turned away from the polls. The Whigs at United States Hall quickly established the propriety or at least the political necessity of launching an election contest. They then turned to a careful scrutiny of the poll books and ballots in each of the district's 20 townships. Someone started a list of volunteers to ride out to the various townships. Many of the volunteers were the same messengers who had just ridden in with the returns. John P. Jeffries, an attorney who had lived in Wooster for ten years, offered to visit Sugar Creek Township the next day. But another Whig pointed out that the sooner the examination could be made the better, so Jeffries rode out that same evening and made his inspection by candlelight. Solomon Bonnewitz, a soft Democrat, rode across the county on Cox's behalf. Bonnewitz, like Jeffries a young Wooster attorney, was one of the county's old residents. He had been born in the county and had held a wide variety of offices over 18 years. In 1846, Bonnewitz had a private legal practice in Wooster and was a future mayor. Within days of the election, Bonnewitz had peeked into the ballot boxes of Wayne, Mohecan, Perry, and Lake townships.[26]

Some Whigs argued that material evidence, such as poll books and ballots, was really unnecessary, that the tie between Whigs and Democrats actually gave Cox a decided advantage. Willford would take his seat in Columbus, but when the Senate considered Cox's challenge Willford must abstain, granting the Whigs a temporary majority of one. But other Whigs countered that if Cox was not legally entitled to a seat they did not want him to have it. Democrats later argued that Cox had orders from Columbus, telling him that he must put up a convincing defense of his claim at all costs. At any rate, Cox himself insisted that if he could not retain his seat "on fair grounds," he did not want it at all. He would not have it said that he had won his seat without a majority of votes. He said testily that if the Whigs wanted him in the Senate they must "make exertions to get him there," because he had not really wanted the office in the first place. As it turned out, Whigs were quite prepared to make those exertions, which meant challenging the ballots of Democratic voters and getting those of disqualified Whigs accepted.[27]

James Irvine, clerk of the election in Wooster Township and a young Cox lieutenant, quietly offered to go anywhere and do what he could. Cox gratefully assented, and another Whig lent Irvine a horse and buggy. Whigs paid Irvine to accompany Bonnewitz on a swing through three townships and to visit Paint Township by himself. Whigs eventually examined the records of every township in the district, sometimes two or three times, with or without the cooperation of the respective township clerks who had collected the ballots and copied out the poll books. In townships with Whig clerks, the party already had possession of the ballot boxes and poll books. Some of the Democratic clerks, however, had taken the ballot boxes home with them, to count the ballots overnight, and so the Whig volunteers had to pay them personal visits. Matthew Pinkerton rode out to Chippewa Township, Lucas Flattery and David H. Howe to Mohecan Township in Ashland County, John Jeffries and C. C. Parsons to Sugar Creek, and Charles T. Leopold and Howe checked the ballots and poll books in Congress Township. The ballots of Wooster Township, however, received the personal attention of John P. Coulter, president of the Bank of Wooster. Coulter, a physician, owned a drugstore in Wooster and had deep roots in local politics. A perpetual trustee of Wooster town and township, Dr. Coulter also served terms as county commissioner and county auditor. In 1845, the Ohio legislature had commissioned Coulter a major general of the Ohio militia. He and William Stitt, a young harness manufacturer in Wooster who was a rising Whig politician, carefully counted and recounted Wooster's 603 ballots in the private offices of Lucius Upham, a local Whig attorney who was the incumbent county auditor.[28]

Within a week of the election, Sprague was already writing in the *Wooster Democrat* that "several errors" had turned up in the voting returns of some of the townships. Democrats, in the meantime, received no official notice of the Whigs' activities. Eugene Pardee, a leading Democratic lawyer, did attend several of the inquiries in the rural townships as Willford's representative. Pardee was a Wooster attorney who described himself pointedly as a *"Hard* Democrat." A native New Yorker, Pardee at age 32 had already served four years as Wayne County's prosecutor. In addition to his legal interests, Pardee was an early booster of the railroads. Settled in a country seat, Grove Hill Place, just outside Wooster, Pardee boasted that, unlike some Whigs, he represented his party without compensation. As late as October 22, Cox still had not decided whether to press his contest. But Sprague assumed that "since it has been ascertained that he has received a clear majority of the vote, he will do so." Sprague's assumption proved correct. Five days later, James Irvine and another young Whig rode out to Willford's farm in Greene Township and handed him an official notice of Cox's contest.[29]

Whigs and Democrats spent the next six weeks preparing for the coming contest, tracking down rumors, interviewing election judges and clerks, rechecking poll books, and taking depositions. The candidates and their representatives met every day to take testimony before two justices of the peace at the law offices of Curtis and Flattery in Wooster. One of the justices was Henry Lehman, a Wooster lawyer of 37. Lehman later defended the "soldier vote" in Ohio during the Civil War and provoked the Ohio Supreme Court's landmark decision in *Lehman v. McBride,* which reaffirmed the volitional foundations of suffrage in Ohio. The young James Irvine represented Cox in the proceedings, and attorney Eugene Pardee represented Willford. Pardee's selection of an assistant counsel unsettled Wayne County Whigs. At age 32, George W. Wasson was the incumbent county prosecutor and was Pardee's successor in that office. The contrast between the young Wasson and Judge Cox was more than Wooster Whigs could stomach. Sprague, for one, believed that Wasson "will do almost anything, and be almost anything," in his own behalf. Worst of all, Wasson seemed ambivalent about the all-important banking issue: "When in company with a *hard,* he was a *hard*; and when with a *soft,* he was a *soft."* But the clannish Whigs of Wooster did not hesitate to give Wasson his due. They acknowledged that, as prosecuting attorney, he had more power than any other man in the county because, they pointed out, he had "the control of all our criminals." Wasson eventually moved on to Columbus.[30]

During the six weeks in late 1846 that Levi Cox, Joseph Willford, and their representatives met in Wooster to listen to the testimony of voters, judges, and clerks in the Wayne County election, they struggled just to make sense out of what they heard. The events of a day took six weeks to unravel. But one fact was clear from the outset. Patterns of migration and conflicting interpretations of Ohio's rules of residence had played an important role in the election and must therefore play a primary role in deciding the contest. There were so many recent migrants in the county that the sequence of challenge, interrogation, and oath taking that greeted new voters recurred time and again in all the townships. Application of residence rules varied greatly from township to township. New voters found that their suffrage often depended on the disposition of the election judges, on local electoral practices, and most especially on their partisan affiliations. The legal and political implications of migration had made it difficult to hold the election in the first place and now, during the contest, made it difficult to interpret the returns. A welter of questions emerged from the testimony, but the question that punctuated the six-week investigation was simply who is a legal voter, and why?

One conclusion went unquestioned: Local party organizations kept firm control over every township. Wayne County was, quite obviously, evenly divided between Democrats and Whigs. In 1846, in fact, only one vote separated the two parties. But below the county level, individual townships went solidly for one party or the other. There were eight Whig townships and eight Democratic townships in the county (Table 7.2). Whigs held their townships with an average vote of 62 percent, while Democrats held theirs with 60 percent. While the two parties struggled to control the district as a whole, each maintained dominance in one-half of the townships. Paul Bourke and Donald DeBats have recently explained this well-known phenomenon by arguing that a political "imprint," stamped on a community at its founding, could persist through decades of political, social, and economic change. Such a durable imprint might maintain the resilient partisan character of local voting units, permit parties to dominate them year after year, and preserve remarkably stable partisan divisions from one election to the next. Most of Wayne County's townships shared such an "imprint" and went either solidly Whig or solidly Democratic.[31]

An urban–rural division was one conspicuous source of such an imprint. Democratic support was scattered throughout the county's rural townships. Whigs, by contrast, managed to hold more heavily populated strongholds, including the city of Wooster. In 1850, for example, the typical Whig township contained more eligible voters, fewer farmers, and more merchants and professionals, practitioners of urban occupations, than did Democratic townships (Table 7.2).

Table 7.2. *Social Characteristics, 1850, of Whig and Democratic townships in Wayne County*

	Whig townships, 1846	Democratic townships, 1846
N	8	8
Majority (%)	62.4	60.2
Mean eligible voters	468	422
Mean age (years)	38.2	38.3
Mean wealth ($)	1,440.87	1,310.09
Farmers (%)	46.8	54.3
Merchants/professionals (%)	8.8	4.6
Native-born (%)	84.6	78.6

Sources: Manuscript U.S. census of population, Wayne County, Ohio, 1850; "Wayne County Case," 24.

The voters in Whig townships also held more wealth, on average, and more of them were native Americans. Whigs also captured a larger share of the vote in Whig strongholds than Democrats did in their own. Wooster Township, the hub of Whig organization, was fully typical of this urban–rural division. Wooster held twice as many voters as the typical township, and Whigs captured it handily with 63 percent of the vote. The influence of Whigs faded, however, with distance from Wooster. The westernmost edge of Wayne District, numbering four townships in eastern Ashland County, was solidly Democratic. Those townships had broken away from Wayne County only a year before, and they now voted against the clique that held Wooster. Beyond local factionalism, Whig philosophy stressed urban values – entrepreneurship, economic opportunity, industrialization, civic improvement – and appealed to the merchant class and the native-born. As one result, Democratic townships were more rural and less heavily populated. Democrats, in fact, captured 12 of Wayne District's 20 townships in 1846 but still won the election by only one vote. It is no coincidence that the *Wooster Democrat* was a Whig newspaper, while the *Wayne County Democrat* was indeed Democratic. Whigs held the town, and Democrats, the country.[32]

An analysis of migration among voters, however, suggests an additional source of "imprinting" in the county's townships. Wayne County's voters, like those in the other study areas, were frequent migrants. As a result, a core community of the most persistent voters could dominate political life in each of the townships, staying put, turning out to vote, and holding office year after year. Congress Township, in the northwest corner of the county, provides a good example of such a persistent core community. Congress Township's poll book is the only such record from the 1846 election to survive. Linking the 1846 poll book with the 1850 manuscript census shows that just fewer than one-half (133 of 276) of the township's voters persisted over those four years. In the meantime, 333 new voters either moved into the township or came of age. The core of persistent voters therefore represented between one-fourth and one-third of the electorate in 1850, and they were quite different from the new voters in Congress Township. They were ten years older than the new voters, 46 years old in 1850. They were much wealthier, holding more than twice as much real property as the new voters – $1,853 as compared to $830. They were more often farmers than were the new voters – 71 percent as compared to only 56 percent. And they were more often native-born – 95 percent as compared to 88 percent. Such a core community of economically successful persisters could retain political control of their township from year to year as more migratory voters moved through the area.[33]

By maintaining a safe partisan majority year after year (Congress was 66 percent Whig in 1846), such a core community could control political life in their township. Political dominance meant that township officers would come from the ranks of a single party, including all three township trustees, who acted as the three election judges on election day. The board of three judges reviewed the eligibility of every challenged voter and, in most instances, ruled unanimously for or against accepting a questionable ballot. By controlling the admission of new voters into the township on election day, the core community and their representatives, the election judges, could keep winning elections and maintain the political character of their township. Election law permitted the core community of persisters to act as a self-perpetuating political majority, and the system of challenging and interrogating new voters was an important and conspicuous element of local party organization.

Most of the testimony taken in the Wayne County case therefore focused on two general questions – first, the residence of each questionable voter and, second, his vote. The latter question was by far the easier to answer. Before the adoption of the secret ballot, parties printed their own tickets, usually on brightly colored paper for easy identification. Additionally, voters handed their ballots to the election judges, who could read them before depositing them in the ballot box. In the era of the party ticket, even in the absence of voice voting, casting a ballot was therefore a public act. The first question was much more challenging. The heavy migration of the mid-nineteenth century and especially the rootless wandering of many Wayne County voters complicated the task of interpreting election laws, both at the polling place and even during the long, drawn-out election contest. New notions of residence, such as volitional belonging, baffled both election judges and the board of inquiry, and throughout the late fall of 1846 they struggled with definitions of community membership. Cox needed to win only two more votes to turn the contest in his favor, and his supporters counted on an examination of migratory voters to make up the deficit. Three-fourths of the voters interviewed in detail were migrants – newcomers to the state, the county, or one of the townships – or foreign immigrants. In challenging the election returns, Whigs tried to invalidate the ballots of migrants who had voted Democratic or, alternatively, to prove that Democratic judges had refused the ballots of migratory Whigs. Democrats charged that Whig judges had joined them in discriminating against migrants.

The new doctrine of domicile, which grounded legal residence in a voter's intentions, was difficult to interpret, not only for many unlettered election judges but also for the board of inquiry, who were all lawyers. The example of Emanuel Hostetter demonstrated at the outset the frustrating difficulties they would face throughout the six-week investigation as they struggled to apply the doctrine. Hostetter was one of the migratory Democrats whose ballots the Whig challengers hoped to invalidate. Hostetter voted in Wooster Township, a Whig stronghold, and then moved away the next day. Hostetter was a hard Democrat, and the Whigs now questioned his eligibility to vote in Wooster. Hostetter was, in fact, a classic local migrant. He was about 25, single, and a millwright. His was a seasonal occupation that took him in constant search of high water. He came from Massillon in Stark County at the beginning of the summer to build a new wheel at a mill just outside Wooster. The wheel took a month, and then he worked by the day. Hostetter had been out of work for a week before the election. He packed his tools into a chest so that he could send them back to Massillon. But before he could go home, Hostetter found work in nearby Chippewa Township. He sent his tools on ahead of him but stayed in Wooster just long enough to cast a ballot in the senatorial election. Did Hostetter's open intention to leave, under the new doctrine of domicile, outweigh his physical presence in Wooster on the day of the election?[34]

The contestants focused on Hostetter's claim to legal residence, and so they interrogated his employer and his foreman at the mill.

David Robison was a leading Whig. Fifty-three years old in 1846, Robison was a transplanted Pennsylvanian who had arrived in Wooster with a brother at the age of 20 in 1813. Robison was a tanner by trade who achieved early success and soon branched out. His fortunes grew with the fledgling town of Wooster, and when the Ohio Canal opened in 1832 he built a flour mill just outside the town to grind wheat on its way to market at Massillon. A Democrat turned Whig, Robison was an early advocate of railroads and a booster of Ohio banking. A former director of the Bank of Wooster, Robison helped to found and then head a rival institution, the Wayne County branch of the State Bank of Ohio, incorporated under the provisions of the Whig Kelley Law of 1845. As a leading Whig, he was at the U.S. Hall the night Cox's supporters started organizing the contest.[35]

Robison joined his foreman, John Crill, on the witness stand to help establish Hostetter's legal residence on election day. Crill was a younger man, only 41, and like Robison, his employer, an active Whig. Crill served as trustee of the town of Wooster off and on for two decades and for another five years as Wooster Township's assessor. Crill agreed with Robison that Hostetter was a hard Democrat and a probable Willford supporter. With Hostetter's politics established, a simple task in this era of party tickets, attention now turned to his claim to residence in Wooster.[36]

The man's physical presence in Wooster on the day of the election was, quite obviously, an undisputed fact. It was his intention to leave the township that called his legal residence into question. Both statute and common law required the intention to remain as an ingredient of domicile or legal residence.[37] But how might the contestants determine Hostetter's intentions? He had no family and no property, so the tribunal turned next to his employment. Both common law and statute located a man's domicile in his "principal place of business."[38]

Why had Hostetter come to Wooster Township in the first place? If he came just for employment, did he lose his legal residence when he lost his position? Crill was noncommittal when pressed about Hostetter's intentions:

> Q: Did said Hostetter, come to said Wooster township, to reside as long as he could get employment; and when he came, did you hear him say or not say, he intended so to stay[?]
> A: I guess he did. I heard him say, if Robison would give him work this winter, he would stay.

And Robison was even more enigmatic than his foreman:

Q: Did he come for the purpose of getting employment in his business as a millwright?

A: I do not know for what purpose, but I employed him as a millwright.

All this, of course, was self-evident. But the clear implication, which favored the Whigs, was that Hostetter had come simply for employment. If so, then his legal residence in Wooster Township ended when he started working elsewhere. Attention now shifted to Hostetter's departure from the township.[39]

The board wanted to establish with precision when Hostetter legally left the township. He stopped working for Robison on the Friday before the election and started working in Chippewa Township at the end of October. For several weeks he had moved piecemeal from Wooster to Chippewa Township. Sometime during that interval he lost his legal residence. Hostetter was a millwright, and the disposition of his tools, his "place of business," now took on political significance. Where were his tools on the day of the election? Willford was specific in his question to Robison:

Q: What day did he pack up his tools; and . . . was it in his usual carpenter's chest?

A: I am not able to say positively, but think it was on the last of that week, and the beginning of the following week [election week], and in his usual carpenter's chest.

And on that day, Willford asked, did Hostetter actually leave for Chippewa Township? No, Robison answered: "He took his tools away the first or second day after the election." Hostetter, it was clear, had packed up his tools in his chest *before* the election but took them away *after* he had voted. What was his intention, and therefore his legal residence, on the day of the election?[40]

Willford probed further to discover from Robison whether Hostetter actually had new employment in Chippewa when he packed up his tools:

Q: When he packed up his tools, did he know whether he could get further employment in his business about Wooster, or in this county?

A: Not to my knowledge; when he packed his tools, he did not know that he could get work in the county, but before he removed his tools, he knew that he could get work at Brown's [in Chippewa].

Hostetter packed up his tools before the election, ending his employment in Wooster Township. When he picked up his tools after the election, he had a new job in Chippewa Township. Sometime during the week that intervened, Hostetter had become a resident of Chippewa and lost his right to vote in Wooster. But only Hostetter himself knew for certain exactly when that happened.[41]

That ambiguity favored Willford and the Democrats and, most of all, Hostetter. Robison could not say exactly when Hostetter found new employment, so the Whigs could prove nothing about his loss of residence. John Crill remained convinced that Hostetter stayed in Wooster simply to vote for Willford, and it was true that he left Wooster the morning after the election. But the Senate Committee on Privileges and Elections, who reviewed all this testimony, pointed out that no Whig challenged Hostetter at the election, and so the final proof of his residence rested on his own actions. His casting of a ballot, in the absence of additional evidence, reflected an intention to remain in the township, if only until the next morning. His participation in the election made him by definition a legal resident. The Whigs' attempt to invalidate Hostetter's hard ballot foundered on the new notion of volitional residence, which placed primary emphasis on the intentions and not the actions of a voter. Hostetter's ballot was legal, according to the doctrine of domicile.[42]

Cox and the Whig challengers struggled with this paradox. Once a migrant successfully cast a ballot, he was a legal voter. Cox could not invalidate the ballot of any Democrat who had actually voted. But the inquiry also focused on migratory Whigs who were denied suffrage in Democratic townships. Were they now unqualified voters, simply by definition? East Union Township produced three glaring examples. Rumors were rampant that the judges of East Union had challenged and disqualified only Whigs and soft Democrats. There was no established Whig elite in this rural township, and the Democratic judges were, like their candidate Joseph Willford, substantial farmers. As elsewhere in Wayne County, the majority party in East Union Township, which was 58 percent Democratic in 1846, could use patterns of migration to keep a firm grip on their political power. Whigs accused the election judges of requiring every challenged voter to swear to future rather than merely present residence. Such a stringent oath of residence, which had no legal foundation, would have made Emanuel Hostetter's vote impossible in East Union Township.[43]

William Immel told the board of inquiry, when they called him to Wooster, that he was about 32 or 33 years old. He was born in Franklin County, Pennsylvania, and had been in Wayne County "near two years." Once in the county, however, Immel became a local migrant. A tailor, he worked for a while in Wooster and then moved to East Union Township at the beginning of September. He knew he was a resident of the state and the county, and any length of residence at all in his new township should have secured him a right to vote there. To make clear his intentions, Immel assured the board of inquiry that he had his "washing, boarding, and lodging" in East Union Township. Cox's first question of this young migrant was designed to pin down his intentions:

> Q: Was it when you went there, and has it ever since been your intention to make that the place of your residence?
> A: Yes it was.

But the judges of East Union turned Immel away from the ballot box because he would not swear to live there for another year. Immel, it turned out, had handed the judges an Independent ticket that carried the name of Levi Cox.[44]

Jason Kail was a wanderer throughout eastern Ohio. A stonecutter by trade, he was going on 25. He had been born in Harrison County, Ohio, and gradually made his way northwestward through Jefferson, Carroll, Stark, and Tuscarawas counties:

> I lived in Tuscarawas county before I came here, some two months, or more; previous to that I lived a short time in Magnolia, on the line between Stark and Carrol counties; previous to that I lived some eight months in Springfield, Jefferson County; after leaving Springfield, I traveled about three months, principally in Jefferson county.

Kail claimed residence in East Union Township only since the beginning of August. He assured the contestants that "at the time of the election, it was, and still is my intention to remain there." Kail offered the judges an Independent ticket, but he too lost his right to vote by refusing to swear to another year's residence.[45]

Samuel Kline was a carpenter from Lancaster County, Pennsylvania. After spending five years in Holmes County, Ohio, Kline arrived in East Union, where his sister lived with her husband. He was only 21. "I came to East Union township for the purpose of making it my residence," he insisted, "as long as I could find employment, and [I] still have the same intention." Kline went to the election, which would have been his first, and handed the judges an Independent ticket. But the judges refused to receive Kline's ballot. They wanted him to swear that he would make the township his permanent residence. Kline refused to make such a promise, and the Wooster Bank faction lost one more vote in East Union Township.[46]

In 1846, therefore, the Democratic farmers of East Union Township turned away a tailor, a stonecutter, and a carpenter who refused to commit themselves to permanent residence. All three were young migrants and newcomers to the township. Their recent arrival made them vulnerable at the ballot box, and their Independent tickets singled them out for close scrutiny. Other voters pledged continuing residence in the township, but these three practiced trades that promised to send them wandering. They refused to make a commitment to residence, and all three did indeed vanish by the end of the decade.[47]

The experiences of Immel, Kail, and Kline illustrate the process of sifting out new voters for political acceptability that was supported by Ohio law and was, presumably, commonplace at elections. The judges called Immel into the polling place, which was a private home, and one of the judges, Bethuel Munn, asked him "how long he had been in the township – what his occupation was – how long he intended to remain – and whether he would be willing to swear he would remain a year in the township." Immel answered merely that he had been in East Union "between one and two months – something like that" and that "he calculated to remain as long as he could get work."[48]

The three rural judges knew full well that Immel had come from Wooster, and now they asked him an important question. Could Immel "get a vote" in Wooster, were he to go there? Immel said he thought he could. The judges then told him "that was the place to go and get it." If Immel could vote in Wooster, then he could not vote in East Union. He should vote, in other words, where he could vote an Independent ticket without a challenge.[49]

Jacob Kail met a similar reception at the polling place. He offered an Independent ticket, but the judges refused to receive it unless he swore to remain in the township for a full year. Kail refused to swear to such an oath but did offer to swear that he had no other residence and intended to stay in East Union as long as he could find work. But the judges insisted that "they would receive my vote under no other circumstances than swearing to remain one year, and exhibiting a receipt for work done on the roads." The judges even read to Kail from the statute book, but when he refused to take the oath, they "threw down the book, and said it would not do; there was no use in listening to such talk, or something to that amount."[50]

During his interrogation, however, Kail compromised his own residence in East Union Township by referring to his birthplace,

Harrison County, as his home. Cox himself was first to notice that blunder and asked Kail to clarify his own notion of "home":

> Q: What did you mean by the word home, as you used it . . . when you spoke of going home?
>
> A: The reason I used the word was, I had formerly resided there and was acquainted there; I was going there merely on business.

That was a satisfactory answer, under Ohio election law, but Cox coaxed Kail to take the point even further. "Since you came to East Union township, have you had your boarding, washing, and lodging there?" he asked Kail. Kail, of course, told the Whig candidate that he had. But Willford's lawyer pounced on Kail's apparent confusion. "Please state," Pardee asked, "what you mean by home?" Kail was obviously squirming: "What I call my home is where I reside, or have been residing; I call East Union my home because I live there." Then he surrendered: "I cannot give a critical definition of the word." The word home had become ambiguous for this young migrant, and many others.[51]

Pardee then asked Samuel Kline a similar question: "Where do you call your home, when you speak of home?" "At my brother-in-law's, when I am about here," Kline answered, "but if I go to Holmes county, my home would be at my father's." But Kline was emphatic on one point: "I have no intention of going there, nor had I on the day of election." He had refused to swear to live permanently in East Union Township, however, because he did not know how long he could get work. As with Immel and Kail, economic uncertainty kept Kline from making a lengthy commitment, and the judges of East Union used his uncertainty to their own advantage. The judges had haggled over Kline's ballot for a full fifteen minutes. Kline, unlike Kail, had actually worked on the roads in lieu of paying township taxes, and his ballot was therefore harder to disqualify. One of the judges wanted to accept Kline's ballot, but the other two told Kline and his friends to read the statute for themselves. And so Kline lost his vote by a two-to-one decision.[52]

One of the judges, Bethuel Munn, remembered Kline, Kail, and Immel, but only vaguely. Munn was a 54-year-old New Yorker and a substantial farmer in the township. His single year as township trustee and therefore as an election judge was his first and only political office. Munn told Kline flatly that he did not "like" to take his vote. Munn recalled that he was not satisfied that Kline's residence was in his township nor did he believe that he intended making one there. Of Kail, Munn would say only that "I did not know there was such a man in the township, till I saw him at the polls." Perhaps Munn expected to know personally every legal voter in his township. Munn went on to deny that the judges had asked any voter to swear to future residence.[53]

The Democratic judges of East Union Township clung tenaciously to an old-fashioned notion of legal residence, one that did not take account of the economic necessity of migration but required a permanent commitment to a single township as home. The judges applied that older standard of residence to the young newcomers in their township whose trades took them wandering. And they applied it exclusively to soft voters. Traditional rules of residence made some voters susceptible to political exclusion, and the township's core community, composed of hard Democrats, applied a political as well as a social conception of residence. Every man had his own "place to vote," as one of the judges put it, and it was the judges' sworn duty to define it. In so doing, they applied both a social definition – the intention to reside – and a political definition – adherence to the majority party. In practice, the right of suffrage required both. And so the picture became familiar – the judges holding a ballot and asking solemnly, "Where do you call your home?" East Union Township remained Democratic in spite of migration because its permanent residents controlled admission to full political membership. And so the Committee on Privileges and Elections found that Immel, Kail, and Kline were not legal voters.

Frequent migration forced on voters the burden of establishing their legal residence. Judges repeatedly asked voters a litany of questions: How long have you been in the township? Are you employed here? Where do you board, and where do you do your laundry? How often do you return to your father's township? Where do you call your home? And these were all questions that many a voter had to ask himself on the morning of an election. Henry Espich was a young businessman who bought a grocery in Wooster a few weeks before the election and sold it a few weeks later. Espich seems to have agonized over his own legal residence before trying to vote in Wooster. His father's farm lay only one-half mile outside Wooster Township, but by leaving it for Wooster, Espich had lost his old residence. He wondered whether he had a new one in Wooster.[54]

The night before the election, Espich consulted John C. Taylor, a minor Whig official in Wooster. Taylor had served as township clerk for five years and therefore should have known something about residence. Espich told Taylor that he had an interest in a grocery in Wooster but continued to have his washing done at his father's farm in Plain Township. Washing was an ingredient of legal residence that had deep roots in common law, going all the way back to the Roman baths. Taylor advised Espich to go back to Plain Township to vote, because he was worried that the judges of Wooster Township would reject him. Espich talked to several other local politicians and received conflicting advice: "Some said to me, this is my place of voting – and some said Plain township. I did not know exactly what to do." Espich made a compromise that was common among migrants. He got up early the next morning to try to vote in Wooster. If he failed in that first attempt, he still had time to ride the eight or nine miles to the polling place in Plain Township. As a local migrant, he knew he had a right to vote somewhere in the county. As it turned out, he got his vote in Wooster. Espich had grown up in Plain Township, which had a Whig majority. Unlike Immel and many other migrants, when Espich crossed township boundaries he remained in Whig territory. The judges accepted his ticket readily, deciding in this instance that "it was not material, that a person should have their washing done in the township in which they voted." It made little difference to the judges of Wooster Township where Espich voted, as long as he voted a Whig ticket.[55]

Matthew Taggart was another young voter whose employment (threshing) took him across township boundaries. Taggart grew up on his father's farm in Baughman Township but, at age 29, crossed over into Sugar Creek Township to work as a thresher. Unlike Espich, Taggart was a rural migrant, but he still faced a similar dilemma: whether he should vote in Baughman or Sugar Creek Township. The most imposing witness against Taggart was Smith Orr, the founder of Orrville. Orr was a Whig and one of the wealthiest men in Wayne County. He was an Irish Protestant who arrived with his family in Delaware at age four in 1801. In 1812 his family settled in Apple Creek in East Union Township, and Orr helped survey the county and taught school until 1837, when he opened his first store in Smithville. He was one of Wayne County's most influential immigrants. The first election in East Union Township took place at his house, and Orr moved quickly into county-level politics as a Whig. He had far-flung commercial interests and helped finance the Wayne County stretch of the Pittsburg, Fort Wayne, and Chicago Railroad. When the Columbus, Mt. Vernon and Cleveland line reached the county, Orr shrewdly purchased land where the two railroads crossed and founded Orrville, which became the county's second-largest city. By the time he died in 1865, Orr had demonstrated convincingly the economic and political opportunities that attended

both long-distance and local migration. He followed those opportunities from Ireland to Delaware to Ohio and, once in Wayne
County, from East Union to Baughman to Greene townships. It is
little wonder that young migrants such as Matthew Taggart eagerly
followed his example in the 1840s and 1850s.[56]

But for the moment, Orr was testifying against Taggart because
the young man was a hard Democrat. Sugar Creek went heavily
Democratic, 55 percent, and Taggart was not even sworn before he
voted there. Orr, who seems to have acted as a sort of authority on
legal residence in his neighborhood, stated flatly that "I have known
Matthew Taggart since he was a boy, and his residence has always
been at his father's in Baughman Township." Orr understood
that Taggart had entered the threshing business, which took him
moving through "different places in the neighborhood," but he
always returned to Baughman Township when through with his
work and should have voted there. Still, Orr had to admit that even
he did not know where Taggart had his washing done before the
election.[57]

A parade of witnesses went on to agree that although Taggart had
voted in Sugar Creek he was a resident of Baughman Township.
Even Taggart's cousin, James R. Taggart, considered him a resident
of Baughman and therefore an illegal voter in Sugar Creek Township. Matthew traveled about during the spring, summer, and fall
threshing but returned to his father's farm every winter. Even when
working, Taggart spent Saturday nights and Sundays with his parents and left his washing there. "He comes home every Saturday
evening, dirty," James Taggart testified, "and goes away on Monday
morning clean, and I have heard his mother complain about his
washing being so hard since he commenced the threshing
business."[58]

Taggart, it turned out, had decided to vote in Sugar Creek Township because of the weather. He told John Clark that "he was going
to try to get a vote in Sugar Creek township, as it was wet and
muddy and he did not like to go to Baughman township." If the
judges did not let him vote, he would go to Baughman Township,
where he knew he was entitled to vote. Like Henry Espich, Taggart
gambled on getting a vote where he worked, to save him the trouble
of riding home on a muddy day. A hard Democrat voting in a
Democratic township, Taggart joined Espich in getting a vote without a challenge. Smith Orr's testimony notwithstanding, the Senate's Committee on Privileges and Elections accepted Taggart's ballot as a legal vote for Willford. They noted that both he and the

judges considered Sugar Creek Township his home and "actual residence" on the day of the election. His casting of a ballot and its ready acceptance by the judges made him, by definition, a legal voter. The circular relationship in which suffrage arose from residence and residence arose from suffrage worked to the advantage of the majority party. Taggart needed a residence to vote in Sugar Creek Township, but once he had voted there he had legal proof of his residence. The Whigs of Sugar Creek had missed their opportunity to challenge Matthew Taggart. Once his ballot was in the box, he had become a legal voter.[59]

Amos Myers was still another voter whose legal residence was unclear in 1846. Myers had come from the East to Greene Township at least five years before, working as a journeyman carpenter. But after three years, Myers's father came out west and settled in neighboring East Union Township. Amos Myers ended up spending so much time at his father's farm that many considered him a resident of East Union, not of Greene Township at all. Myers was a Whig, and Greene was a Whig township. East Union was Democratic, and so Myers chose to vote where he worked, in Greene. Joseph Willford had the misfortune to live in Greene Township, a Whig stronghold, and so he attended the polls to challenge Whig voters. Willford himself objected to Amos Myers's ballot on the grounds of residence and, as one witness remembered, "There was a dispute about the law of the matter." Willford spoke about the meaning of the election law, and "there was a great deal of talking."[60]

The judges intervened in the personal dispute between Willford and Myers. One of the judges asked Myers where he "had his home." Myers said he lived with his father but then reconsidered and said his home was "wherever he was, or something to that amount." One of the judges asked him where he had his washing, and Myers mentioned three or four different places. After some more haggling, during which Willford threatened Myers with the penalty of the law, the judges accepted the Whig ballot. But Myers, like Espich and Taggart, really had little to fear from the election law. Although their claims to residence were questionable, they had in fact cast their ballots, which was the best proof of legal residence in any voting unit. As members of the majority party in their respective townships, the door was open for them to establish legal residence if they wanted it. Once their ballots were in the box, the weight of responsibility shifted to the judges. Nonresident voting was, in this sense, a crime of election judges rather than voters. As Amos Myers stated so clearly, "it was the judges fault" if they accepted his ballot illegally. As representatives of the community, the judges alone accepted or rejected a ballot once it was offered. The majority party controlled that gateway into the community. Immel, Kline, and Kail all lost their votes, and legal residence, by presenting soft ballots in a Democratic township. But by the same token, migrants such as Espich, Taggart, and Myers gained access to the ballot box by presenting tickets that the local judges welcomed.[61]

Partisan interpretation of residence rules was so flexible, in fact, that even noncitizens could vote if they had the right political connections. Foreign immigrants represented about one-fifth of all adult males in Wayne County. These most conspicuous of all migrants faced the severest handicap to political participation, because Ohio law always demanded U.S. citizenship of its voters and public officials. And yet citizenship was far easier to demonstrate than legal residence in the state or in a county or township, because every naturalized citizen received a certificate, his "final papers." Election law demanded proof of naturalization at the polling place, and so the board of inquiry should not have had to review the ballots of any foreign immigrants. In fact, however, they examined the qualifications of six such immigrants who managed to vote without proving their citizenship. In practice, it turned out, immigrants could "get their votes" as long as they went unchallenged and as long as the election judges were willing to accept their ballots.

Noncitizens who voted in Wayne County did so with the help, the encouragement, and the endorsement of the local party organizations. A vocal Democrat might vote for years in a Democratic township without challenge even if known to be a noncitizen. In Plain Township, for example, two aliens, father and son, voted for years with the complicity of local Democratic judges. George F. Wilden was in his early forties in 1846, his father in his seventies. They were German immigrants, and they had come from York County, Pennsylvania, in 1834. The father and son lived together for many years in Reedsburgh in the northwest corner of the township and then moved to Mansfield, on the canal in neighboring Stark County. After two or three years in Mansfield, the Wildens came back to Plain Township, where they lived for about a year before the election.[62]

The Wildens' right to vote did not depend on their final papers, because they had none. It rested instead on their vocal support of the Democratic Party. The younger Wilden had served as Reedsburgh's postmaster for six years, and so his politics were public knowledge. He was considered an uncompromising Democrat. His commitment to his party was so intense that he voted the hard ticket in spite of his public support for banking. As Wilden expressed it, he and his father "voted the hard ticket, and he did not care a DAMN who knows it." The older Wilden, especially, wore his party label as a badge of honor. On the day of the election, he had walked, despite his age, the whole distance to the polling place. "The old man told me," George Stough remembered, that "he had come all the way on foot, and that Lightner would not let him ride in his wagon, because he was a democrat, and that Lightner had said if he was a whig or a 'soft,' he would let him ride." Lightner later assured Stough that he had only been joking with Wilden but "the old man . . . got offended and would not ride with him."63

No one in Plain Township questioned the citizenship of such vocal Democrats. During Cox's challenge, however, several Whig officials goaded the Wildens into proving their naturalization. George Wilden would say only that he and his father were both naturalized but had lost their papers. Then he changed his story. The older Wilden was naturalized, and the son, when still a minor, had acquired his citizenship from his father. But those papers were missing too. When pressed to produce papers, Wilden retorted angrily that he had been a voter for 22 years and had never been challenged. That was just as good as citizenship, as he saw it.64

That was just as good as citizenship as most Democrats saw it, too. The Wildens got their votes precisely because they had been so vociferous about supporting Joseph Willford. The Democratic majority on the Senate's Committee on Privileges and Elections took pains to note that the Wildens were recognized members of their community. While their claim to citizenship stood unproven, it had never before been challenged. They "have long been residents of Wayne County, and it appears by common consent, have enjoyed all the rights and privileges of citizenship." As old residents of Plain Township, the Wildens enjoyed full legal residence by "common consent," voting even though they were suspected aliens.65

Daniel Marklinger was another alien who voted regularly in Plain Township. In contrast to the Wildens, however, Marklinger earned his suffrage not by courting one of the local parties but rather both of them. Marklinger, a German immigrant, succumbed to the influence of two competing party organizations and tried to turn each one to his own advantage. No one knew for certain how Marklinger voted and, as it turned out, neither did Marklinger himself. On the day of the election, three of Marklinger's friends gave him tickets – one Democratic, one Mixed, and one "genuine Whig." But Marklinger refused to reveal his actual vote because he was a tailor and wanted to do business with customers of all parties. Both Whigs and Democrats in Plain Township, as a result, considered him "doubtful." Some of them passed Marklinger with silent contempt on the streets of Blachleyville because of his political ambivalence.[66]

Marklinger, who spoke little English, could read and write none at all and, as a result, relied heavily for advice on his political friends. As one acquaintance remarked, "Politically he was anything and everything." William B. Anderson, a hard Democrat, escorted Marklinger to the polls in 1846. "I met Daniel Marklinger near the polls," Anderson remembered. "I took him by the arm, and we walked to the window, and he voted." Anderson assumed that Marklinger had cast a Democratic ticket, but he was not certain. Another tailor challenged Marklinger's ballot. The two tailors had an old grudge going that apparently found political expression. The judges held Marklinger's ballot, which he had shrewdly folded, all during the challenge. The judges talked to Marklinger, let him swear to legal residence, and then accepted his ballot.[67]

During the contest, the board of inquiry questioned Marklinger's citizenship. Marklinger was not a citizen, as it turned out, and everyone in town had known that all along. Both parties had acquiesced in his suffrage, each hoping to win his ballot. But still no one knew how the German had voted. A friend warned Marklinger that he faced up to five years in prison as an illegal voter and advised him to reveal the nature of his vote so that it might be thrown out. "After hearing the different stories about his vote," he recalled, "I concluded to caution him, as people would suppose he was more 'knave than fool.'" But in fact Marklinger proved to be more fool than knave: He had cast a folded ballot without ever looking at it. Democrats and Whigs in Plain Township had knowingly permitted an alien to vote because each party wanted to secure his support. Marklinger himself did not, in fact could not, read his ticket before casting it. An election board of two Whigs and one Democrat had accepted the folded ballot, each expecting it to hold the name of his own party's candidate. But still no one, not even Marklinger himself, knew for certain how he had voted.[68]

The majority Democrats of the Senate Committee, who reviewed all this testimony, decided somewhat illogically that Marklinger had voted for Cox as senator. They invalidated the immigrant's right of suffrage and then threw out one Whig ballot. But during the election, informal recognition of residence by the community – or at least by one or both political parties – ensured even aliens the right to vote in Plain Township. Political criteria of residence in the township could outweigh legal standards of suffrage. In particular, the complicity of local party officials could secure almost anyone a legal suffrage, even in a divided township.[69]

The heavy migration of voters during the mid-nineteenth century and the doctrine of domicile that was embodied in Ohio election law reinforced the majority party in each of Wayne County's townships. The right of election judges to screen new voters – and old ones – for legal residence gave local party organizations immense authority in defining the boundaries of the local electorate. By applying political criteria before awarding suffrage, judges could disqualify adherents of the opposing party, rack up outsized majorities at the local level, and preserve the political character of their townships in the wake of wholesale migration. Migration, in fact, enhanced the authority of such core communities of persisters by enlarging the pool of new or suspect voters for challenge and interrogation. Rules of residence and their enforcement at the polling place represented an important element in party strategy and organization. No matter what their numbers, new voters could make little impression in an election that was run by members of the opposing party.

No one was above twisting election rules or courting questionable voters in Wayne County, not even the powerful directors of the Bank of Wooster. Thirty-four years old in 1846, Constant Lake was a director of the Bank of Wooster and a substantial merchant whose interests stretched across northern Ohio. Lake was almost a lifelong resident. He was born in Trumbull County, Ohio, but arrived in Wooster with his family within a year of his birth. He opened his first grocery with his older brother Joseph at age 14. Lake never held elective office, but his extensive business pursuits provoked a natural interest in local politics. At age 24, Lake married the only daughter of Benjamin Jones, another director of the Bank of Wooster, giving him firm economic, political, and family connections among the town's elite. His eldest son, Constant Lake, Jr., went on to marry the youngest daughter of Dr. William Blachley, one of the earliest settlers in Wayne County and founder of Blachleyville in Plain Township. The Lake brothers and Jones, all directors of the Bank of Wooster, were leading soft Democrats whose political connections stretched well beyond Columbus, to the Senate and even the White House.[70]

In light of Lake's business and political credentials, it seems ludicrous at first sight to picture him pulling a drunken immigrant by the elbow along the streets of Wooster. But this is precisely what he did on election day in 1846. Godfrey Kibler was a long-time resident who had been gone for a year and a half and whose residence was now suspect. During Cox's contest, Kibler's name turned up on the Wooster poll books, and Democrats charged the Bank of Wooster with direct responsibility for putting it there. Peter Wilhelm, a Democrat, had seen Lake and Kibler together. Kibler, a German immigrant, met Lake in a barroom before 9:00 a.m. on the day of the election. Christian Younger, the bar's owner, kept two bundles of ballots that he distributed to customers – Democratic tickets for hard Democrats and Independent tickets for softs. Younger, who preferred the soft ticket but also stocked hard ones as a courtesy to his customers, offered Kibler an Independent ticket and led him into the privacy of the bar's entry. But as soon as Kibler took the ballot, Lake appeared and led him out onto the town square.[71]

Outside on the square, Henry Wolford saw Kibler leave Younger's tavern and head for the polls. Wolford himself stopped to offer Kibler a ticket, but he refused to take it, saying Wolford "carried water on both shoulders." Wolford's stand on banking was evidently ambiguous. Then the bank director reappeared, took Kibler by the arm, and walked him around the corner of the courthouse in the direction of the polls. Lake himself testified that Kibler went with him to the polls and voted. But Lake later learned, according to his own testimony, that Kibler had not voted the Independent ticket. Kibler voted a ballot he had picked up at Winters', a hard Democratic tavern in Wooster. If the Democrats threw out Kibler's ticket, according to Lake, Willford and not Cox would lose another ballot.[72]

But Kibler's friend Wilhelm claimed that Kibler had indeed cast a soft ballot. Wilhelm met Kibler back in Younger's tavern on the evening of the election. "I said to him, you used to be a good Democrat, and you have now voted the Whig ticket." Kibler replied that he had indeed cast a hard ticket, that Constant Lake gave it to him, and Lake was a Democrat. Wilhelm told Kibler, who had been gone for some time from Wooster, that Lake had been a good Democrat, but now he was a "soft." Kibler, according to Wilhelm, was only "mad a little." And so Cox and the bank faction had an unwitting supporter. When Lake became a soft, he dragged Godfrey Kibler, literally, along with him.[73]

In defense of his residence, under interrogation, Kibler argued shrewdly that he must be a legal resident. Some of Wooster's most prominent citizens had offered him ballots. These men included Constant Lake, director of the Bank of Wooster; Christian Younger, who ran a Whig tavern in Wooster; John Larwill, one of the fathers of the county who would later defend volitional suffrage in Ohio's constitutional convention; Charles Greater, a local bookseller and future mayor; and Dr. John P. Coulter, president of the Wooster Bank "who knew him this twelve years." With connections such as these, Kibler's claim to residence – and his unwitting vote for Cox – stood up at the ballot box, and he was not even challenged. As Kibler told the board of inquiry, he "thought these men would not offer him a ticket, unless he had a right to vote." Kibler defined his own right of suffrage as he understood it and as he saw it in practice: open acceptance by the township's core community.[74]

Wooster went so heavily Whig because the Wooster Bank faction dominated the township's core community. The town's merchants, bankers, and lawyers, with but a few exceptions, were Whigs and soft Democrats. Interlocking relationships of business, family, and friendship linked Wooster's merchants in a tight network of politics. Political organization centered on the Bank of Wooster. Figure 7.2 shows graphically the intensive network that went into action on election day to bring only one voter, Godfrey Kibler, to the polling place with a Whig ballot. The bank faction's growing influence spread further through a network of economic and political connections at the local, state, and even national levels. But the center of that network still remained rooted firmly within Wooster, which made Cox's defeat a blow of such stunning proportions. Willford's victory shook the alliance between Whigs and soft Democrats at its very foundation and even challenged Whig domination of the Ohio Senate. But as the testimony in the Wayne County case made clear, electoral victory at the local level could hinge not merely on politics and parties but on patterns of migration and legal definitions of residence. Parties could use high rates of migration, in combination with flexible rules of residence, to dominate local voting units. The stalemate in the Ohio Senate had to await a painstaking reexamination of ambiguous rules of residence.

In fact, the Wayne County testimony trickled into the hands of the Senate Committee all through December and early January. Senate Whigs wanted badly to print the testimony for distribution on the floor of the Senate, believing that it contained enough evidence of fraud to prove their case and return Levi Cox to the Senate. Democrats initially resisted but then reluctantly consented. But the Democrats, who had managed to organize the Senate in a compromise between soft Democrats and Whigs, had a majority on the Committee on Privileges and Elections. Neither soft nor hard Democrats wanted to give Whigs a majority by seating Cox. They

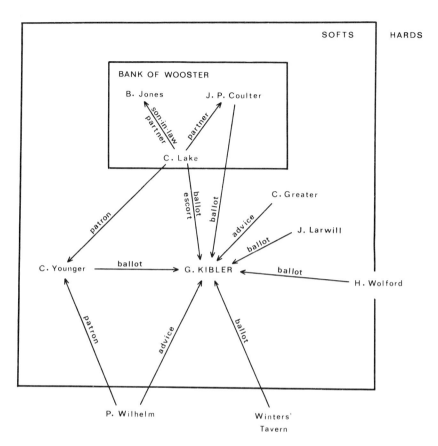

Figure 7.2. Godfrey Kibler and the Wooster Bank faction. *Source:* "Wayne County Case," 143–45, 202–5, 208, 216.

now heeded the call of party and reported unfavorably against the Whig's challenge, largely overlooking the testimony painstakingly accumulated during six weeks in Wooster. The committee argued, in effect, that in general a township could select its own legal voters. In early January, the issue left the committee and headed toward the floor of the Senate.[75]

It was at this moment that the Whigs lost their best hope of sustaining their contest. Proving himself a scoundrel in the eyes of Whigs and even some Democrats, Willford challenged the rules of parliamentary procedure by insisting on voting in his own case. Willford's refusal to withdraw from the Senate floor preserved the tie between Democrats and Whigs and brought Cox's carefully prepared challenge to a standstill. Willford appealed to party loyalty in his determination to preserve the 17-to-17 tie. According to the Columbus *Ohio State Journal*, he rose to the floor of the Senate and "declared that he was not to be deterred from voting by any objections that Whig Senators might raise, or by any precedents from parliamentary rules that they might quote." Willford now stunned senators of both parties by challenging them to remove him from the Senate chambers by force. "He had received quite a number of letters from his political friends in Wayne county, insisting that he should force his vote upon the contest," he explained, "and he certainly should do so, unless removed from the bar of the Senate by *brute force*." Willford then turned away from his Senate colleagues to launch a personal threat against his opponent. "So far as Mr. Cox and himself were concerned, there was nothing personal between them," he promised, but "If there was, there was a way of settling that too." Willford was insistent: He had instructions to defend his seat, and he would obey them.[76]

Whigs and even Democrats across the state were astounded by Willford's open show of bravado. The *Ohio State Journal* labeled him a brute and remarked that "no person possessed of the ordinary sensibilities of a man, could be induced to give utterance to sentiments like the above, on the floor of a deliberative body." Even the *Ashland Standard*, a soft Democratic press, claimed that "There are not twenty farmers in Wayne County *less* qualified for the station." The *Standard*'s editor believed that he had found just the proper employment for Joseph Willford. "If he *is* to be retained at Columbus," he suggested, "wouldn't it be a good idea to have him change places with the man who makes fires in the Senate chambers?" Privately, a fellow senator asked John Larwill, a Wooster Democrat, to "Keep Willford straight it may be he will say two much [*sic*]."[77]

But Willford did not have the chance to say much more. During the next week, a Democratic senator retired suddenly with a serious illness, breaking the tie in the Senate that Willford had been so defiantly and even recklessly defending. The sudden Whig majority of one not only lent renewed vigor to Cox's challenge but actually threatened Willford with prosecution for his actions. Prompted by Cox's reluctance to reclaim his Senate seat, Wayne County Whigs settled for a compromise – Willford's resignation, which they had worked so hard to achieve, and his replacement at a by-election. In the spirit of popular rule that permeated antebellum politics, the choice between Whig and Democrat, soft and hard, went back to the voters of Wayne County.[78]

But as the contest between Willford and Cox makes clear, the choice was not nearly so simple. Wayne County voters were caught up in a web of competing party organizations, core communities of old residents who worked hard to bring supporters to the polls on election day and to keep their opponents away. Part of that organization included a shrewd understanding and application of rules of residence amid an electorate that was on the move. Commercial activity and agricultural development attracted many long-distance migrants to Wayne County and sent many other voters moving locally. Most newcomers remained temporarily in a voting unit and then moved on again. On the day of the election, recent migrants had to decide for themselves where it was that they lived and then convince the local election judges to accept their ballots. That decision was always a political gamble, because a rejection at the ballot box could bring temporary disfranchisement – nonresidence until the next election. Newcomers needed political and social acceptance by their township's core communities to secure a reliable suffrage.

Historians have noted a remarkable persistence of political divisions at the local level over long periods, even in the face of extreme population turnover. That robust persistence finds partial explanation in the self-perpetuation of a core community that could use elections as an institution for recruiting new members. Members of the core community reached out, through their political organizations, to newcomers and migrants. Local parties had a perfect motive to put the popular theory of political equality to the test. Political parties were much more inclusive than other local institutions. Associations such as churches and voluntary associations tended to be exclusive: they discriminated in selecting their members. Parties, by contrast, were by definition inclusive. Every white adult male possessed something of potential value to each political party – his vote. Parties continually sought out new members, in some instances scouring the township for new voters. As part of the intensive political organization they practiced before the Civil War, local parties not only recruited newcomers to the community but actually competed for them. In their maintenance of political control and their recruitment of new members, local parties presaged the more elaborate urban machines of the late nineteenth century. Both organized local society in their pursuit and exercise of political power.[79]

Local politicians had an institutional imperative to control the admission of newcomers into full political membership in their communities, recruiting adherents of their own parties and challenging members of the opposition. Each of Ohio's 2,000 townships reserved the right to define the boundaries of its own electorate. In the face of widespread migration, that political task was even more difficult than historians have imagined. Ohio's policymakers used demographic criteria in sorting out legal from fraudulent voters, and local party leaders had to apply those criteria to define the political boundaries of their communities. In the process, politicians defended the bounds of their communities and then had to work within them. Townships chose their members at the polling place, and so successful party leaders had to be experts at interpreting and applying ambiguous rules of residence.

Conclusion

Ohio's political system evolved amid a mobile, unsettled electorate. During the early decades of statehood, especially, the westward movement carried hundreds of thousands of settlers into and through Ohio. Later, the growth of cities, rapid innovations in transportation, and foreign immigration dominated patterns of movement within and through the state. At first glance, the residents of Ohio's townships succeeded quite well in maintaining political order in the face of widespread migration. But on closer examination that political stability proves to have been superficial only. The local political continuity so often displayed in election returns was actually the end result of a complex set of suffrage rules, election practices, partisan tactics, and personal relationships designed to make partisan politics workable in the midst of migration. Ohio's antebellum political system evolved over several generations during which rapid and frequent population turnover was a political as well as social fact of life. It would be surprising indeed if the aggressive national expansion that drew millions of migrants westward through Ohio did *not* help to direct the state's political development.

Ohio's initially simple political practices had to change gradually to accommodate the burgeoning streams of migrants moving through and within the state. The formal mission of any political system is, of course, to choose public officials and to make decisions. But Ohio's political system, like all political systems, had to do more. It had to perform the additional, informal function of maintaining political order in the wake of social change. Widespread migration represented, in this sense, not only a social problem but also an important political problem. Ohio's policymakers faced the challenge of creating a political system that both preserved political order and recognized the rights of migrants to participate freely in their new communities. The political challenge of migration, the incessant arrival of new voters year after year, forced a choice between democracy and order, between the rights of individual migrants to vote and the rights of their new communities to enjoy political stability.[1]

Because migration did not abate after the westward movement

171

through Ohio crested, that dilemma did not characterize merely a frontier area or a frontier period but in fact deepened as the nineteenth century unfolded. At statehood in 1803, Ohio's rules of suffrage included only one criterion of residence, which required one year in the state before voting. By the outbreak of the Civil War, however, the state possessed a wide array of complicated residence rules as well as elaborate mechanisms for their interpretation and application. The problems of maintaining stability while most voters moved provoked both new rules of suffrage and a new doctrine of legal residence. By the end of the century, migrants were largely free to move about without suffering political and legal disabilities. But the intervening decades were a transitional period. Slowly, a political system emerged that was designed to dampen the effects of widespread migration by sorting out legitimate newcomers from fraudulent voters and balancing the rights of individuals against the needs of their communities.

Overall, Ohio policymakers solved this dilemma by restricting political participation. Residence was only one of a wide array of demographic characteristics that subjected most Ohioans to disfranchisement. Sex, race, citizenship, age, and propertyholding were added to residence as demographic qualifications for political participation. Ohio, of course, restricted the franchise to men, and this qualification went virtually unchallenged until the twentieth century. Like most other states, antebellum Ohio also restricted suffrage to whites. This qualification, too, went largely unchallenged until a constitutional amendment, the Fifteenth, ratified in 1870, required a change. Ohio's first constitution did not require voters to be U.S. citizens. But an early statute, passed in 1809, initiated that qualification, which has never been revoked. Age was another obvious demographic qualification. Ohio's first constitution required voters to be 21, state representatives to be 25, and state senators and the governor to be 30 years old. A fifth demographic qualification, taxpaying, also restricted political participation. Ohio's first constitution required voters to pay a county or township tax, limiting the franchise to propertyholders. This taxpaying qualification, however, was easy to meet and so probably disfranchised few potential voters. Ohio's second constitution, adopted in 1851, revoked the taxpaying qualification altogether.[2]

Even before experiencing the full effects of internal migration, therefore, Ohio's political leaders had already severely limited the franchise. In fact, a venerable political rule of thumb held that only one-seventh of the total population were eligible voters. Some of these suffrage restrictions, such as age and citizenship, reflected sound judgments during the period and still stand in modified form. Others were simply political expressions of unreasonable but common, and therefore largely unchallenged, prejudices. Such demographic qualifications were designed to limit the franchise to those whom prevalent ideology, popular prejudices, or simply the common sense of the age labeled legitimate voters. It is therefore not surprising that as migrants gradually became a political problem, policymakers responded to them in much the same way, by restricting the franchise.

At statehood, Ohio adopted simple rules of suffrage modeled largely after the experiences of the older states. Residence in Ohio was consensual: The voters of a township themselves decided, by common consent, who was a legal voter. The Constitution of 1802 did not even require voters to be citizens. That restriction appeared within a decade, however, and the revolution in legal definitions of residence that took place after 1815 provoked political restrictions on internal migrants as well. Ohio courts gradually extended full legal and political rights to migrants, shifting primary authority in awarding legal residence away from townships and increasingly granting migrants the right to reside legally wherever they chose. Reacting to their experiences with migration, Ohioans gradually altered their state's suffrage rules to accommodate increasing numbers of migrants. Reflecting national legal trends, particularly the emergence of the doctrine of domicile, Ohio jurists gradually broadened rules of suffrage for internal migrants as the century progressed. They gave migrants more freedom to participate in their communities even as relative newcomers.

Jurists responded to a new wave of judicial individualism after 1815 by extending new rights to migrants to select their own legal residence. Between 1803 and 1878, Americans' increasing mobility contributed heavily to a new theory of suffrage that emphasized the needs and intentions of individual voters rather than the political integrity of their communities. By 1878, migrants had the right to vote wherever they chose, and indeed, through the doctrine of domicile, voting itself became a crucial test of legal residence. Voters were free to move within the state without suffering even temporary disfranchisement. Suffrage was now volitional, resting in the intentions of the voter to become a settled resident. The colonial meeting had withered away and the modern election, better suited to the needs of a modern, mobile electorate, had appeared in its place.

While the courts were liberalizing rules of suffrage for migrants, however, the legislature was wrestling with new definitions of legal residence. New suffrage rules were designed to respond to the novel volitional suffrage without endangering the stability of Ohio's political system. Beginning in 1831, the legislature tightened rules of residence. Voters now had to reside in the townships where they voted, not just within the county. A local board of election judges received new authority to review the qualifications of prospective voters, including their legal residence, and to reject their ballots. In 1841, in a comprehensive election law that governed electoral practices until the Civil War, the legislature drew detailed rules of residence in Ohio for the first time. The local election judges could now interrogate challenged voters to determine their eligibility. Voters could also declare legal residence in a voting unit by swearing to an election oath, and so newcomers could participate in elections as "sworn" voters. Finally, in 1857, the legislature stipulated a fixed term of residence not only in the state but in counties and townships, for the first time. Voters now had to reside in a county for 30 days before an election and in a township for 20 days. As the locus of suffrage shifted gradually from the township to the individual, rules of residence grew more specific.

On the eve of the Civil War, therefore, Ohio residents faced a hierarchy of demographic qualifications for political participation (Table C.1). Ohio's constitutions and statutes set up a series of six demographic hurdles that its residents had to overcome in succession before participating in politics – sex, race, citizenship, age, property, and residence. The first four criteria for voting (sex, race, citizenship, and age) survived the antebellum period intact. Several of the restrictions were revoked, however, including the taxpaying qualification for voting and the age qualifications for holding office. Significantly, every qualification that was added after statehood dealt with migration and residence. The most important changes in the suffrage reflected policymakers' experiences with migrants.

Residence itself contained an internal hierarchy of demographic hurdles. By 1860, suffrage demanded U.S. citizenship, one year's residence in Ohio, 30 days' residence in the county, and 20 days' residence in the township. The final hurdle for the voter was, of course, convincing the local board of election judges that he was indeed a legal resident. This was perhaps the most difficult hurdle of all, because all of the other qualifications could be documented in the form of a public record – a birth certificate, naturalization papers, a tax receipt, or a receipt for work on the public roads, which substituted for payment of taxes. The ambiguity of legal residence

Table C.1. *A hierarchy of political qualifications in antebellum Ohio*

Qualifications	Changes before 1860
1. Sex: Male	None
2. Race: White	None
3. Citizenship: United States	Established in 1809
4. Age: 21 for voting	None
25 for state representatives	Revoked in 1851
30 for state senators, governor	Revoked in 1851
5. Property: Taxpayer	Revoked in 1851
6. Residence: One year in state	None
30 days in county	Established in 1857
20 days in township	Established in 1857

Sources: Ohio Constitution (1802), art. 1, secs. 4, 7, art. 2, sec. 3,art. 4, sec. 1; Chase, ed., *Statutes of Ohio*, 3: chap. 834, sec. 5, 1740; *Ohio Constitution* (1851), art. 2, art. 3, art. 5, sec. 1; *Ohio Laws*, 54 v 136 (1857).

was, indeed, the reason for the elaborate system of challenge, oath, interrogation, and a second oath that greeted many migrants at the polling place.

In theory, Americans considered equal access to the ballot box an essential ingredient in the participant politics that they saw awakening around them. In practice, however, migrants were underrepresented at the ballot box, partially disfranchised by both law and practice. Most obviously, election laws, which were grounded in residence, disfranchised migrants temporarily. Every time a voter moved across a political boundary he lost his right of suffrage for up to one year. The sheer frequency of migration during the nineteenth century therefore meant extended or frequent periods of disfranchisement for many voters. Further, rootlessness meant that most voters' impact on the affairs of any single community could be only temporary. The majority of newcomers voted only once or twice in a community before moving on, enhancing the political influence of the minority who remained.

Antebellum election laws tended to give broad discretionary powers to settled residents, particularly local party officials, in accepting or rejecting the ballots of migratory voters. Those broad powers ensured that a minority of persistent voters, organized into local parties, might control the local political process. Formal and informal disfranchisement of newcomers blunted the political disruption that might have arisen from the potent combination of heavy migration and a broadening suffrage, concentrating unusual political power in the hands of a persistent core community. The legislature, in short, reacted to the new volitional conception of suffrage by concentrating new political power within the hands of settled persisters and their representatives. Election judges could, and frequently did, interrogate newcomers at the polling place before ruling on their eligibility to vote. A core community of economically successful persisters therefore had the right to define the legal boundaries of the local electorate. Local parties, in effect, dispensed suffrage selectively to newcomers.

Widespread migration, the new volitional theory of suffrage, and the statutory authority of persisters to screen newcomers all combined to complicate the casting of ballots in antebellum elections. Most obviously, the transience of most voters produced complex and subtle patterns of political participation at the local level. Poll books show that the local electorate was not a stable cadre of long-term participants consistently turning out in elections year after year. Instead, the majority of voters participated in only one or two elections in any single township before moving on.

At the other extreme stood the core community, a relative handful of each township's voters, no more than 5 to 10 percent. They participated in as many as ten consecutive elections or even more. Persisters tended to possess greater wealth and occupational status than migrants and to be middle-aged. They represented a persistent political and economic elite. The most frequent voters and officeholders, in other words, were the wealthiest and most persistent. The local electorate, as a result, was dominated numerically by newcomers and transients but politically by a small core of economic leaders. Members of the core community used their persistence to win exaggerated influence both at the ballot box and in political office.

Ohio elections were won and lost at the local level, within thousands of communities. During the Second Party Period, Ohio politics presented a clear picture of intense partisan competition at the state level. From 1832 to 1853, the Ohio electorate was almost evenly divided between Democrats and Whigs. Ohio Democrats commanded a slight plurality of 48.9 percent in the typical election, with Whigs garnering an average of 47.3 percent. Neither party dominated the state, and every statewide election therefore provoked a bitter and hard-fought campaign. Such partisan competitiveness bred political instability, and the Ohio statehouse and legislature swung unpredictably from one election to the next.[3]

But the partisan balance at the state level merely reflected and largely obscured political continuity within thousands of local political units. Majorities were both larger and more consistent at the local level. Residence requirements, with their provisions for interrogating voters at the polling place, put a premium on local partisan organization. Local party leaders rose to that challenge magnificently. Settled Ohioans gradually met the challenge of migration by altering their state's political practices to turn the transiency of voters to their own advantage. A minority of persisters used election laws to promote political continuity by concentrating political power within their own hands. Electoral practices were designed, in part, to resolve political conflicts between migrants and persisters, in many instances before the actual casting of ballots. Election returns therefore displayed to outsiders – and to historians – a deceptive image of relative stability. Antebellum voting returns therefore do not do justice to the rich complexity of local political life. In Ohio, state-level returns reveal a precarious balance between Democrats and Whigs. But they obscure political stability within townships, the state's basic political units. Each local political system was in fact designed to promote stability. Local politicians were committed to delivering their townships on election day, and they used every resource at their disposal to do just that. Those resources included the unsettled movement of voters through the township, rules of residence that were still in transition on their way to modernity and were therefore ambiguous, and, finally, the settled persistence of party leaders.

In the wake of migration, local politicians and party organizations performed a much more difficult and important task than historians have realized. The electorates they managed were far less settled, socially and politically, than aggregate voting returns alone could ever suggest. Routine migration among voters presented an organizational challenge of immense proportions. Local leaders represented a stable political elite in the midst of a constantly moving electorate. After every election, up to one-third of all voters might leave a community, only to be replaced before the next election by as many or more new voters. Over an entire decade, the local electorate might turn over almost completely. Electoral victory therefore required of local parties the incessant repetition of the same, well-practiced organizational routine – identifying new voters, keeping the issues before them, winning their involvement, and most especially bringing them out to the polls on election day. In the face of migration, and given the frequency of antebellum elections, those tasks were literally never-ending.

It is little wonder that local political leaders, especially the partisan press, kept up a steady drumbeat that seems excessive by modern standards. During this period, too, parties had every incentive to cultivate emotional issues and to shift the focus of voters' allegiances upward in the political hierarchy, to the state and national levels. Migrants who were already emotionally involved in a national party system required less coaxing to participate within their new communities. Routine migration put a premium on intensive party organization. A stable and ordered community, amid an electorate in motion, was no accident; it was a considerable political achievement.[4]

In their deceptive simplicity, aggregate voting returns can therefore conceal the impact of migration on local political organization – the coming and going of thousands of voters every decade, the application of ambiguous rules of suffrage that focused on residence, the persistence of a powerful social and political elite, and the public give-and-take between migrants and judges at the polling place. As a result, historians should use great care in interpreting aggregate voting returns. Election outcomes could reflect the interaction of a wide variety of social, economic, personal, and demographic, as well as political, processes. Historians must look beneath voting returns and examine closely the political and social organization of the communities that reported them.

Because of their relative scarcity and selective survival, individual-level voting records can never replace aggregate voting returns as a basic resource for nineteenth-century political history. During the past two decades, in fact, historians have made crucial methodological breakthroughs that promise a strikingly thorough analysis of aggregate electoral records. Sophisticated procedures such as ecological inference permit historians to link voting returns with other records, such as the U.S. census, that are organized according to geographical units (counties, townships, and wards). Historians can therefore link voting behavior directly with personal characteristics of the electorate, such as socioeconomic status, ethnic background, and religious orientation. They can also use voting returns to chart abrupt or subtle changes in participation and partisanship from one election to the next.[5]

Such estimates of individual-level behavior, however, should remain firmly grounded within the context of community political life. Their knowledge of patterns of migration and of turnover within the electorate will help historians to interpret aggregate voting returns within a broader social setting. Historians may, for example, prefer county-level rather than township-level voting records. Because an important minority of voters were local-level migrants, township-level voting returns are more susceptible to the disruptive impact of migration on political behavior. Historians may also want to place more confidence in ecological estimates of individual-level behavior in long-settled areas. Changes in patterns of participation and partisanship in regions that were experiencing less geographical mobility are more likely to reflect the influence of political rather than demographic processes. Because the local electorate turned over so rapidly in the wake of migration, estimates of partisan transitions between elections will be more reliable when restricted to elections separated by only a year or two. Tempered by a more detailed portrait of local political organization, interpretation of aggregate voting returns promises even more precision and sophistication.[6]

Indeed, any thorough analysis of elections, local parties, or voting returns during the mid-nineteenth century should include an intensive social analysis of the local electorate. Historians cannot take voting returns at face value as an accurate and unbiased reflection of the popular political will of any community. Some social, economic, demographic, and even geographical groups within the community were consistently overrepresented both at the ballot box and in office. Moreover, because of selective persistence and migration, historians cannot even view census data as an accurate portrait of the local electorate from one year to the next. A close analysis of migration and persistence must therefore play a role in any study of local political life. A full appreciation of voting returns must take into account how elections were held, who controlled voting units, how parties were organized, how rules of suffrage were actually applied, and above all who persisted and who did not. Historians must, in short, bring to every analysis of local political behavior a complete understanding of what politics meant in a time and in a place, within the context of a particular community.[7]

In antebellum Ohio, migration was a complex social phenomenon that provoked a complex political reaction. Migration could mean, on the one hand, the annual arrival of hundreds of anonymous newcomers, each seeking enfranchisement at the polling place and then moving on again before the next election. But the impact of migration could, on the other hand, be much more personally and keenly felt, as when an early antislavery society reported that "Our meeting at this place was a failure. The person to whom we wrote to make the appointment had moved away."[8] From either perspective, the restless movement of voters played an important role in the organization of local political life.

Notes

Introduction

1   John Mason Peck, *A New Guide to the West* (Cincinnati, 1848), 121; Frederick Jackson Turner, *The Frontier in American History* (New York: Henry Holt, 1920), 1, 259.

2   Richard S. Alcorn, "Leadership and Stability in Mid-Nineteenth-Century America: A Case Study of an Illinois Town," *Journal of American History*, 61 (December 1974), 685–702; and Don H. Doyle, "Social Theory and New Communities in Nineteenth-Century America," *Western Historical Quarterly*, 8 (April 1977), 151–65, offer historiographical reviews that gauge the impact of recent migration studies on the Turnerian controversy over the sources of order and disorder in nineteenth-century communities.

3   Two important and very suggestive essays hypothesize that spatial and occupational mobility inhibited a sense of class solidarity and the development of effective political organizations among nineteenth-century workers; Stephan Thernstrom, "Socialism and Social Mobility," in *Failure of a Dream? Essays in the History of American Socialism*, ed. Peter Laslett and Seymour M. Lipset (New York: Doubleday, 1974), 509–25; and Charles Stephenson, "A Gathering of Strangers? Mobility, Social Structure, and Political Participation in the Formation of Nineteenth-Century American Workingclass Culture," in *American Workingclass Culture: Explorations in American Labor and Social History*, ed. Milton Cantor (Westport, Conn.: Greenwood, 1979), 31–60.

4   James C. Malin, "The Turnover of Farm Population in Kansas," *Kansas Historical Quarterly*, 4 (November 1935), 339–72.

5   William L. Bowers, "Crawford Township, 1850–1870: A Population Study of a Pioneer Community," *Iowa Journal of History*, 58 (January 1960), 1–30; Mildred Throne, "A Population Study of an Iowa County in 1850," *Iowa Journal of History*, 57 (October 1959), 305–30; Merle Curti, *The Making of an American Community: A Case Study of Democracy in a Frontier County* (Stanford, Calif.: Stanford University Press, 1959), 65–77; Peter J. Coleman, "Restless Grant County: Americans on the Move," *Wisconsin Magazine of History*, 46 (Autumn 1962), 16–20. Earlier in the 1950s, the "Owsley school" of Southern social historians produced many population studies that focused, in part, on migration; see especially Frank L. Owsley, *Plain Folk of the Old South* (Baton Rouge: Louisiana University Press, 1949), 23–77. Stephan Thernstrom, *The Other Bostonians: Poverty*

and *Progress in the American Metropolis, 1880–1970* (Cambridge, Mass.: Harvard University Press, 1973), 221–32, reviews American migration studies.

6 Stephan Thernstrom, *Poverty and Progress: Social Mobility in a Nineteenth Century City* (Cambridge, Mass.: Harvard University Press, 1964), 84–90. Subsequent persistence studies have confirmed the general relationship between persistence and economic success during the nineteenth century; see, for example, Thernstrom, *Other Bostonians*, 9–44; Richard J. Hopkins, "Occupational and Geographic Mobility in Atlanta, 1870–1876," *Journal of Southern History*, 34 (May 1968), 200–13; Michael B. Katz, Michael J. Doucet, and Mark J. Stern, "Migration and the Social Order in Erie County, New York: 1855," *Journal of Interdisciplinary History*, 8 (Spring 1978), 669–701; Howard M. Gitelman, *Workingmen of Waltham: Mobility in American Urban Industrial Development, 1850–1890* (Baltimore: Johns Hopkins University Press, 1974), 23–49; Clyde Griffen and Sally Griffen, *Natives and Newcomers: The Ordering of Opportunity in Mid-Nineteenth-Century Poughkeepsie* (Cambridge, Mass.: Harvard University Press, 1978); Gordon W. Kirk, Jr., and Carol Tyirin Kirk, "Migration, Mobility and the Transformation of the Occupational Structure in an Immigrant Community: Holland, Michigan, 1850–80," *Journal of Social History*, 7 (Winter 1974), 142–64; and Michael B. Katz, Michael J. Doucet, and Mark J. Stern, *The Social Organization of Early Industrial Capitalism* (Cambridge, Mass.: Harvard University Press, 1982), 102–30. Stanley L. Engerman, "Up or Out: Social and Geographic Mobility in the United States," *Journal of Interdisciplinary History*, 3 (Winter 1975), 469–89, offers an important theoretical review.

7 Stephan Thernstrom and Peter R. Knights, "Men in Motion: Some Data and Speculations about Urban Population Mobility in Nineteenth-Century America," *Journal of Interdisciplinary History*, 1 (Autumn 1970), 7–35, were first to alert historians to the need to examine annual rates of persistence and migration. Thernstrom, *Other Bostonians*, 221–32, reviews most studies of migration up to 1973.

8 Richard P. McCormick, "New Perspectives on Jacksonian Politics," *American Historical Review*, 65 (January 1960), 288–301; Chilton Williamson, *American Suffrage: From Property to Democracy, 1760–1860* (Princeton, N.J.: Princeton University Press, 1960); Ronald P. Formisano, "Deferential-Participant Politics: The Early Republic's Political Culture, 1789–1840," *American Political Science Review*, 68 (June 1974), 473–87; David Donald, "An Excess of Democracy: The American Civil War and the Social Process," in *Lincoln Reconsidered: Essays on the Civil War Era*, 2d ed. (New York: Random House, 1956), 209–35; William E. Gienapp, "'Politics Seem to Enter into Everything': Political Culture in the North, 1840–1860," in *Essays on American Antebellum Politics, 1840–1860*, ed. Stephen E. Maizlish and John J. Kushma (College Station: Texas A & M University Press, 1982), 14–69.

9 John Higham, *From Boundlessness to Consolidation: The Transformation of American Culture, 1848–1860* (Ann Arbor, Mich.: William L. Clements Library, 1969). See also Robert H. Wiebe, *The Opening of American Society: From the Adoption of the Constitution to the Eve of Disunion* (New York: Random House, 1984). Kenneth A. Lockridge, *A New England Town: The First Hundred Years: Dedham, Massachusetts, 1636–1736* (New York: Norton, 1970), describes the erosion of the "closed corporate community" in eighteenth-century New England. Other discussions include Richard L. Bushman, *From Puritan to Yankee: Character and the Social Order in Connecticut, 1690–1765* (New York: Norton, 1967), 235–88; James A. Henretta, "Families and Farms: *Mentalité* in Pre-Industrial America," *William and Mary Quarterly*, 3d ser., 35 (January 1978), 3–32; and Christopher Clark, "Household Economy, Market Exchange and the Rise of Capitalism in the Connecticut Valley, 1800–1860," *Journal of Social History*, 13 (Winter 1979), 169–89.

10 R. W. B. Lewis, *The American Adam: Innocence, Tragedy, and Tradition in the Nineteenth Century* (Chicago: University of Chicago Press, 1955), quote from 5; James Willard Hurst, *Law and the Conditions of Freedom in the Nineteenth-Century United States* (Madison: University of Wisconsin Press, 1956), 3–32; Thomas R. Hietala, *Manifest Design: Anxious Aggrandizement in Late Jacksonian America* (Ithaca, N.Y.: Cornell University Press, 1985); Donald, "Excess of Democracy"; Stanley M. Elkins, *Slavery: A Problem in American Institutional and Intellectual Life* (Chicago: University of Chicago Press, 1959), 27–37, 140–57; George M. Fredrickson, *The Inner Civil War: Northern Intellectuals and the Crisis of the Union* (New York: Harper & Row, 1965), 36–50.

11 Paul F. Bourke and Donald A. Debats, "Identifiable Voting in Nineteenth-Century America: Toward a Comparison of Britain and the United States before the Secret Ballot," *Perspectives in American History*, 11 (1977–1978), 259–88, and "Individuals and Aggregates: A Note on Historical Data and Assumptions," *Social Science History*, 4 (Spring 1980), 229–50; David A. Bohmer, "The Maryland Electorate and the Concept of a Party System in the Early National Period," in *The History of American Electoral Behavior*, ed. Joel H. Silbey, Allan G. Bogue, and William H. Flanigan (Princeton, N.J.: Princeton University Press, 1978), 146–73; Melvyn Hammarberg, *The Indiana Voter: The Historical Dynamics of Party Allegiance During the 1870s* (Chicago: University of Chicago Press, 1977); and Kenneth J. Winkle, "The Voters of Lincoln's Springfield: Community and Politics in the Antebellum Midwest," unpub. paper presented at Organization of American Historians meeting, 1986.

12 Residence and registration requirements, although more stringent in the U.S. than in most Western democracies, have relaxed in recent decades. Still, political scientists estimate that a thorough liberalization of such restrictions would increase voter turnout by 3 to 9 percent. See Angus Campbell, Philip E. Converse, Warren E. Miller, and Donald E. Stokes, *The American Voter* (New York: Wiley, 1960), 276–86; Stanley

Kelley, Jr., Richard E. Ayres, and William G. Bowen, "Registration and Voting: Putting First Things First," *American Political Science Review*, 61 (June 1967), 359–77; Lester W. Milbrath and M. L. Goel, *Political Participation: How and Why Do People Get Involved in Politics?*, 2d ed. (Chicago: Rand McNally, 1977), 128–32; and Raymond E. Wolfinger and Steven J. Rosenstone, *Who Votes?* (New Haven, Conn.: Yale University Press, 1980), 61–88.

13 J. D. B. DeBow, *Statistical View of the United States, 1850: Compendium of the Seventh Census* (Washington, D.C., 1854), 114–18. Important ethnocultural studies of antebellum political behavior include Ronald P. Formisano, *The Birth of Mass Political Parties: Michigan, 1827–1861* (Princeton, N.J.: Princeton University Press, 1971); and Michael F. Holt, *Forging a Majority: The Formation of the Republican Party in Pittsburgh, 1848–1860* (New Haven, Conn.: Yale University Press, 1969). A good review of ethnocultural studies is Robert P. Swierenga, "Ethnocultural Political Analysis: A New Approach to American Ethnic Studies," *Journal of American Studies*, 5 (April 1971), 59–79.

1. The tide of emigration

1 "Report of the Standing Committee on Privileges and Elections," *Ohio Senate Journal, Appendix, 1846–1847*, 95, 100–102; John H. Klippart, *The Wheat Plant* (Cincinnati, 1860).

2 Don E. Fehrenbacher, *The Era of Expansion, 1800–1848* (New York: Wiley, 1969); Ray Allen Billington and Martin Ridge, *Westward Expansion: A History of the American Frontier*, 5th ed. (New York: Macmillan, 1982); and David Ward, *Cities and Immigrants: A Geography of Change in Nineteenth-Century America* (New York: Oxford University Press, 1971), provide an overview of westward expansion and urban growth during the nineteenth century.

3 *Report of the Ohio Board of Agriculture, 1855*, 12; "Annual Report of the Commissioner of Statistics, 1860," *Ohio Executive Documents, 1861*, 30; Ralph H. Brown, *Historical Geography of the United States* (New York: Harcourt, Brace, 1948), 197–99, 256–64; Billington and Ridge, *Westward Expansion*, 293–308; Archer Butler Hulbert, "The Old National Road – The Historic Highway of America," *Ohio Archaeological and Historical Publications*, 9 (1901), 405–519.

4 *Report of the Ohio Board of Agriculture, 1855*, 12; "Commissioner of Statistics Report, 1860," 30; Joseph C. G. Kennedy, *Population of the United States in 1860: Compendium of the Eighth Census* (Washington, D.C., 1864), xxxiii; "Annual Report of the Commissioner of Statistics, 1857," *Ohio Executive Documents, 1857*, Part 2, 489–90; Henry S. Shryock, Jacob S. Siegel, and Associates, *The Methods and Materials of Demography* (Washington, D.C.: U.S. Department of Commerce, 1973), 2: 618–19; Richard K. Vedder and Lowell E. Gallaway, "Migration and the Old North-

west," in *Essays in Nineteenth Century Economic History: The Old North-west*, ed. David C. Klingaman and Richard K. Vedder (Athens: Ohio University Press, 1975), 165.

5 "Commissioner of Statistics Report, 1857," 490; "Sixth Annual Report of the Commissioner of Statistics, 1862," *Ohio Executive Documents, 1863*, 45; *Cincinnati Gazette*, November 24, 1849, February 6, 1850; Daniel Drake, *Physician to the West: Selected Writings of Daniel Drake on Science and Society*, ed. Henry D. Shapiro and Zane L. Miller (Lexington: University Press of Kentucky, 1970), 245; *The Traveller's Directory and Emigrant's Guide* (Buffalo: Steele & Faxon, 1832), 32; William D. Gallagher, *Facts and Conditions of Progress in the North-West* (Cincinnati: H. W. Derby, 1850), 14.

6 J. D. B. DeBow, *Statistical View of the United States, 1850: Compendium of the Seventh Census* (Washington, D.C., 1854), 114–18. The following discussion of interstate migration is based on these census tables unless otherwise indicated. Peter D. McClelland and Richard J. Zeckhauser, *Demographic Dimensions of the New Republic: American Interregional Migration, Vital Statistics, and Manumissions, 1800–1860* (Cambridge, Eng.: Cambridge University Press, 1982), studied rates of migration, corrected for mortality and natural increase, among six regions but not individual states.

7 DeBow, *Statistical View, 1850*, 116–17, provides a summary table of migration among 32 states and the territories as a whole. The number of possible migration streams in 1850 was therefore 33 × 33 − 33 or 1056. The summary table is the source for Figure 1.1 and the following analysis of migration streams.

8 McClelland and Zeckhauser, *Demographic Dimensions*, 6–7; John D. Barnhart, "The Southern Influence in the Formation of Ohio," *Journal of Southern History*, 3 (February 1937), 28–42, and "Sources of Southern Migration into the Old Northwest," *Mississippi Valley Historical Review*, 22 (June 1935), 49–62.

9 In national perspective, 30.2 percent of all Americans, but 38.4 percent of all Ohioans, were interstate migrants or foreign immigrants in 1850.

10 *Report of the Ohio Board of Agriculture, 1846*, 11; Drake, *Selected Writings*, 235; Elfrieda Lang, "Ohioans in Northern Indiana before 1850," *Indiana Magazine of History*, 49 (December 1953), 391–404; Gregory S. Rose, "Hoosier Origins: The Nativity of Indiana's United States-Born Population in 1850," *Indiana Magazine of History*, 81 (September 1985), 201–32; Allan G. Bogue, *From Prairie to Corn Belt: Farming on the Illinois and Iowa Prairies in the Nineteenth Century* (Chicago: University of Chicago Press, 1963), 13–15.

11 Drake, *Selected Writings*, 235.

12 "Commissioner of Statistics Report, 1857," 488; Richard Easterlin, "Population Change and Farm Settlement in the Northern United States," *Journal of Economic History*, 36 (March 1976), 53, cites 1845 as the beginning of net emigration from Ohio.

13   Kennedy, *Eighth Census*, xxxiii; "Commissioner of Statistics Report, 1860," 7; Vedder and Gallaway, "Migration and the Old Northwest," 161–62, 165; J. Potter, "The Growth of Population in America, 1700– 1860," in *Population in History: Essays in Historical Demography*, ed. D. V. Glass and D. E. C. Eversley (Chicago: Aldine, 1965), 635. Easterlin, "Population Change and Farm Settlement," 54, estimates natural increase as 20 percent in the antebellum U.S. and therefore considers a growth rate of less than 20 percent a general indication of net emigration. This seems to have been true of antebellum Ohio.

14   Kennedy, *Eighth Census*, xxxiii; *Statistics of the United States, 1860* (Washington, D.C., 1866), lxi, lxii; Frederick Jackson Turner, *The United States, 1830–1850: The Nation and Its Sections* (New York: Holt, Rinehart, and Winston, 1935), 259. The 1850s were the decade of greatest immigration for the rest of the Midwest; McClelland and Zeckhauser, *Demographic Dimensions*, 51.

15   Caleb Atwater, *A History of the State of Ohio*, 2d ed. (Cincinnati, 1838), 350; "Annual Report of the Secretary of State, 1855," *Ohio Executive Documents, 1855*, Part 2, 360.

16   *Report of the Ohio Board of Agriculture, 1860*, 22; *Report of the Ohio Board of Agriculture, 1858*, xvii–xviii; *Ohio Cultivator*, March 1, 1855; "Second Annual Report of the Commissioner of Statistics, 1858," *Ohio Executive Documents, 1859*, 15–16; Louis Bernard Schmidt, "The Westward Movement of the Wheat Growing Industry in the United States," *Iowa Journal of History and Politics*, 18 (July 1920), 396–412; Paul W. Gates, *The Farmer's Age: Agriculture, 1815–1860* (New York: Holt, Rinehart and Winston, 1960), 160; Eugene H. Roseboom, *The Civil War Era: 1850– 1873*, Vol. 4 of *A History of the State of Ohio*, ed. Carl Wittke (Columbus: Ohio State Archaeological and Historical Society, 1944), 72. John H. Klippart provided a contemporary analysis of "depopulation" in *Report of the Ohio Board of Agriculture, 1857*, 44–45. Compare the attitudes of New Englanders toward emigrants discussed in Hal S. Barron, *Those Who Stayed Behind: Rural Society in Nineteenth-Century New England* (Cambridge, Eng.: Cambridge University Press, 1984), 31–50.

17   *Ohio Cultivator*, September 1, 1857; (Cleveland) *Family Visitor*, March 21, 1850; *Report of the Ohio Board of Agriculture, 1855*, 138; *Report of the Ohio Board of Agriculture, 1857*, 277–78; *Report of the Ohio Board of Agriculture, 1860*, 22.

18   Frederick Kuhne, "History and Review of the Condition of Agriculture in Ohio," *Report of the Ohio Board of Agriculture, 1859*, 450–581, quote from 515; John H. Klippart, "Agricultural Statistics," *Report of the Ohio Board of Agriculture, 1860*, 11–21, quote from 21; *Report of the Ohio Board of Agriculture, 1855*, 138; *Report of the Ohio Board of Agriculture, 1857*, 44.

19   *Report of the Ohio Board of Agriculture, 1857*, 44; *Report of the Ohio Board of Agriculture, 1856*, 315; *Ohio Cultivator*, March 1, 1850. The *Ohio Cultivator*, a leading agricultural journal, mounted a campaign to keep prospective migrants in Ohio, urging readers to welcome newcomers and

reprinting poems such as Frances D. Gage's "Don't Go to California"; see *Ohio Cultivator*, May 15, 1852, September 1, 1854. McClelland and Zeckhauser, *Demographic Dimensions*, 7, found that most emigrants from the Northeast were between 20 and 40 years old; Lang, "Ohioans in Northern Indiana," 398, found that 82 percent of Ohio's emigrants to Indiana were under 30.

20 J. D. B. Debow, *Seventh Census of the United States, 1850* (Washington, D.C., 1853), 817–18; Kennedy, *Eighth Census*, 364–73. Because of changes in county boundaries between 1840 and 1850, Figure 1.2 required the joining of several counties into larger units. *Report of the Ohio Board of Agriculture, 1848*, 58, 94; John G. Clark, *The Grain Trade in the Old Northwest* (Urbana: University of Illinois Press, 1966), 57–59; and Allan R. Pred, *Urban Growth and City-Systems in the United States, 1840–1860* (Cambridge, Mass.: Harvard University Press, 1980), 99–100, discuss the rapid growth of the Lake Erie ports during the 1840s and 1850s.

21 "Commissioner of Statistics Report, 1858," 15–16; "Fifth Annual Report of the Commissioner of Statistics, 1861," *Ohio Executive Documents, 1862*, 27–28; Wilbur Zelinsky, "Changes in the Geographic Patterns of Rural Population in the United States, 1790–1960," *Geographical Review*, 52 (October 1962), 498–99, 500. Easterlin, "Population Change and Farm Settlement," applies population growth of less than 20 percent as an indicator of net emigration. Easterlin argues that natural increase declined in settled areas, and so the emigration threshold may have been lower in eastern Ohio. To be on the safe side, I have therefore used a more conservative index of less than 10 percent population increase to signify net emigration.

22 DeBow, *Seventh Census*, 817–18; Kennedy, *Eighth Census*, 364–73; DeBow, *Statistical View, 1850*, 284–85, 290–91; Vedder and Gallaway, "Migration and the Old Northwest," 161–62.

23 Debow, *Seventh Census*, 818–51; Kennedy, *Eighth Census*, 373–96; "Commissioner of Statistics Report, 1857," 491.

24 Harry N. Scheiber, *Ohio Canal Era: A Case Study of Government and the Economy, 1820–1861* (Athens: Ohio University Press, 1969), 187–211; Chester E. Finn, "The Ohio Canals: Public Enterprise on the Frontier," *Ohio State Archaeological and Historical Quarterly*, 51 (January-March 1942), 1–41; C. P. McClelland and C. C. Huntington, *History of the Ohio Canals: Their Construction, Cost, Use and Partial Abandonment* (Columbus: Ohio State Archaeological and Historical Society, 1905); Harvey H. Segal, "Cycles of Canal Construction," in *Canals and American Economic Development*, ed. Carter Goodrich (New York: Columbia University Press, 1961), 169–215.

25 Clark, *Grain Trade*, 52–79, 124–46; Scheiber, *Ohio Canal Era*, 187–211, 227; Edward K. Muller, "Selective Urban Growth in the Middle Ohio Valley, 1800–1860," *Geographical Review*, 66 (April 1976), 178–99; Albert Fishlow, *American Railroads and the Transformation of the Ante-Bellum*

Economy (Cambridge, Mass.: Harvard University Press, 1965), 289–90; Harry N. Scheiber, "Urban Rivalry and Internal Improvements in the Old Northwest, 1820–1860," *Ohio History*, 71 (October 1962), 227–39; John W. Weatherford, "The Short Life of Manhattan, Ohio," *Ohio Historical Quarterly*, 65 (October 1956), 376–98; Margaret Walsh, "The Spatial Evolution of the Mid-western Pork Industry, 1835–75," *Journal of Historical Geography*, 4 (January 1978), 1–22; Harvey H. Segal, "Canals and Economic Development," in Goodrich, ed., *Canals and American Economic Development*, 216–48.

26 DeBow, *Statistical View, 1850*, 284–85, 290–91. Figure 1.4 does not reveal migration among Ohio natives. See also Turner, *United States, 1830–1850*, 265.

27 DeBow, *Statistical View, 1850*, 284–85, 290–91; "Commissioner of Statistics Report, 1857," 490–91.

28 *Report of the Ohio Board of Agriculture, 1849*, 187. Harold E. Davis, "The Economic Basis of Ohio Politics, 1820–1840," *Ohio State Archaeological and Historical Quarterly*, 47 (October 1938), 288–318; Eugene O. Porter, "Financing Ohio's Pre-Civil War Railroads," *Ohio State Archaeological and Historical Quarterly*, 57 (July 1948), 215–36; and John F. Stover, *Iron Road to the West: American Railroads in the 1850s* (New York: Columbia University Press, 1978), 131, discuss the feverish pursuit of market outlets in antebellum Ohio.

29 *Report of the Ohio Board of Agriculture, 1850*, 429, 436; *Marietta Intelligencer*, quoted in *American Railroad Journal*, January 3, 1852, 28.

30 Scheiber, "Urban Rivalry"; Stover, *Iron Road to the West*, 131; Fishlow, *American Railroads*, 190–91; Porter, "Financing Ohio's Railroads." See Stover, *Iron Road to the West*, 122–39, for a review of Ohio railroad construction before the Civil War and Finn, "Ohio Canals," 29, for a schedule of annual railroad construction.

31 *Report of the Ohio Board of Agriculture, 1847*, 60; *Report of the Ohio Board of Agriculture, 1848*, 47; *Report of the Ohio Board of Agriculture, 1852*, 169, 333. Other expressions of satisfaction with the new railroads appear in *Report of the Ohio Board of Agriculture, 1851*, 250, 272, 326; *Report of the Ohio Board of Agriculture, 1852*, 240–49; *Report of the Ohio Board of Agriculture, 1855*, 113; *Report of the Ohio Board of Agriculture, 1856*, 218. Fishlow, *American Railroads*, discusses "anticipatory settlement" along the projected paths of railroads.

32 *Report of the Ohio Board of Public Works, 1849*, 144–45; *Report of the Ohio Board of Public Works, 1851*, 294–95; *Report of the Ohio Board of Public Works, 1852*, 217, 228–34; *Report of the Ohio Board of Public Works, 1854–1855*, 439–40. George Rogers Taylor, *The Transportation Revolution, 1815–1860* (New York: Rinehart, 1951), 45–48; Clark, *Grain Trade*, 224–25; and Finn, "Ohio Canals," discuss the competition between canals and railroads during the 1850s.

33 DeBow, *Seventh Census*, 818–51; Kennedy, *Eighth Census*, 373–96;

"Commissioner of Statistics Report, 1858," 23–29; Douglass C. North, *The Economic Growth of the United States, 1790–1860* (New York: Norton, 1966), 142; Clark, *Grain Trade*, 59–65, 124–31, 217, 223–25, 228; Stover, *Iron Road to the West*, 122, 131, 133; Fishlow, *American Railroads*, 289–91; Muller, "Selective Urban Growth"; Edward K. Muller, "Early Industrialization in the Ohio Valley: A Review Essay," *Historical Geography Newsletter*, 3 (Fall 1973), 19–30; Pred, *Urban Growth and City-Systems*, 44–49; Walsh, "Mid-Western Pork Industry"; Sherry O. Hessler, "'The Great Disturbing Cause' and the Decline of the Queen City," *Bulletin of the Historical and Philosophical Society of Ohio*, 20 (July 1962), 169–85. For an early contemporary recognition of the shift in trade from the Ohio River to Lake Erie, see *Report of the Ohio Board of Agriculture, 1851*, 406–7.

34 DeBow, *Seventh Census*, 818–51; Kennedy, *Eighth Census*, 373–96. Transportation networks were reconstructed from *Phelps' Travelers' Guide through the United States* (New York: Horace Thayer, 1853), 51–55. See Pred, *Urban Growth and City-Systems*, for antebellum "city-systems." Fishlow, *American Railroads*, 207–15; and Clarence H. Danhof, *Change in Agriculture: The Northern United States, 1820–1870* (Cambridge, Mass.: Harvard University Press, 1965), 13–26, discuss the role of railroads in the commercialization of agriculture. Robert Higgs, "The Growth of Cities in a Midwestern Region, 1870–1900," *Journal of Regional Science*, 9 (December 1969), 369–75, discounts the role of situation on the American railroad network as a contributor to urban growth. In Ohio, towns and cities that were situated on only one transportation link, whether canal, stage, or railroad, did indeed lose population during the 1850s, declining 8.2 percent. Towns and cities that lay on two routes grew moderately during the decade (14.1 percent). The fastest growth (54.6 percent) was restricted to the six cities situated at intersections among all three transportation routes. The railroad did not stimulate urban growth by itself but enhanced the locational advantages of cities and towns already served by a major transportation route.

35 DeBow, *Seventh Census*, 818–51; Kennedy, *Eighth Census*, 373–96.

36 DeBow, *Seventh Census*, 818–51; Kennedy, *Eighth Census*, 373–96; *Phelps' Travelers' Guide*, 51–55.

2. An electorate in motion

1 *Ohio Cultivator*, May 15, 1855. Mrs. Bateham's husband, M. B. Bateham, was editor of the *Ohio Cultivator*. A transplanted New Yorker, M. B. Bateham was a former editor of the *Genesee Farmer*.

2 Stephan Thernstrom, *The Other Bostonians: Poverty and Progress in the American Metropolis, 1880–1970* (Cambridge, Mass.: Harvard University Press, 1973), 221–32, provides the most thorough inventory of American migration studies. Pathbreaking studies that helped to alert historians to

high levels of mobility in rural areas include James C. Malin, "The Turn-over of Farm Population in Kansas," *Kansas Historical Quarterly*, 4 (November 1935), 339–72; Frank L. Owsley, *Plain Folk of the Old South* (Baton Rouge: Louisiana State University Press, 1949), 23–77; William L. Bowers, "Crawford Township, 1850–1870: A Population Study of a Pi-oneer Community," *Iowa Journal of History*, 58 (January 1960), 1–30; Mildred Throne, "A Population Study of an Iowa County in 1850," *Iowa Journal of History*, 57 (October 1959), 305–30; Merle Curti, *The Making of an American Community: A Case Study of Democracy in a Frontier County* (Stan-ford, Calif.: Stanford University Press, 1959); and Peter J. Coleman, "Restless Grant County: Americans on the Move," *Wisconsin Magazine of History*, 46 (Autumn 1962), 16–20. One of the most succinct and influen-tial of the traditional portraits of a settled rural society during the nine-teenth century is Robert Wiebe's discussion of the "island community" in *The Search for Order, 1877–1920* (New York: Hill & Wang, 1967), 1–10.

3 Quadrennial Enumerations of White Adult Males, Shelby County, Ohio, 1851 and 1855, Wright State University Archives, Wright State Univer-sity, Dayton, Ohio. The enumerations were compiled by county as-sessors at the same time that they assessed taxable property; *Ohio Laws*, 25 v 16 (1827). The quadrennial enumerations are records of potential voters or "electoral registers." For the use of such electoral registers in the analysis of European political behavior, consult Jorgen Elklit, "Nomi-nal Record Linkage and the Study of Non-Secret Voting: A Danish Case," *Journal of Interdisciplinary History*, 15 (Winter 1985), 422–23.

4 *Combination Atlas Map of Shelby County, Ohio* (Philadelphia: Page and Smith, 1875), 13, 15; *History of Shelby County, Ohio* (Philadelphia: R. Sutton & Company, 1883), 348; J. D. B. DeBow, *Seventh Census of the United States, 1850* (Washington, D.C., 1853), 817–18, 862–68; Joseph C. G. Kennedy, *Population of the United States in 1860: Compendium of the Eighth Census* (Washington, D.C., 1864), 364–67. For purposes of analy-sis, Ohio's Miami Valley includes the 15 counties in the state's south-western corner – Brown, Butler, Champaign, Clark, Clermont, Clinton, Darke, Greene, Hamilton, Logan, Miami, Montgomery, Preble, Shelby, and Warren.

5 *Combination Atlas Map of Shelby County*, 13, 15; *History of Shelby County*, 348; Randolph C. Downes, "Evolution of Ohio County Boundaries," *Ohio Archaeological and Historical Publications*, 36 (1927), 472–73; Edward K. Muller, "Selective Urban Growth in the Middle Ohio Valley, 1800–1860," *Geographical Review*, 66 (April 1976), 178–99; Harry N. Scheiber, *Ohio Canal Era: A Case Study of Government and the Economy, 1820–1861* (Athens: Ohio University Press, 1969), 187–211, 227; John G. Clark, *The Grain Trade in the Old Northwest* (Urbana: University of Illinois Press, 1966), 52–79, 124–31.

6 DeBow, *Seventh Census*, 817–18; Kennedy, *Eighth Census*, 364–67; Joseph C. G. Kennedy, *Agriculture of the United States in 1860: Compendium of the*

Eighth Census (Washington, D.C., 1864), 112–19; Muller, "Selective Urban Growth"; Clark, *Grain Trade*, 124–31; Clarence H. Danhof, *Change in Agriculture: The Northern United States, 1820–1870* (Cambridge, Mass.: Harvard University Press, 1969), 13–26; Albert Fishlow, *American Railroads and the Transformation of the Ante-Bellum Economy* (Cambridge, Mass.: Harvard University Press, 1965), 289–90; Margaret Walsh, "The Spatial Evolution of the Mid-western Pork Industry, 1835–75," *Journal of Historical Geography*, 4 (January 1978), 1–22; Harry N. Scheiber, "Urban Rivalry and Internal Improvements in the Old Northwest, 1820–1860," *Ohio History*, 71 (October 1962), 227–39.

7 DeBow, *Seventh Census*, 846. This study labels Clinton Township an urban township and employs Clinton Township as a surrogate for an urban area. The city of Sidney contained 63.0 percent of Clinton Township's population in 1850 and 78.2 percent in 1860. Sidney grew 57.8 percent between 1850 and 1860, from 1,302 to 2,055 residents, while the rural portions of the township grew only .4 percent, from 764 residents in 1850 to 767 in 1860. Fully 99.6 percent of Clinton Township's growth, therefore, was urban; DeBow, *Seventh Census*, 846; Kennedy, *Eighth Census*, 392.

8 Most students of migration who consider the sources of population change have found that rates of immigration and not rates of natural increase or emigration determined patterns of growth and decline during the nineteenth century. Hal S. Barron, *Those Who Stayed Behind: Rural Society in Nineteenth-Century New England* (Cambridge, Eng.: Cambridge University Press, 1984), 88, for example, found that population decline in Vermont arose from low immigration and not high emigration. Similarly, Gordon W. Kirk, Jr., and Carol Tyirin Kirk, "Migration, Mobility and the Transformation of the Occupational Structure in an Immigrant Community: Holland, Michigan, 1850–80," *Journal of Social History*, 7 (Winter 1974), 152, discovered that rates of persistence and emigration remained constant but rates of immigration varied widely and were responsible for net population change. Surveying American migration studies, Thernstrom, *Other Bostonians*, 225, concluded that "Communities differed enormously in their power to attract outsiders into them; they varied hardly at all in their ability to hold on to their existing population." A student of modern migration concluded similarly that there is "no evidence that labor-market conditions at the origin had any influence on the rate of out-migration" and that population loss reflected low rates of immigration; Ira S. Lowry, *Migration and Metropolitan Growth: Two Analytical Models* (San Francisco: Chandler Publishing Company, 1966), 94–95. At the same time, fertility seems to have played little role in determining rates of growth and decline, particularly in rural areas. See especially Wilbur Zelinsky, "Changes in the Geographic Patterns of Rural Population in the United States, 1790–1960," *Geographical Review*, 52 (October 1962), 517.

9   See Everett S. Lee, "A Theory of Migration," *Demography*, 3 (Number 1, 1966), 47–57, for "push" and "pull" factors in migration.
10 Donald H. Parkerson and Jo Ann Parkerson, "Estimating the Population Dynamics of New York State, 1845–1855," unpub. paper presented at Social Science History Assocation meeting, 1985, introduced the powerful concept of a "two-dimensional migration profile."
11 A regression of the 14 townships' rates of immigration with their rates of growth showed a nearly perfect relationship, yielding a regression coefficient (b) of .96 and a correlation coefficient (r) of .92. A similar regression of rates of emigration with rates of growth, however, yielded a b of only .22 and an r of only .05.
12 See Parkerson and Parkerson, "Estimating Population Dynamics," for the properties of a "migration profile."
13 See Michael P. Conzen, "Local Migration Systems in Nineteenth-Century Iowa," *Geographical Review*, 64 (July 1974), 339–61; John C. Hudson, "Migration to an American Frontier," *Annals of the Association of American Geographers*, 66 (June 1976), 242–65; and Roberta Balstad Miller, *City and Hinterland: A Case Study of Urban Growth and Regional Development* (Westport, Conn.: Greenwood, 1979), for discussions of "migration hinterlands."
14 This discussion divides the sample into "long-distance" and "local" migrants on the basis of persistence in the seven-township study area or migration from it. The lack of migration between Clinton Township and the outer ring suggests that the six townships of the inner ring represent the boundaries of Clinton Township's "migration field" in Shelby County. In other words, migrants from Clinton Township who did not enter an adjacent township almost invariably left the county entirely, becoming "long-distance" migrants. Every township, by definition, possessed its own migration field, and this study focuses on the field of only one township, Clinton. For a definition of migration fields, see Lawrence A. Brown, John Odlund, and Reginald G. Golledge, "Migration, Functional Distance, and the Urban Hierarchy," *Economic Geography*, 46 (July 1970), 472–85, esp. 474.
15 The difference between the percentages of emigrants from Clinton Township and from the rural townships was not significant at the .05 level. The difference in the distances traveled by those emigrants, however, was significant. Barron, *Those Who Stayed Behind*, 101, 106, similarly found that nonfarmer migrants traveled greater distances than did farmers.
16 Manuscript U.S. Census of Population, Shelby County, Ohio, 1850.
17 E. G. Ravenstein, "The Laws of Migration," *Journal of the Royal Statistical Society*, 48 (1885), 167–227. Lee, "Theory of Migration," provides the best modern discussion of Ravenstein's laws. D. B. Grigg, "E. G. Ravenstein and the 'Laws of Migration,'" *Journal of Historical Geography*, 3 (January 1977), 41–54, compares the laws to empirical evidence of mi-

gration. See also Allan Pred, "The External Relations of Cities during 'Industrial Revolution,'" University of Chicago, Department of Geography, *Research Paper No. 76* (Chicago: University of Chicago, 1962), 57–68, for an intriguing discussion of refinements in the gravity model.

18 In 1851, Clinton Township claimed 20.5 percent of the area's adult males but received 27.9 percent of all eligible voters arriving from outside the study area. This difference was significant at the .05 level.

19 Manuscript U.S. Census of Population, Shelby County, Ohio, 1850.

20 This difference was not significant at the .05 level.

21 See Brown, Odlund, and Golledge, "Urban Hierarchy," for a discussion of migration hierarchies.

22 The net shift in population from the rural townships to Clinton Township was not significant at the .05 level. Miller, *City and Hinterland*, 114–15, similarly found that 9 percent of all household heads living in Syracuse, New York, in 1855 had immigrated from within the county.

23 See Michael P. Conzen, *Frontier Farming in an Urban Shadow: The Influence of Madison's Proximity on the Agricultural Development of Blooming Grove, Wisconsin* (Madison: State Historical Society of Wisconsin, 1971), for the impact of an "urban shadow" on a growing city's rural hinterland.

24 Table 2.6 is based on Manuscript U.S. Census of Agriculture, Shelby County, Ohio, 1850 and 1860, Wright State University Archives, Wright State University, Dayton, Ohio. Farms were more highly developed in urban areas throughout Ohio during the 1850s. Farms in urban areas contained a greater proportion of improved acreage than those in rural areas, and farmland was 50 percent more valuable. See Danhof, *Change in Agriculture*, 13–26, for the early transition from subsistence to commercial agriculture near urban centers and along transportation routes. Agricultural historians generally recognize wheat culture as an indicator of agricultural development and commercialization. Wheat, as a "money crop," played the greatest role in western commerce. See, for example, Paul W. Gates, *The Farmer's Age: Agriculture, 1815–1860* (New York: Holt, Rinehart and Winston, 1960), 167; Louis Bernard Schmidt, "The Internal Grain Trade of the United States, 1850–1860," *Iowa Journal of History and Politics*, 18 (January 1920), 94–124; and Robert Leslie Jones, *History of Agriculture in Ohio to 1880* (Kent, Ohio: Kent State University Press, 1983), 59. "Second Annual Report of the Commissioner of Statistics, 1858," *Ohio Executive Documents, 1859*, 15–16, provides a contemporary analysis of the rise of wheat culture in the Miami Valley.

25 *Combination Atlas Map*, 13, 15, 16, 20; George W. Hawes, *Ohio State Gazetteer and Business Directory for 1859 and 1860* (Cincinnati, 1859), 475–76. Many recent studies of regional development emphasize the economic, social, and demographic complementarity of growing cities and their rural hinterlands before the Civil War. Growing cities usually

enhanced agricultural development in the surrounding countryside but inhibited urban growth nearby. See, for example, James T. Lemon, *The Best Poor Man's Country: A Geographical Study of Early Southeastern Pennsylvania* (Baltimore: Johns Hopkins University Press, 1972), 131; Diane Lindstrom, *Economic Development in the Philadelphia Region, 1810–1850* (New York: Columbia University Press, 1978), 24, 173; Miller, *City and Hinterland*, 116–17; Conzen, *Frontier Farming in an Urban Shadow*, 50; Muller, "Selective Urban Growth"; and John Modell, "The Peopling of a Working-Class Ward: Reading, Pennsylvania, 1850," *Journal of Social History*, 5 (Fall 1971), 71–95. Robert Higgs, "The Growth of Cities in a Midwestern Region, 1870–1900," *Journal of Regional Science*, 9 (December 1969), 369–75, challenges the idea of urban development feeding on a stagnating rural economy in the nineteenth-century Midwest. Higgs found that city growth and regional agricultural development varied positively during the late nineteenth century. The present study confirms Higgs's interpretation by revealing the complementarity of urban and rural development at the local level. Sidney's growth enhanced agricultural development in its rural hinterland but stifled urban growth nearby. A contemporary observer concluded, correctly, that "the village is an offspring of the country"; *Ohio Cultivator*, January 15, 1858.

26   DeBow, *Seventh Census*, 846; Kennedy, *Eighth Census*, 392; *Combination Atlas Map*, 13, 14, 16, 20; Thomas H. Smith, *The Mapping of Ohio*, (Kent, Ohio: Kent State University Press, 1977), 220. Port Jefferson's population in 1860 was drawn from Manuscript U.S. Census of Population, Shelby County, Ohio, 1860. Muller, "Selective Urban Growth," provides an excellent review of urban growth patterns in Ohio's Miami Valley.

27   Manuscript U.S. Census of Agriculture, Shelby County, Ohio, 1850 and 1860.

3. From meeting to election: migration and suffrage

1   Quote from *Shapiro v. Thompson*, 394 U.S. 629 (U.S. Supr. Ct. 1968), which struck down a one-year residence requirement for eligibility for welfare payments. *Edwards v. California*, 314 U.S. 160 (U.S. Supr. Ct. 1944), established the right of all migrants to travel from state to state without legal impediments. *Dunn v. Blumstein*, 405 U.S. 330 (U.S. Supr. Ct. 1972), mandated a state residence requirement for voting of 30 days or less, which has been met by almost all the states. A table describing modern residence requirements and registration laws appears in Raymond E. Wolfinger and Steven J. Rosenstone, *Who Votes?* (New Haven, Conn.: Yale University Press, 1980), 68–70. Jacobus tenBroek, *The Constitution and the Right of Free Movement* (New York: National Travelers Aid Association, 1955), provides a succinct review of the legal rights of mod-

ern migrants and their development. Ronald L. Rowland, "Voter Residency Requirements in State and Local Elections," *Ohio State Law Journal*, 32 (1971), 600–17, examines the erosion of state authority in setting lengthy residence requirements.

2 Before passage of the Fourteenth Amendment, migrants and travelers depended largely on the Privileges and Immunities Clause of the Constitution when crossing state boundaries. The Articles of Confederation denied such interstate "privileges and immunities" to "paupers, vagabonds, and fugitives from justice," but the idea of comity is a central ingredient in the Constitution's federal system; *Articles of Confederation and Perpetual Union*, Art. 4. In *City of New York v. Miln*, 11 Pet. 102 (U.S. Supr. Ct. 1837), the U.S. Supreme Court permitted New York City to impede immigration but eventually reversed itself, beginning with the Passenger Cases, 7 How. 283 (U.S. Supr. Ct. 1849). Migrants did not receive an absolute guarantee of their rights to interstate movement, however, until *Edwards v. California* in 1944. Paul Finkelman, *An Imperfect Union: Slavery, Federalism, and Comity* (Chapel Hill: University of North Carolina Press, 1981), 9–10, briefly discusses these issues and, overall, admirably reviews the specific rights of blacks and white slaveholders to travel and migrate before the Civil War.

3 *Ohio Laws*, 2 v 63 (1804), 5 v 53 (1807). At one time or another, Ohio, Michigan Territory, Indiana, Illinois, and Iowa all excluded blacks outright or required them to post bonds before immigrating. Illinois and Indiana actually wrote exclusion clauses into their constitutions in 1848 and 1851, respectively. Most of Ohio's "Black Laws" were repealed in 1849. Consult Leon F. Litwack, *North of Slavery: The Negro in the Free States, 1790–1860* (Chicago: University of Chicago Press, 1961), 70–73; Carter G. Woodson, *A Century of Negro Migration* (Washington, D.C.: Association for the Study of Negro Life and History, 1918), 51–52; and Leonard Erickson, "Politics and Repeal of Ohio's Black Laws, 1837–1849," *Ohio History*, 82 (Summer-Autumn 1973), 154–75. Eugene H. Berwanger, *The Frontier Against Slavery: Western Anti-Negro Prejudice and the Slavery Extension Controversy* (Urbana: University of Illinois Press, 1967), 7–59, reviews the history of black exclusion in the antebellum Midwest.

4 Randolph C. Downes, *Frontier Ohio, 1788–1803* (Columbus: Ohio State Archaeological and Historical Society, 1935), 149–50, discusses the legal foundations of the Ohio township. Common law held that "the original domicil [legal residence] is not gone until a new one has been actually acquired"; Joseph Story, *Commentaries on the Conflict of Laws*, 2d ed. (London, 1841), 52. By 1878, residence in the state of Ohio rested entirely on legal residence in a particular township within the state: "A residence in the state includes a residence at some particular place therein. Until a person coming into the state begins to acquire a residence in some township or election precinct of the state, he does not begin to acquire a

residence in the latter"; *Esker v. McCoy*, 5 Dec. Rep. 702 (Ross Common Pleas 1878). Although both arose through residence in a particular township, the right to vote and the right to poor relief represented two distinct kinds of legal residence, and inhabitants of a township might be residents for one purpose but not for the other; *Smith v. Dalton*, 1 Cincinnati 152–53 (Cin. Super. Ct. 1871).

5   *Statutes of Ohio and the Northwestern Territory Adopted or Enacted from 1788 to 1833 Inclusive*, ed. Salmon P. Chase (Cincinnati, 1833), 1: chap. xvi, sec. 1, 107–9; William T. Utter, *The Frontier State: 1803–1825*, Vol. 2 of *A History of the State of Ohio*, ed. Carl Wittke (Columbus: Ohio State Archaeological and Historical Society, 1942), 35. In some parts of Ohio, such as the Western Reserve, townships were 25 square miles, and sizes and shapes varied widely throughout the Virginia Military District, which never adopted a rectangular survey; Norman J. W. Thrower, *Original Survey and Land Subdivision: A Comparative Study of the Form and Effect of Contrasting Cadastral Surveys* (Chicago: Rand McNally, 1966), 135. There was a long tradition in English and New England law of drawing township boundaries to suit the convenience of inhabitants. See, in particular, Hildegard Binder Johnson, *Order Upon the Land: The U.S. Rectangular Land Survey and the Upper Mississippi Country* (New York: Oxford University Press, 1976), 36; and J. S. Wood, "Elaboration of a Settlement System: The New England Village in the Federal Period," *Journal of Historical Geography*, 10 (October 1984), 331–56. For a contemporary description of the structure and functions of Ohio townships, see John Kilbourn, *The Ohio Gazetteer or Topographical Dictionary*, 11th ed. (Columbus, 1833), xiv–xviii.

6   For a review of "consensual" membership in the New England town, consult Albert Edward McKinley, *The Suffrage Franchise in the Thirteen English Colonies in America* (Philadelphia: University of Pennsylvania Press, 1905), quote from 477–78; Michael Zuckerman, *Peaceable Kingdoms: New England Towns in the Eighteenth Century* (New York: Knopf, 1970), 85–122, quote from 110; Thomas Bender, *Community and Social Change in America* (Baltimore: Johns Hopkins University Press, 1978), 62–78; and Douglas Lamar Jones, "The Strolling Poor: Transiency in Eighteenth-Century Massachusetts," *Journal of Social History*, 8 (Spring 1975), 28–54. Kenneth A. Lockridge, *A New England Town: The First Hundred Years: Dedham, Massachusetts, 1636–1736* (New York: Norton, 1970), 37–56; and Michael Zuckerman, "The Social Context of Democracy in Massachusetts," *William and Mary Quarterly*, 3d ser., 25 (October 1968), 523–44, present the fullest, although perhaps overdrawn, discussion of the consensual foundations of the New England town. The classic portrait of life in the antebellum township remains Alexis de Tocqueville, *Democracy in America*, ed. Phillips Bradley (New York: Random House, 1945), 1: 62–71. James H. Kettner, *The Development of American Citizenship, 1608–*

1870 (Chapel Hill: University of North Carolina Press, 1978), traces a similar transition from consensual, which he labels "perpetual," to volitional allegiance in the notion of American citizenship.

7 Chase, ed., *Statutes of Ohio*, 1: chap. xv, secs. 2, 14, 364–68; Utter, *Frontier State*, 33.

8 *Ohio Constitution* (1802), art. 4, sec. 1; Chase, ed., *Statutes of Ohio*, 1: chap. xv, secs. 2, 14, 364–68; 1: chap. 185, sec. 11, 622–23; 3: chap. 834, sec. 5, 1740; *Ohio Cultivator*, April 1, 1856. Examples of elections that were held in private homes, included as few as 18 voters, and were called "meetings" as late as the 1830s include William L. Curry, *History of Union County, Ohio* (Indianapolis: B. F. Bowen, 1915), 467, 485–86; *History of Morgan County, Ohio* (Chicago: L. H. Watkins & Co., 1886), 379, 462; *History of Ross and Highland Counties, Ohio* (Cleveland: W. W. Williams, 1880), 520; Crisfield Johnson, *History of Cuyahoga County, Ohio* (Cleveland: D. W. Ensign, 1879), 405, 438, 492; and A. Banning Norton, *A History of Knox County, Ohio* (Columbus: Richard Nevins, 1862), 45, 362, 365, 366. The Constitution of 1802 imposed a taxpaying qualification, which any eligible voter could satisfy by performing work on township or county roads; *Ohio Constitution* (1802), art. 4, secs. 1, 5. The taxpaying qualification seems to have served, in practice, as a mere formality. See Andrew W. Young, *First Lessons in Civil Government* (Cleveland: M. C. Younglove, 1846), 35: "In this state, every white male citizen of the age of twenty-one years, who has paid, or is charged with, a state or county tax, may become a voter. A highway tax is a tax of this kind; and as nearly every man is liable to labor on the roads, very few are denied the right to vote." Chilton Williamson, *American Suffrage: From Property to Democracy, 1760–1860* (Princeton, N.J.: Princeton University Press, 1960), 136: "With taxation of adult males almost universal, a taxpaying suffrage was almost universal suffrage." The Constitution of 1851 revoked the taxpaying qualification.

9 Chase, ed., *Statutes of Ohio*, 1: chap. liv, sec. 16, 175–83. For a discussion of legal settlement in New England, consult the classic study by Josiah Henry Benton, *Warning Out in New England* (Boston: W. B. Clarke, 1911); and Jones, "Strolling Poor." J. R. Pole, *Political Representation in England and the Origins of the American Republic* (London: Macmillan, 1966), 141–42, labels property and residence the two essential ingredients of colonial suffrage. Aileen Elizabeth Kennedy, *The Ohio Poor Law and Its Administration* (Chicago: University of Chicago Press, 1934), provides an indispensable institutional review of the development of Ohio's poor law.

10 Chase, ed., *Statutes of Ohio*, 1: chap. liv, secs. 18, 20, 175–83. For Connecticut's system of certificates and removal, see Edward Warren Capen, *The Historical Development of the Poor Law of Connecticut* (New York: Columbia University Press, 1905), 23–34, 68–74, 97–115, 172–80.

11 *Ohio Laws*, 3 v 272, sec. 4 (1805); Daniel Drake, *Physician to the West:*

Selected Writings of Daniel Drake on Science and Society, ed. Henry D. Shapiro and Zane L. Miller (Lexington: University Press of Kentucky, 1970), 103. Pole, *Political Representation*, 40–41; Zuckerman, *Peaceable Kingdoms*, 112–13; and Benton, *Warning Out*, 5–8, cite warning out as an expression of the consensual nature of communities in colonial New England.

12 *Ohio Laws*, 14 v 197, sec. 4 (1816); Ray Allen Billington and Martin Ridge, *Westward Expansion: A History of the American Frontier*, 5th ed. (New York: Macmillan, 1982), 289–95; Douglass C. North, *The Economic Growth of the United States, 1790–1860* (New York: Norton, 1966), 180–81.

13 See Williamson, *American Suffrage*, for suffrage extension before the Civil War. In an influential contribution to American legal history, James Willard Hurst, *Law and the Conditions of Freedom in the Nineteenth-Century United States* (Madison: University of Wisconsin Press, 1956), 3–32, argued that antebellum jurists, in a wave of "judicial activism," pursued a "release of creative energy" that favored change rather than stability and sought to free individuals from the restraints of communal responsibilities. Similarly, John Higham, *From Boundlessness to Consolidation: The Transformation of American Culture, 1848–1860* (Ann Arbor, Mich.: William L. Clements Library, 1969), noted a more general cultural and intellectual "boundlessness" after 1815 that stressed individualism at the expense of tradition and stability.

14 *Jefferson Township v. Letart Township*, 3 Ohio 100 (Ohio Supr. Ct. 1827).

15 *Jefferson Township v. Letart Township*, 3 Ohio 102 (Ohio Supr. Ct. 1827). The court ruled that a minor derives his legal residence from that of his father. Because Jackson fell into poverty while living with his father, he was a legal resident of Lebanon Township.

16 *Wayne Township v. Stock Township*, 3 Ohio 172 (Ohio Supr. Ct. 1827). See Hurst, *Conditions of Freedom*, 3–32, for the judicial pursuit of individual freedoms in antebellum America.

17 *Wayne Township v. Stock Township*, 3 Ohio 172 (Ohio Supr. Ct. 1827).

18 *Wayne Township v. Stock Township*, 3 Ohio 172–78 (Ohio Supr. Ct. 1827).

19 *Wayne Township v. Stock Township*, 3 Ohio 173 (Ohio Supr. Ct. 1827). Consult Hurst, *Conditions of Freedom*, 3–32, for judicial activism. See also Morton J. Horwitz, *The Transformation of American Law, 1780–1860* (Cambridge, Mass.: Harvard University Press, 1977), for the increasing use of law as an "instrument" of public policy in antebellum America.

20 *Wayne Township v. Stock Township*, 3 Ohio 173–75 (Ohio Supr. Ct. 1827). Warning out lingered in Ohio's poor laws until 1854; *Ohio Laws*, 52 v 88 (1854); Kennedy, *Ohio Poor Law*, 27.

21 *Wayne Township v. Stock Township*, 3 Ohio 176 (Ohio Supr. Ct. 1827).

22 *Wayne Township v. Stock Township*, 3 Ohio 177 (Ohio Supr. Ct. 1827); *Ohio Laws*, 27 v 54, sec. 1 (1829); Kennedy, *Ohio Poor Law*, 25. The poor law of 1829 clearly distinguished between legal residence for poor relief and legal residence for voting, establishing a harsher racial barrier for

relief than for suffrage. In *Jeffries v. Ankeny*, 11 Ohio 372 (Ohio Supr. Ct. 1842), the Ohio Supreme Court enfranchised a voter who was not white but was less than one-half black. There is no indication that the court ever applied such a lenient racial standard to the poor laws, and in any case the court reversed itself in *Van Camp v. Logan*, 9 Ohio State 407 (Ohio Supr. Ct. 1858). Ohio's poor law discriminated against blacks until 1865, long after most of the "Black Laws" were repealed in 1849. Stephen E. Maizlish, *The Triumph of Sectionalism: The Transformation of Ohio Politics, 1844–1856* (Kent, Ohio: Kent State University Press, 1983), 5–9, 16–17, discusses partisan attitudes toward this issue.

23   Kettner, *Development of American Citizenship*, discusses the increasingly "volitional" nature of American citizenship in statutory and case law during this period, and I have applied that immensely useful concept to legal residence in Ohio.

24   *Ohio Laws*, 29 v 320, secs. 1, 2 (1831).

25   *Cincinnati Township v. Aaron Ogden*, 5 Ohio 23–25 (Ohio Supr. Ct. 1831). Richard P. McCormick, *The History of Voting in New Jersey: A Study of the Development of Election Machinery, 1664–1911* (New Brunswick, N.J.: Rutgers University Press, 1953), 131–32, notes a similar distinction between "residents" and "inhabitants" in New Jersey.

26   Ohio's commissioner of statistics estimated that during the late 1850s an average of 20,000 Ohioans depended on poor relief every year. There is no way to estimate how many of them were migrants, but they represented about 1 percent of the state's population; "Fourth Annual Report of the Commissioner of Statistics, 1860," *Ohio Executive Documents, 1861*, 44.

27   *Ohio Laws*, 29 v 44, sec. 9 (1831). The act of 1831 stipulated no taxpaying qualification for voting in a particular township.

28   *Ohio Laws*, 39 v 13, sec. 2 (1841). See McCormick, *Voting in New Jersey*, 122–23, for a similar discussion of the social sources of electoral reform during the 1840s: "Voting was no longer to be a small-town affair where most individuals were known to their neighbors. It now involved masses of persons whose individual identities were little regarded."

29   *Ohio Laws*, 39 v 13, sec. 2 (1841).

30   *Ohio Laws*, 39 v 13, secs. 2, 13–15 (1841).

31   Story, *Commentaries*, 44–54, wrote an entire chapter on the development of domicile; quote from 47. Domicile was established in law as early as 1813 in Massachusetts in *Putnam v. Johnson*, 10 Mass. 488 (Mass. Supr. Ct. 1813). The doctrine became a national trend and was enunciated by the U.S. Supreme Court in *Ennis v. Smith*, 14 How. 422–23 (U.S. Supr. Ct. 1852). Ohio jurists derived their conception of domicile from Joseph Story and often quoted Story's *Commentaries* verbatim.

32   *Henrietta Township v. Brownhelm Township*, 9 Ohio 76–78 (Ohio Supr. Ct. 1839).

33   *Henrietta Township v. Oxford Township*, 2 Ohio State 32–36 (Ohio Supr.

Ct. 1853); *Egan v. Lumsden and McGovern*, 2 Disney 168 (Cincinnati Super. Ct. 1859).

34 A review of *Century Edition of the American Digest* (St. Paul: West, 1900), 17: 1043–1101, provides a good indication of the rapid acceptance and broad applicability of domicile throughout the United States during the nineteenth century.

35 *Ohio Laws*, 39 v 13, secs. 2, 13, 15 (1841). The Constitution of 1851 retained the one-year residence requirement for interstate migrants but still did not define "residence" in townships; *Ohio Constitution* (1851), art 5.

36 *Ohio Laws*, 61 v 80 (1863); *Lehman v. McBride*, 15 Ohio State 573 (Ohio Supr. Ct. 1863). Josiah Henry Benton, *Voting in the Field: A Forgotten Chapter of the Civil War* (Boston: Privately printed, 1915), provides a general discussion of "soldier voting" in the northern states; consult 73–79 for a brief review of Ohio's experience. Rather than setting up a ballot box in the field, some states adopted "proxy voting," which was a true absentee ballot. Arnold Shankman, "Soldier Votes and Clement L. Vallandigham in the 1863 Ohio Gubernatorial Election," *Ohio History*, 82 (Winter-Spring 1973), 88–104, reviews the partisan roots and implications of soldier voting.

37 *Lehman v. McBride*, 15 Ohio State 583 (Ohio Supr. Ct. 1863).

38 *Lehman v. McBride*, 15 Ohio State 582–84 (Ohio Supr. Ct. 1863).

39 *Lehman v. McBride*, 15 Ohio State 578 (Ohio Supr. Ct. 1863).

40 *Lehman v. McBride*, 15 Ohio State 579 (Ohio Supr. Ct. 1863).

41 *Lehman v. McBride*, 15 Ohio State 579 (Ohio Supr. Ct. 1863). See Pole, *Political Representation*, 205–14; McCormick, *Voting in New Jersey*, 50–51; and Rowland Berthoff, "Independence and Attachment, Virtue and Interest: From Republican Citizen to Free Enterprise, 1787–1837," in *Uprooted Americans: Essays to Honor Oscar Handlin*, ed. Richard L. Bushman et al. (Boston: Little, Brown, 1979), 97–124, for the emergence of "political individualism."

42 *Lehman v. McBride*, 15 Ohio State 594–95, 597, 601 (Ohio Supr. Ct. 1863). The majority, which included Chief Justice Jacob Brinkerhoff, Justices Horace Wilder and William White, and Justice Josiah Scott, who wrote the opinion, were all Republicans; Joseph P. Smith, *History of the Republican Party in Ohio* (Chicago: Lewis, 1898), 45–46, 66–67, 197–98. Pole, *Political Representation*, 54–55, discusses virtual representation in the American colonies. Alfred De Grazia, *Public and Republic: Political Representation in America* (New York: Knopf, 1951), 113–45, provides the most thorough discussion of the rise of direct democracy during the nineteenth century.

43 *Lehman v. McBride*, 15 Ohio State 600, 607 (Ohio Supr. Ct. 1863).

44 *Lehman v. McBride*, 15 Ohio State 629–31, 633–34, 649–50 (Ohio Supr. Ct. 1863). Ranney came to Ohio from Massachusetts at age 11 in 1813. A former law partner of Benjamin F. Wade, Ranney was known as an

"out and out Democrat" or an "old-time Democrat." He was Democratic nominee for governor in 1859; *The Democratic Party of the State of Ohio*, ed. Thomas E. Powell (Columbus: Ohio Publishing Company, 1913), 1: 125–26, 168; Eugene H. Roseboom, *The Civil War Era: 1850–1873*, Vol. 4 of *A History of the State of Ohio*, ed. Carl Wittke (Columbus: Ohio State Archaeological and Historical Society, 1944), 348.

45 *Lehman v. McBride*, 15 Ohio State 629–31, 633–34, 649–50 (Ohio Supr. Ct. 1863).

46 *Ohio Laws*, 107 v 52 (1917).

47 *Blair v. Western Female Seminary*, 1 Bond 578 (Ohio Cir. Ct., S.D. 1864). The Blair decision rested on *Shelton v. Tiffin*, 6 How. 185 (U.S. Supr. Ct. 1852), which declared that "On a change of domicile from one State to another, citizenship may depend upon the intention of the individual. But this intention may be shown more satisfactorily by acts than declarations. An exercise of the right of suffrage is conclusive on the subject."

48 *Esker v. McCoy*, 5 Dec. Rep. 698 (Ross Common Pleas 1878).

49 *Esker v. McCoy*, 5 Dec. Rep. 701 (Ross Common Pleas 1878); *Lehman v. McBride*, 15 Ohio State 649 (Ohio Supr. Ct. 1863). Compare volitional residence with the "community of limited liability" posed by Morris Janowitz, *The Community Press in an Urban Setting: The Social Elements of Urbanism*, 2d ed. (Chicago: University of Chicago Press, 1967), 210–13.

4. The defended community: migration and elections

1 "Report of the Committee on Privileges and Elections in the Medina County Case," *Ohio House Journal, Appendix, 1848–1849*, 143–46.

2 *Lehman v. McBride*, 15 Ohio State 582 (Ohio Supr. Ct., 1863); George Sidney Camp, *Democracy* (New York: Harper and Brothers, 1841), 185–86; "Governor's Message," *Ohio Executive Documents, 1856*, Part 1, 456; Samuel Jones, *A Treatise on the Right of Suffrage* (Boston: Otis, Broaders and Company, 1842), 48–49; Chilton Williamson, *American Suffrage: From Property to Democracy, 1760–1860* (Princeton, N.J.: Princeton University Press, 1960), 290; Rush Welter, *The Mind of America, 1820–1860* (New York: Columbia University Press, 1975), 173–89.

3 Andrew W. Young, *First Lessons in Civil Government* (Cleveland: M. C. Younglove, 1846), 35; "Governor's Message," *Ohio Executive Documents, 1852*, Part 1, 24. Modern arguments for lengthy residence requirements are quite similar; Ronald L. Rowland, "Voter Residency Requirements in State and Local Elections," *Ohio State Law Journal*, 32 (1971), 604.

4 Jones, *Right of Suffrage*, 125, 126–27, 172; Williamson, *American Suffrage*, 290.

5 *Ohio Constitution* (1802), art. 1, secs. 4, 7, art. 2, sec. 3; *Report of the Debates and Proceedings of the Convention for the Revision of the Constitution of the State of Ohio, 1850–51*, ed. Joseph V. Smith (Columbus: Medary, 1851), 2:

9. Illinois required state representatives, state senators, and the governor to live in the state for three, five, and ten years, respectively; *Illinois Constitution* (1848), art. 3, secs. 3, 4, art. 4, sec. 4.

6 *Ohio Constitution* (1802), art. 4, secs. 1, 5; *Statutes of Ohio and the Northwestern Territory Adopted or Enacted from 1788 to 1833 Inclusive*, ed. Salmon P. Chase (Cincinnati, 1833), 1: chap. 185, sec. 11, 622–23; *Ohio Laws*, 29 v 44, secs. 6, 9 (1831); Young, *First Lessons*, 35; Chilton Williamson, *American Suffrage: From Property to Democracy, 1760–1860* (Princeton, N.J.: Princeton University Press, 1960), 136. Any eligible voter could satisfy Ohio's taxpaying qualification by working on county or township roads, which does not seem to have imposed a very heavy burden on voters. As one Ohio farmer complained, "The two days labor which the law prescribes, is considered a penalty that has to be endured, and they seek its mitigation by working as little as possible. And those that let them off with the least amount of work, are considered the best supervisors, and are frequently elected on that account"; *Ohio Cultivator*, March 1, 1850. Only five states did not impose the corvée or labor tax; Hildegard Binder Johnson, *Order Upon the Land: The U.S. Rectangular Survey and the Upper Mississippi Country* (New York: Oxford University Press, 1976), 169.

7 *Ohio Laws*, 29 v 44, secs. 6, 9 (1831).

8 *Ohio Laws*, 39 v 13, sec. 2 (1841); *Ohio Constitution* (1802), art. 4, sec. 1.

9 *Ohio Laws*, 39 v 13, sec. 13 (1841). The election board was traditional in Ohio but acquired new powers in 1841.

10 *Ohio Laws*, 39 v 13, sec. 13 (1841).

11 The law of 1841 required election clerks to note "sworn" voters in the poll books; *Ohio Laws*, 39 v 13, secs. 15, 17 (1841). From 1841 to 1849, 797 voters cast ballots in Clinton Township, and 71, or 8.9 percent, "swore" to the election oath. During the 1850s, the proportion fell to 3.8 percent, or 54 of 1,413 voters; Poll Books, Clinton Township, Shelby County, Ohio, 1841–60, Wright State University Archives, Wright State University, Dayton, Ohio.

12 *Ohio Laws*, 39 v 13, sec. 16 (1841). According to the law of 1831, "the trustees of the several townships shall serve as judges"; *Ohio Laws*, 29 v 44, sec. 6 (1831). The act of 1841 retained this provision. See also Young, *First Lessons*, 36: "Elections are conducted by the trustees in the several townships, who are called judges of election. . . . If any of the trustees or the clerk are not present, the electors may choose, *viva voce*, suitable persons in their places." Liverpool Township was 68.8 percent Democratic in 1848; "Medina County Case," 102.

13 *Ohio Laws*, 29 v 44, sec. 9 (1831); *Ohio Laws*, 39 v 13, secs. 4, 5, 7 (1841).

14 Jones, *Right of Suffrage*, 172. Jones advocated the adoption of registry laws by the states and described their operation in minute detail; *Right of Suffrage*, 170–73.

15 Cincinnati *Daily Gazette*, February 5, 1841; *Cincinnati Gazette*, October 13, 1847; *Ohio Laws*, 43 v 116, secs. 1, 2, 4, 9 (1845). Williamson, *Ameri-*

can Suffrage, 272–77, argues that Whigs were the greatest advocates of residence requirements before the Civil War. Ohio Democrats complained bitterly that Whigs misused the new election law to disfranchise Democratic voters. See, for example, Columbus *Daily Ohio Statesman*, April 4, 1850.

16   *Ohio Laws*, 43 v 116, secs. 1, 2, 4, 9 (1845). Between 1840 and 1860, the population of the canal counties rose 56.8 percent as compared to 48.8 percent in the rest of Ohio. The difference between 1840 and 1850 was even greater, 39 percent vs. 25.7 percent. In 1850 and 1860, 17.8 percent and 24.3 percent, respectively, of the canal counties' residents were foreign-born. The comparable proportions were 6.8 percent and 8.6 percent in the other counties; J. D. B. DeBow, *Seventh Census of the United States, 1850* (Washington, D.C., 1853), 818–51; Joseph C. G. Kennedy, *Population of the United States in 1860: Compendium of the Eighth Census* (Washington, D.C., 1864), 373–96.

17   *Wooster Democrat*, January 9, 1845.

18   Columbus *Ohio Statesman*, December 14, 1846; "Medina County Case," 87, 117.

19   Smith, *Convention Proceedings*, 2: 9.

20   Smith, *Convention Proceedings*, 1: 3–6, lists every delegate's age and length of residence in Ohio. The 39 Whig delegates had resided for a mean of 34.8 years in the state, the 67 Democratic delegates only 29.5 years. The typical Whig delegate was also five years older than the typical Democrat (48.5 years vs. 43.1 years, for a grand mean of 45.1 years). Both the typical Whig and the typical Democrat arrived in Ohio at the age of 13. The members of the 1845–46 Ohio legislature had resided in Ohio for a mean of only 26.5 years, arriving at age 15; Columbus *Semi-Weekly Ohio Statesman*, December 26, 1845.

21   Smith, *Convention Proceedings*, 2: 8.

22   Smith, *Convention Proceedings*, 1: 4, 5; 2: 8, 9. There is no record of roll-call votes in the convention, and further analysis of partisan, ethnic, or regional divisions is therefore impossible.

23   Smith, *Convention Proceedings*, 1: 3, 5; 2: 8.

24   Smith, *Convention Proceedings*, 1: 5; 2: 9; Eugene H. Roseboom, *The Civil War Era: 1850–1873*, Vol. 4 of *A History of the State of Ohio*, ed. Carl Wittke (Columbus: Ohio State Archaeological Society, 1844), 401.

25   Smith, *Convention Proceedings*, 1: 5; 2: 9.

26   Smith, *Convention Proceedings*, 1: 4; 2: 9.

27   Smith, *Convention Proceedings*, 1: 3, 4; 2: 9, 10.

28   Smith, *Convention Proceedings*, 1: 3; 2: 10; *Esker v. McCoy*, 5 Dec. Rep. 698 (Ross Common Pleas 1878). Dorsey, a 37-year-old physician, was a native Ohioan who later became a Republican and was a delegate to the Ohio Constitutional Convention of 1873; Joseph P. Smith, *History of the Republican Party in Ohio* (Chicago: Lewis, 1898), 143.

29   *Ohio Laws*, 54 v 136 (1857). In 1861, the legislature exempted local mi-

grants who were household heads from disfranchisement; *Ohio Laws*, 58 v 17 (1861). See *Ohio Laws*, 61 v 91 (1864); *Ohio Laws*, 64 v 151 (1867); and *Ohio Laws*, 73 v 155 (1876), for codification and later refinements.

30 In 1877 a registration law singled out recent migrants for registration, requiring of voters 360 days' residence in a county and 355 days' residence in a township or precinct before voting. This stringent residence requirement, however, could be overcome through registration 30 days before an election. In effect, only newcomers arriving within one year of an election needed to register; *Ohio Laws*, 74 v 211 (1877). An 1885 law established general registration of voters in Ohio's largest cities, Cincinnati and Cleveland; *Ohio Laws*, 82 v 232 (1885). This law was struck down, however, as too stringent in *Daggett v. Hudson*, 43 Ohio State 548 (1885). In 1921 the legislature established annual registration of voters in all cities of 100,000 or more residents and quadrennial registration in all cities of 11,800 to 100,000 residents. This law also made legal residence dependent on registration, stating that "No person shall have acquired a legal residence in a ward or election precinct . . . for the purpose of voting" unless registered; *Ohio General Code* (1921), secs. 4870–72. In 1972 registration became mandatory in cities of 16,000 or more residents and voluntary for towns smaller than 16,000; *Ohio General Code* (1972), sec. 3503.06. Beginning in 1977, all Ohio voters must register; *Ohio Revised Code* (1985), sec. 3503.06. Ohio lowered the residence requirement for newcomers to the state from one year to six months in 1970 and to 30 days in 1977; *Ohio General Code* (1972), sec. 3503.01; *Ohio Revised Code* (1985), sec. 3503.01.

31 Quotes from Alexis de Tocqueville, *Democracy in America*, ed. Phillips Bradley (New York: Random House, 1945), 1: 62; and Lewis Atherton, *Main Street on the Middle Border* (Bloomington: Indiana University Press, 1954), 181, 185. The classic portrait of communities rising spontaneously during the nineteenth century is Daniel J. Boorstin, *The Americans: The National Experience* (New York: Random House, 1965), 49–112. The modern debate over the prevalence of conflict or cooperation in the building of American communities began with Stanley Elkins and Eric McKitrick, "A Meaning for Turner's Frontier," *Political Science Quarterly*, 69 (September and December 1954), 321–53, 565–602; and Rowland Berthoff, "The American Social Order: A Conservative Hypothesis," *American Historical Review*, 65 (April 1960), 495–514.

32 Gerald D. Suttles, *The Social Construction of Communities* (Chicago: University of Chicago Press, 1972), contrasts "natural" with "defended" or "contrived" communities. Portraits of community building that emphasize conflict and competition within formal organizations and power structures include Allan G. Bogue, "Social Theory and the Pioneer," *Agricultural History*, 34 (January 1960), 21–34; Robert R. Dykstra, *The Cattle Towns* (New York: Knopf, 1968); Richard S. Alcorn, "Leadership and Stability in Mid-Nineteenth-Century America: A Case Study of an

Illinois Town," *Journal of American History*, 61 (December 1974), 685–702; Don H. Doyle, "Social Theory and New Communities in Nineteenth-Century America," *Western Historical Quarterly*, 8 (April 1977), 151–65, and "The Social Functions of Voluntary Associations in a Nineteenth-Century American Town," *Social Science History*, 1 (Spring 1977), 333–55; and Walter S. Glazer, "Participation and Power: Voluntary Associations and the Functional Organization of Cincinnati in 1840," *Historical Methods Newsletter*, 5 (September 1972), 151–68. From this perspective, community building often required hard work, compromise, and even confrontation. John C. Hudson, *Plains Country Towns* (Minneapolis: University of Minnesota Press, 1985), 121–30, argues, for example, that some railroad towns on the northern plains never developed a sense of community because their promoters never took the time and trouble to create one.

33 "Medina County Case," 134.
34 "Medina County Case," 155.
35 "Medina County Case," 114–15.

5. "A movable column": migration and voting

1 "Annual Report of the Commissioner of Statistics, 1857," *Ohio Executive Documents, 1857*, Part 2, 489.

2 Lester W. Milbrath and M. L. Goel, *Political Participation: How and Why Do People Get Involved in Politics?*, 2d ed. (Chicago: Rand McNally, 1977), inventory the conclusions of the extensive survey literature. Sidney Verba and Norman H. Nie, *Participation in America: Political Democracy and Social Equality* (New York: Harper & Row, 1972), present the most systematic model of participation, but for more recent refinements, consult Raymond E. Wolfinger and Steven J. Rosenstone, *Who Votes?* (New Haven, Conn.: Yale University Press, 1980).

3 Jorgen Elklit, "Nominal Record Linkage and the Study of Non-Secret Voting: A Danish Case," *Journal of Interdisciplinary History*, 15 (Winter 1985), 419–43, provides the best introduction to the political analysis of poll books. There is as yet no published review of the conclusions of American poll-book research, but earlier studies include Paul F. Bourke and Donald A. DeBats, "Identifiable Voting in Nineteenth-Century America: Toward a Comparison of Britain and the United States before the Secret Ballot," *Perspectives in American History*, 11 (1977–78), 259–88, and "Individuals and Aggregates: A Note on Historical Data and Assumptions," *Social Science History*, 4 (Spring 1980), 229–50; David A. Bohmer, "The Maryland Electorate and the Concept of a Party System in the Early National Period," in *The History of American Electoral Behavior*, ed. Joel H. Silbey, Allan G. Bogue, and William H. Flanigan (Princeton, N.J.: Princeton University Press, 1978), 146–73; John M. Rozett, "The Social Bases of Party Conflict in the Age of Jackson: Individual Voting

Behavior in Greene County, Illinois, 1838–1848," unpub. Ph.D. diss., University of Michigan, 1974; Paul F. Bourke and Donald A. DeBats, "Society and Politics in a New Community: Washington County, Oregon, in the 1850s," unpub. paper presented at Social Science History Association meeting, 1980; and Kenneth J. Winkle, "The Voters of Lincoln's Springfield: Politics and Community in the Antebellum Midwest," unpub. paper presented at Organization of American Historians meeting, 1986. Poll-book analysts have focused on partisan affiliation to the near exclusion of participation. A notable exception is David H. Bohmer, "Voting Behavior During the First American Party System: Maryland, 1796–1816," unpub. Ph.D. diss., University of Michigan, 1974, 116–68.

4 Poll Books, Shelby County, Ohio, 1822–60, and Auglaize County, Ohio, 1850–60, Wright State University Archives, Wright State University, Dayton, Ohio; Poll Books, Highland County, Ohio, 1850–60, University of Cincinnati Archives, Cincinnati, Ohio; Poll Books, Portage County, Ohio, 1856–66, Kent State University Archives, Kent State University, Kent, Ohio. For a description of the poll books, see *Ohio Laws*, 29 v 44, secs. 19, 20, 21 (1831). The best contemporary definition of poll books comes from a textbook on Ohio government: "Each of the clerks has a poll-book, in which he keeps a list of the name and number of every elector voting at the election. *Poll* is a Saxon word, signifying head, and has come to mean person. Hence, so much 'a head' means, so much for every person. And by a still farther change, it is made to signify an election, because the persons there voting are numbered. Thus, 'going to the polls' has obtained the same meaning as going to an election, or to the place of voting; and the poll-list is the list of the names and number of voters"; Andrew W. Young, *First Lessons in Civil Government* (Cleveland: M. C. Younglove, 1846), 36. European poll-book analysts label poll books that do not reveal partisanship "voting lists"; Elklit, "Nominal Record Linkage," 422–23; J. R. Vincent, *Pollbooks: How Victorians Voted* (Cambridge, Eng.: Cambridge University Press, 1967). In law and practice, Ohioans referred to their voting lists as "poll books."

5 Poll Books, Shelby County, Ohio, 1836, 1844, 1852, 1854, 1856, 1857, 1860. Robert A. Mahan, an election clerk in Medina County, described the process of comparing and cross-checking poll books at an election: "There were 165 names recorded on the poll books that I kept. We discovered, on comparing my poll books with Mr. Perkins', the other clerk, that the name of John Hull, was on my poll book, but not on his. His poll book was corrected by mine." Mahan later discovered a discrepancy of only one vote between the two poll books; "Report of the Committee on Privileges and Elections in the Medina County Case," *Ohio House Journal, Appendix, 1848–1849*, 112.

6 Poll Books, Shelby County, Ohio, 1834, 1854; "Report of the Standing Committee on Privileges and Elections," *Ohio Senate Journal, Appendix, 1846–1847*, 1–272. Other investigations include "Medina County Case,"

83–184; "Report of the Committee on Privileges and Elections," *Ohio House Journal, Appendix, 1848–1849*, 35–81; "Reports of the Majority and Minority of the Committee on Privileges and Elections," *Ohio Senate Journal, Appendix, 1848–1849*, 81–144; and "Report of the Committee on Privileges and Elections, on the Morgan County Case," *Ohio House Journal, Appendix, 1851–1852*, 9–33. The authors of these documents reproduced and scrutinized dozens of poll books. Because of the precision of election clerks in distinguishing among voters with common names, very few voters shared identical names, which greatly facilitated record linkage. Whenever I was confronted with identical names, I made a link and may therefore be guilty of "mu" errors, the construction of false links. I believe, however, that I have minimized "lambda" errors, the failure to make true links, and so have avoided overestimating rates of migration among voters. See Elklit, "Nominal Record Linkage," 427–30, for a discussion of mu and lambda errors.

7   Manuscript U.S. Census of Population, Shelby County, Ohio, 1850 and 1860. To be on the conservative side in estimating rates of migration, I selected the highest rates of mortality that are available, Table C–9 in Peter D. McClelland and Richard J. Zeckhauser, *Demographic Dimensions of the New Republic: American Interregional Migration, Vital Statistics, and Manumissions, 1800–1860* (Cambridge, Eng.: Cambridge University Press, 1982), 151.

8   Stephan Thernstrom and Peter R. Knights, "Men in Motion: Some Data and Speculations about Urban Population Mobility in Nineteenth-Century America," *Journal of Interdisciplinary History*, 1 (Autumn 1970), 7–35, were first to demonstrate the importance of estimating population turnover between censuses.

9   The figures in Table 5.1 and all estimates of political participation are based on "recovered votes" and "recovered voters." Voters whose names were illegible in the poll books were not included in the analysis. Such underenumeration was slight and is considered random. See Rozett, "Social Bases of Party Conflict," 226–31.

10   Manuscript U.S. Census of Population, Highland County, Ohio, 1850 and 1860; *History of Ross and Highland Counties, Ohio* (Cleveland: W. W. Williams, 1880), 93, 153–54.

11   Manuscript U.S. Census of Population, Portage County, Ohio, 1850 and 1860; *History of Portage County, Ohio* (Chicago: Warner, Beers, 1885), 192, 289, 290–92. Table 5.4 presents rates of participation in ten annual elections in Ravenna Township between 1856 and 1866 instead of during the 1850s.

12   Manuscript U.S. Census of Population, Portage County, Ohio, 1850 and 1860; *History of Portage County*, 531.

13   In addition to Clinton, Paint, and Ravenna townships, the eight townships include Goshen, Moulton, Pusheta, Salem, and Union townships, Auglaize County, located just north of Shelby County. Consult

Kenneth J. Winkle, "The Politics of Community: Migration and Politics in Antebellum Ohio," unpub. Ph.D. diss., University of Wisconsin, 1984, 198–211, for an analysis of participation in these additional townships.

14   Poll Books, Clinton Township, Shelby County, Ohio, 1822–60, Wright State University Archives, Wright State University, Dayton, Ohio.

15   Compare Douglass C. North's characterization of the period 1837–45 as a lull in western development and 1850–56 as a peak period; Douglass C. North, *The Economic Growth of the United States, 1790–1860* (New York: Norton, 1966), 136.

16   Manuscript U.S. Census of Population, Shelby County, Ohio, 1850, 281; *Combination Atlas Map of Shelby County, Ohio* (Philadelphia: Page and Smith, 1875), 349; Poll Books, Shelby County, Ohio, 1822–60.

6. The core community: migration and leadership

1   Angus Campbell, Philip E. Converse, Warren E. Miller, and Donald E. Stokes, *The American Voter* (New York: Wiley, 1960); Lester W. Milbrath and M. L. Goel, *Political Participation: How and Why Do People Get Involved in Politics?*, 2d ed. (Chicago: Rand McNally, 1977); Sidney Verba and Norman H. Nie, *Participation in America: Political Democracy and Social Equality* (New York: Harper & Row, 1972); Raymond E. Wolfinger and Steven J. Rosenstone, *Who Votes?* (New Haven, Conn.: Yale University Press, 1980).

2   Manuscript U.S. Census of Population, Auglaize County, Ohio, 1850 and 1860; Poll Books, Auglaize County, Ohio, 1850–60, Wright State University Archives, Wright State University, Dayton, Ohio.

3   Manuscript U.S. Census of Population, Shelby County, Ohio, 1850 and 1860. Stephan Thernstrom, *The Other Bostonians: Poverty and Progress in the American Metropolis, 1880–1970* (Cambridge, Mass.: Harvard University Press, 1973), 221–32, reviews studies of migration in both urban and rural areas.

4   Stephan Thernstrom and Peter R. Knights, "Men in Motion: Some Data and Speculations about Urban Population Mobility in Nineteenth-Century America," *Journal of Interdisciplinary History*, 1 (Autumn 1970), 7–35.

5   Poll Books, Clinton Township, Shelby County, Ohio, 1850–60, Wright State University Archives, Wright State University, Dayton, Ohio.

6   Estimates of mortality drawn from Table C–9 in Peter D. McClelland and Richard J. Zeckhauser, *Demographic Dimensions of the New Republic: American Interregional Migration, Vital Statistics, and Manumissions, 1800–1860* (Cambridge, Eng.: Cambridge University Press, 1982), 151.

7   Merle Curti, *The Making of an American Community: A Case Study of Democracy in a Frontier County* (Stanford, Calif.: Stanford University Press, 1959), 65–77; Stephan Thernstrom, *Poverty and Progress: Social Mobility in a Nineteenth Century City* (Cambridge, Mass.: Harvard University Press,

1964), 84–90; Richard J. Hopkins, "Occupational and Geographic Mo-
bility in Atlanta, 1870–1876," *Journal of Southern History*, 34 (May 1968),
200–13; Thernstrom, *Other Bostonians* 9–44, 221–32; Michael B. Katz,
Michael J. Doucet, and Mark J. Stern, "Population Persistence and Ear-
ly Industrialization in a Canadian City: Hamilton, Ontario, 1851–1871,"
Social Science History, 2 (Winter 1978), 208–29; Gordon W. Kirk, Jr., and
Carol Tyirin Kirk, "Migration, Mobility and the Transformation of the
Occupational Structure in an Immigrant Community: Holland, Michi-
gan, 1850–80," *Journal of Social History*, 7 (Winter 1974), 142–64; Howard
M. Gitelman, *Workingmen of Waltham: Mobility in American Urban Indus-
trial Development, 1850–1890* (Baltimore: Johns Hopkins University
Press, 1974), 23–49; Michael B. Katz, *The People of Hamilton, Canada
West: Family and Class in a Mid-Nineteenth-Century City* (Cambridge,
Mass.: Harvard University Press, 1975), 94–175; Michael B. Katz, Mich-
ael J. Doucet, and Mark J. Stern, *The Social Organization of Early Industrial
Capitalism* (Cambridge, Mass.: Harvard University Press, 1982), 102–30.
Stanley Engerman, "Up or Out: Social and Geographic Mobility in the
United States," *Journal of Interdisciplinary History*, 5 (Winter 1975), 469–
89, offers a theoretical review of this evidence.

8   Charles Stephenson, "A Gathering of Strangers? Mobility, Social Structure, and Political Participation in the Formation of Nineteenth-Century
American Workingclass Culture," in *American Workingclass Culture: Explorations in American Labor and Social History*, ed. Milton Cantor (Westport, Conn.: Greenwood, 1979), 31–60.

9   Table 6.1 uses chi-square ($p < .05$) to determine the statistical significance of these relationships. Relationships that are not significant
should not be generalized outside Clinton Township. Table 6.1 includes males 11–20 years old ($N = 87$) only in analyzing the relationship
between age and persistence.

10 For a theoretical discussion of this issue that presents a practical application, consult J. Morgan Kousser, Gary W. Cox, and David W. Galenson, "Log-Linear Analysis of Contingency Tables: An Introduction for
Historians with an Application to Thernstrom on the 'Floating Proletariat,'" *Historical Methods*, 15 (Fall 1982), 152–69.

11 Guides to conducting and interpreting log-linear analyses include, in
order of their usefulness as introductions, Kousser, Cox, and Galenson,
"Log-Linear Analysis"; David Knoke and Peter J. Burke, *Log-Linear Mod-
els* (Beverly Hills: Sage, 1980); Stephen E. Fienberg, *The Analysis of Cross-
Classified Categorical Data* (Cambridge, Mass.: MIT Press, 1977); and
Yvonne M. M. Bishop, Stephen E. Fienberg, and Paul W. Holland,
Discrete Multivariate Analysis: Theory and Practice (Cambridge, Mass.:
MIT Press, 1975).

12 Log-linear contingency table analysis tests the independence of
categorical variables. Unlike regression, it does not distinguish between
independent and dependent variables. The log-linear equation includes

a grand mean effect, an effect for each variable, and terms for all possible interactions among variables. The initial hierarchical log-linear model ($p < .05$) in this analysis tested for sixth-order interaction and all lower-order interactions. It produced a saturated model that, by including all variables, shows that all the variables were closely related. A second log-linear analysis tested for only second-order interactions. It produced as a final model {PO} {AW} {AN} {AR} {OR} {WR} {NR}, where P, O, A, W, N, and R stand for the initial letters of each variable. The final log-linear analysis also tested for second-order interactions but excluded N and R. It produced a final model of {PO} {OW} {OA} {WA}, suggesting that O, W, and A were all closely related but that only O had a direct relationship with P. W and A acted on P only indirectly through O.

13   Richard S. Alcorn, "Leadership and Stability in Mid-Nineteenth-Century America: A Case Study of an Illinois Town," *Journal of American History*, 61 (December 1974), 685–702; Curti, *Making of an American Community*, 338–44, 416–27; Don H. Doyle, "The Social Functions of Voluntary Associations in a Nineteenth-Century American Town," *Social Science History*, 1 (Spring 1977), 333–55; Robert R. Dykstra, *The Cattle Towns* (New York: Knopf, 1968); Walter S. Glazer, "Participation and Power: Voluntary Associations and the Functional Organization of Cincinnati in 1840," *Historical Methods Newsletter*, 5 (September 1972), 151–68; Edward Pessen, *Riches, Class, and Power before the Civil War* (Lexington, Mass.: Heath, 1973), 281–301; Whitman H. Ridgway, *Community Leadership in Maryland, 1790–1840: A Comparative Analysis of Power in Society* (Chapel Hill: University of North Carolina Press, 1979); Robert A. Dahl, *Who Governs? Democracy and Power in an American City* (New Haven, Conn.: Yale University Press, 1961), 11–86; Ralph A. Wooster, *Politicians, Planters and Plain Folk: Courthouse and Statehouse in the Upper South, 1850–1860* (Knoxville: University of Tennessee Press, 1975); Harry L. Watson, *Jacksonian Politics and Community Conflict: The Emergence of the Second American Party System in Cumberland County, North Carolina* (Baton Rouge: Louisiana State University Press, 1981), 198–245; Don H. Doyle, "Social Theory and New Communities in Nineteenth-Century America," *Western Historical Quarterly*, 8 (April 1977), 151–65. David C. Hammack, "Problems in the Historical Study of Power in the Cities and Towns of the United States, 1800–1960," *American Historical Review*, 83 (April 1978), 323–49, provides the best review of historical studies of power in America.

14   Alcorn, "Leadership and Stability," introduced the idea of "core leaders," whose persistence helped to bring social, economic, and political organization to midwestern communities. For the historiographical development of this idea, see Kenneth J. Winkle, "The Politics of Community: Migration and Politics in Antebellum Ohio," unpub. Ph.D. diss., University of Wisconsin, 1984, 255–68. The concept of a "core" electo-

rate was first advanced by Angus Campbell, "Surge and Decline: A Study of Electoral Change," in Angus Campbell, Philip E. Converse, Warren E. Miller, and Donald E. Stokes, *Elections and the Political Order* (New York: Wiley, 1966), 40–62, and has gained wide acceptance among political scientists.

15 Alcorn, "Leadership and Stability"; Doyle, "Social Functions of Voluntary Associations"; Doyle, "Social Theory and New Communities"; R. A. Burchell, "The Character and Function of a Pioneer Elite: Rural California, 1848–1880," *Journal of American Studies*, 15 (December 1981), 377–89; Kenneth J. Winkle, "A Social Analysis of Voter Turnout in Ohio, 1850–1860," *Journal of Interdisciplinary History*, 13 (Winter 1983), 411–35, and "Political Friends: Migration and Officeholding in Lincoln's Springfield," unpub. paper presented at Social Science History Association meeting, 1986.

16 Information on officeholding was obtained from *Combination Atlas Map of Shelby County, Ohio* (Philadelphia: Page and Smith, 1875), 12; *History of Shelby County, Ohio* (Philadelphia: R. Sutton & Company, 1883), 346, 349.

17 Relationships that are not significant should not be generalized outside Clinton Township.

18 The final model, achieved in a manner similar to that discussed in note 12, was {EO} {ER} {OR} {OA} {AN} {ON}, where E stands for elected office.

19 Basil G. Zimmer, "Participation of Migrants in Urban Structures," *American Sociological Review*, 20 (April 1955), 218–24, found that today migrants with "high status personal characteristics" become most quickly involved in community affairs.

20 The other communities are Ravenna Township, Portage County, Ohio; Paint Township, Highland County, Ohio; Goshen, Moulton, Pusheta, Salem, and Union townships, Auglaize County, Ohio; Middleton Township, Dane County, Wisconsin; and Springfield, Illinois. See, for example, Kenneth J. Winkle, "The Voters of Lincoln's Springfield: Politics and Community in the Antebellum Midwest," unpub. paper presented at Organization of American Historians meeting, 1986.

21 Thomas Bender, *Community and Social Change in America* (Baltimore: Johns Hopkins University Press, 1978), 93; Frederick Grimké, *The Nature and Tendency of Free Institutions*, ed. John William Ward (Cambridge, Mass.: Harvard University Press, 1968), 181.

22 Over 30 years ago the sociologist George A. Hillery proposed a simple empirical definition of community after uncovering 94 working definitions among sociologists: "Persons in social interaction within a geographic area and having one or more additional common ties"; George A. Hillery, Jr., "Definitions of Community: Areas of Agreement," *Rural Sociology*, 20 (June 1955), 111–23. Bender, *Community and Social Change*, 7, proposed a definition that depends less on geographic criteria and

more on social interaction: "a network of social relations marked by mutuality and emotional bonds."

23 *Statutes of Ohio and the Northwestern Territory Adopted or Enacted from 1788 to 1822 Inclusive,* ed. Salmon P. Chase (Cincinnati, 1833), 1: chap. xv, sec. 2, 364; *Lehman v. McBride,* 15 Ohio State 629–31 (Ohio Supr. Ct. 1863).

24 The differences in mean turnout among the three regions were statistically significant at the .05 level. In Clinton Township, the differences were not significantly related to any of the social and economic variables considered, including the urban-rural and farmer-nonfarmer distinctions. Poll Books, Shelby County, Ohio, 1858 and 1860, linked with Plat Book, Shelby County, Ohio, 1859, Office of the Shelby County Engineer, Sidney, Ohio; Poll Books, Portage County, Ohio, 1858 and 1860, Kent State University Archives, Kent State University, Kent, Ohio, linked with Plat Book, Portage County, Ohio, 1859, Office of the Portage County Engineer, Ravenna, Ohio. Quote from "Report of the Standing Committee on Privileges and Elections," *Ohio Senate Journal, Appendix, 1846–1847,* 77.

7. Migration and local politics: an antebellum election

1 "Report of the Standing Committee on Privileges and Elections," *Ohio Senate Journal, Appendix, 1846–1847,* 219, 220–21, 221–22 [hereafter cited as "Wayne County Case"]. Wayne Senatorial District consisted of all 16 townships in Wayne County and four in Ashland County – Jackson, Lake, Mohecan, and Perry.

2 "Wayne County Case," 219–22.

3 *Ohio Senate Journal, 1846–1847,* 13, 23, 47, 58, 62, 171; *Wooster Democrat,* January 7, 1847.

4 Ben Douglass, *History of Wayne County, Ohio* (Indianapolis: Robert Douglass, 1878), 262; *Report of the Ohio Board of Agriculture, 1846,* 69; *Report of the Ohio Board of Agriculture, 1849;* Eugene H. Roseboom, *The Civil War Era: 1850–1873,* Vol. 4 of *A History of the State of Ohio,* ed. Carl Wittke (Columbus: Ohio State Archaeological and Historical Society, 1944), 72–73; Robert Leslie Jones, *History of Agriculture in Ohio to 1880* (Kent, Ohio: Kent State University Press, 1983), 61–62. In 1850, Wayne County's population density was 58.5 / sq. mi., compared to Ohio's 48.0 / sq. mi.; J. D. B. DeBow, *Statistical View of the United States, 1850: Compendium of the Seventh Census* (Washington, D.C., 1854), 290–93.

5 The sources for Table 7.1 are J. D. B. DeBow, *Seventh Census of the United States, 1850* (Washington, D.C., 1853), 862–68; DeBow, *Statistical View,* 290–93.

6 *Sixth Census of the United States, 1840* (Washington, D.C., 1841), 337; DeBow, *Seventh Census,* 850.

7 DeBow, *Seventh Census,* 850; Joseph C. G. Kennedy, *Population of the*

United States in 1860: Compendium of the Eighth Census (Washington, D.C., 1864), 373, 395; *Wooster Democrat,* July 31, 1845, September 3, 1846; Wooster *Republican Advocate,* November 16, 1837. See Michael P. Conzen, *Frontier Farming in an Urban Shadow: The Influence of Madison's Proximity on the Agricultural Development of Blooming Grove, Wisconsin* (Madison: State Historical Society of Wisconsin, 1971), for the impact of an "urban shadow" on a growing city's rural hinterland.

8 Edgar Allan Holt, *Party Politics in Ohio, 1840–1850* (Columbus: Ohio Archaeological and Historical Society, 1931), 60–62, 66–68, 72–73, 75, 82; Francis P. Weisenberger, *The Passing of the Frontier, 1825–1850,* Vol. 3 of *A History of the State of Ohio,* ed. Carl Wittke (Columbus: Ohio State Archaeological and Historical Society, 1941), 415–16; Delmer J. Trester, "David Tod and the Gubernatorial Campaign of 1844," *Ohio State Archaeological and Historical Quarterly,* 62 (April 1953), 162–78. For a broad discussion of the banking issue during the 1840s, consult William G. Shade, *Banks or No Banks: The Money Issue in Western Politics, 1832–1865* (Detroit: Wayne State University Press, 1972); and James Roger Sharp, *The Jacksonians versus the Banks: Politics in the States after the Panic of 1837* (New York: Columbia University Press, 1970). See Sharp, *Jacksonians versus the Banks,* 123–89, for the banking issue in Ohio and, 142–47, for the role of the Bank of Wooster.

9 Holt, *Party Politics,* 88–89, 94–96, 98; Weisenberger, *Passing of the Frontier,* 416; Charles C. Huntington, "A History of Banking and Currency in Ohio before the Civil War," *Ohio Archaeological and Historical Quarterly,* 24 (July 1915), 419; Shade, *Banks or No Banks,* 104–5.

10 Holt, *Party Politics,* 96, 102–3, 112; Huntington, "History of Banking," 413, 419; Trester, "David Tod."

11 Huntington, "History of Banking," 413. Sharp, *Jacksonians versus the Banks,* 143, labeled the Bank of Wooster a "rallying point for conservative Democratic strength in Ohio" and noted that "Stockholders and officers in the bank included both Whigs and Democrats who, despite their different political affiliations, worked extremely well together when banking matters became political problems."

12 Holt, *Party Politics,* 114, 115, quoted from 115; Sharp, *Jacksonians versus the Banks,* 143, 145–46; Weisenberger, *Passing of the Frontier,* 417–18; Stephen E. Maizlish, *The Triumph of Sectionalism: The Transformation of Ohio Politics, 1844–1856* (Kent, Ohio: Kent State University Press, 1983), 48–49.

13 Holt, *Party Politics,* 116–22; Weisenberger, *Passing of the Frontier,* 418–20.

14 Weisenberger, *Passing of the Frontier,* 422–24, 428; Huntington, "History of Banking," 421; Holt, *Party Politics,* 123–33; Shade, *Banks or No Banks,* 107–9.

15 Holt, *Party Politics,* 134–35, 142, 144, 146; Weisenberger, *Passing of the*

Frontier, 428–31; Maizlish, *Triumph of Sectionalism*, 48. Samuel Lewis, the Liberty Party candidate for governor, won 4 percent of the vote in 1846. See Maizlish, *Triumph of Sectionalism*, 40–50, for a discussion of the banking issue in the elections of 1845 and 1846. Maizlish, 45–46, labeled the election of 1846 "one last crusade against the state's banking system." Whigs retained control of the Ohio legislature for the rest of the decade, but hard Democrats captured the constitutional convention of 1850–51. In a moderate compromise between hards and softs, Ohio's second constitution, like most new constitutions during this period, initiated general incorporation or "free banking." But in a nod toward hard Democrats, the new constitution reinstated individual liability for holders of bank stocks. This constitutional compromise governed Ohio banking until passage of the federal Banking Act of 1863, and it eliminated banking as a popular political issue. See Holt, *Party Politics*, 152; Sharp, *Jacksonians versus the Banks*, 321. Consult Roseboom, *Civil War Era*, 124–46, for a discussion of the constitutional convention and the banking issue during the 1850s.

16 Weisenberger, *Passing of the Frontier*, 430–31.

17 "Wayne County Case," 24; *Wooster Democrat*, September 10, 1846, October 7, 1847. Maizlish, *Triumph of Sectionalism*, 22–24, 43–45, 48–49. Robert Taggart, the Abolition candidate for senator from Wayne District, won 1.5 percent of the ballots.

18 *Wooster Democrat*, April 25, October 3, 1844, April 9, 1846.

19 *Wooster Democrat*, April 25, 1844; J. A. Caldwell, *Caldwell's Atlas of Wayne County* (Sunbury, Ohio: J. A. Caldwell, 1877), 7.

20 *Wooster Democrat*, May 16, August 8, August 22, September 12, September 26, December 12, 1844, September 3, 1846.

21 *Wooster Democrat*, January 4, October 3, 1844, October 22, 1846.

22 *Wooster Democrat*, September 19, 1844, September 16, 1847.

23 Douglass, *History of Wayne County*, 245, 247, 249, 349, 351, 356–57, 728; *History of Wayne County, Ohio* (Indianapolis: B. F. Bowen & Company, 1910), 305; Manuscript U.S. Census of Population, Wayne County, Ohio, 1850, 507 [hereafter cited as Wayne County Census]; Columbus *Semi-Weekly Ohio Statesman*, December 26, 1845.

24 Officeholding information from Douglass, *History of Wayne County*, 245–51, 292–94, linked with the Wayne County Census; "Wayne County Case," 24. According to a contemporary business directory, all 19 of Wayne County's lawyers were practicing in Wooster in 1853; W. W. Reilly & Co.'s *Ohio State Business Directory* (Cincinnati: Morgan and Overend, 1853), 50.

25 Douglass, *History of Wayne County*, 245–46; Wayne County Census, 375; Columbus *Semi-Weekly Ohio Statesman*, December 26, 1845; Joseph Willford to John Larwill, February 13, 1846, *Larwill Family Papers*, Collection 154, Box 8, Ohio State University Archives, Columbus, Ohio;

William A. Taylor, *Ohio Statesmen and Annals of Progress* (Columbus: Westbote, 1899), 2: 31. Willford returned to the Ohio Senate for the 1856–57 term.

26 "Wayne County Case," 207–8, 219, 221, 228, 229; Douglass, *History of Wayne County*, 294, 809–10; Wayne County Census, 418.

27 "Wayne County Case," 207–8, 219, 221, 228, 229.

28 "Wayne County Case," 65, 78, 110, 111, 206, 220, 259, 260; Douglass, *History of Wayne County*, 249, 250, 292–94, 533; *Wooster Democrat*, December 18, 1845; Wayne County Census, 477.

29 "Wayne County Case," 77, 260, 261, 262; Douglass, *History of Wayne County*, 250, 292–94; *Wooster Democrat*, August 27, October 22, November 19, 1846; Columbus *Ohio State Journal*, October 31, 1846; Wayne County Census, 475.

30 Douglass, *History of Wayne County*, 247; *History of Wayne County*, 311; *Wooster Democrat*, October 9, 1845. Apparently Wasson's reputation stretched across northeast Ohio. An editor in Salem, 60 miles to the east, publicly labeled him a "braying Ass"; Salem *Anti-Slavery Bugle*, November 6, 1846.

31 Table 7.2 presents the 1846 voting returns listed in "Wayne County Case," 24, linked with the Wayne County Census; see Paul F. Bourke and Donald A. DeBats, "Society and Politics in a New Community: Washington County, Oregon, in the 1850s," unpub. paper presented at Social Science History Association meeting, 1980, for the concept of a political "imprint."

32 Daniel Walker Howe, *The Political Culture of the American Whigs* (Chicago: University of Chicago Press, 1979), offers the most thorough review of Whig ideology.

33 Congress Township poll book in "Wayne County Case," 40–42, linked with the Wayne County Census.

34 "Wayne County Case," 87, 88, 89, 92. As Justice Joseph Story remarked of domicile, "It is sometimes a matter of no small difficulty to decide in what place a person has his true or proper domicil"; Joseph Story, *Commentaries on the Conflict of Laws*, 2d ed. (London, 1841), 48.

35 "Wayne County Case," 68; Douglass, *History of Wayne County*, 264, 470, 571, 726, 730–31; Wooster *Republican Advocate*, June 8, 1837; Wayne County Census, 543.

36 "Wayne County Case," 88, 90, 92; Douglass, *History of Wayne County*, 293–94, 728; *Wooster Democrat*, March 28, 1844; Wayne County Census, 663.

37 Story, *Commentaries*, 47, concluded that "Two things, then, must concur to constitute domicil: first, residence; and secondly, the intention of making it the home of the party. There must be the fact, and the intent." The Ohio election law of 1841 incorporated this union of physical presence and intention in its definition of legal residence; *Ohio Laws*, 13 v 39, sec. 2 (1841).

38 Story, *Commentaries*, 44, noted that "In a strict and legal sense that is properly the domicil of a person where he has his true and fixed permanent home and principal establishment, and to which, whenever he is absent, he has the intention of returning." Under Roman law, "every person has his domicil in that place which he makes his family residence and principal place of business"; Story, *Commentaries*, 45. Under the Ohio election law of 1841, "If a married man has his family fixed in one place, and he does his business in another, the former shall be considered and held to be the place of his residence"; *Ohio Laws*, 13 v 39, sec. 2 (1841).

39 "Wayne County Case," 90, 92–93.

40 "Wayne County Case," 89, 90.

41 "Wayne County Case," 90.

42 "Wayne County Case," 15–16, 91–92.

43 "Wayne County Case," 24.

44 "Wayne County Case," 74–75.

45 "Wayne County Case," 71–72, 72–73.

46 "Wayne County Case," 68–69.

47 Immel, Kail, and Kline were not listed in the Wayne County Census as residents of Wayne County.

48 "Wayne County Case," 74, 76, 77; Douglass, *History of Wayne County*, 770.

49 "Wayne County Case," 76.

50 "Wayne County Case," 72. The Ohio Constitution of 1802 permitted nontaxpayers to vote if they performed work on township or county roads; *Ohio Constitution*, (1802), art. 4, sec. 5.

51 "Wayne County Case," 72–73, 73, 73–74.

52 "Wayne County Case," 69, 71.

53 "Wayne County Case," 69, 180, 183; Douglass, *History of Wayne County*, 614, 616; Wayne County Census, 421.

54 "Wayne County Case," 136; Wayne County Census, 454.

55 "Wayne County Case," 24, 136, 136–37, 217, 218; Douglass, *History of Wayne County*, 728. Roman law applied attendance at the public baths as one criterion of legal residence; Story, *Commentaries*, 45. Henry Espich did not appear in the Wayne County Census as a resident of Wayne County.

56 "Wayne County Case," 84; Wayne County Census, 341; Douglass, *History of Wayne County*, 247, 267, 270, 677, 681, 686–87, 688–91, 699; *History of Wayne County*, 377; *Wooster Democrat*, January 4, 1844. According to the Wayne County Census, Orr owned real estate worth $19,300 in 1850.

57 "Wayne County Case," 24, 61, 84, 85, 86.

58 "Wayne County Case," 84, 85.

59 "Wayne County Case," 15, 59.

60 "Wayne County Case," 174, 176, 178, 239.

61 "Wayne County Case," 176, 177, 179.
62 "Wayne County Case," 16, 119, 123, 129, 152, 272.
63 "Wayne County Case," 114–15, 117, 129, 150–51.
64 "Wayne County Case," 150–51.
65 "Wayne County Case," 16–17, 151.
66 "Wayne County Case," 24, 114, 121, 123, 192.
67 "Wayne County Case," 111, 112–13, 115, 118, 121, 191; Douglass, *History of Wayne County*, 647.
68 "Wayne County Case," 112, 116, 118, 119, 120, 191.
69 "Wayne County Case," 16.
70 "Wayne County Case," 209; Douglass, *History of Wayne County*, 285, 436–38, 643, 647; Wayne County Census, 485.
71 "Wayne County Case," 204–5, 205, 216.
72 "Wayne County Case," 202, 203–4, 204.
73 "Wayne County Case," 208.
74 "Wayne County Case," 143–44, 144–45, 211–12.
75 *Ohio Senate Journal, 1846–1847*, 13, 23, 47, 58, 62, 171; *Wooster Democrat*, January 7, 1847.
76 Columbus *Ohio State Journal*, January 11, 1847; *Wooster Democrat*, January 14, 1847.
77 Columbus *Ohio State Journal*, January 11, 1847; *Ashland Standard*, January 7, 1847, quoted in Columbus *Ohio State Journal*, January 11, 1847; [?] to John Larwill, January 19, 1847, *Larwill Family Papers*, Collection 154, Box 8. Samuel Medary countered with the accusation that "The editor of the 'Ashland Standard,' body and breeches, is owned by the Wooster Bank"; Columbus *Ohio Statesman*, January 12, 1847.
78 *Wooster Democrat*, January 28, 1847; Columbus *Ohio State Journal*, January 19, 1847; *Cleveland Herald*, quoted in *Wooster Democrat*, January 28, 1847; *Ohio Senate Journal, 1846–1847*, 308–9; Columbus *Ohio Statesman*, January 19, 1847; John Larwill to Joseph Larwill, June 20, 1847, *Larwill Family Papers*, Collection 154, Box 8. Willford resigned his seat, effective at the end of the current session, and the Senate accepted his resignation by a purely partisan vote. Cox withdrew his challenge but continued to draw his legislative salary as if he were a sitting member. Democrats reestablished their traditional majority in Wayne County and went on to win the by-election in October 1847 by a large margin.
79 Bourke and DeBats, "Society and Politics in a New Community." The best example of intensive political organization in the antebellum Midwest is Lincoln's plan of organization for the campaign of 1840 in Illinois; Abraham Lincoln, *Collected Works*, ed. Roy P. Basler (New Brunswick, N.J.: Rutgers University Press, 1953), 1: 180–81, 201–3. For a good review of antebellum political organization, consult William E. Gienapp, "'Politics Seem to Enter into Everything': Political Culture in the North, 1840–1860," in *Essays on American Antebellum Politics, 1840–1860*, ed. Stephen E. Maizlish and John J. Kushma (College Station:

Texas A & M University Press, 1982), 14–69. Studies of the role of urban machines in social organization include Robert K. Merton, *Social Theory and Social Structure*, rev. ed. (New York: Free Press, 1957), 72–82; Samuel P. Hays, "The Politics of Reform in Municipal Government in the Progressive Era," *Pacific Northwest Quarterly*, 55 (October 1964), 157–69; and Eric L. McKitrick, "The Study of Corruption," *Political Science Quarterly*, 72 (December 1957), 502–14.

Conclusion

1 Debate over the sources of conflict and consensus in American communities has typically focused on new communities on the frontier; see, for example, Stanley Elkins and Eric McKitrick, "A Meaning for Turner's Frontier," *Political Science Quarterly*, 69 (September and December 1954), 321–53, 565–602; Allan G. Bogue, "Social Theory and the Pioneer," *Agricultural History*, 34 (January 1960), 21–34; Robert R. Dykstra, *The Cattle Towns*, (New York: Knopf, 1968); Richard S. Alcorn, "Leadership and Stability in Mid-Nineteenth-Century America: A Case Study of an Illinois Town," *Journal of American History*, 61 (December 1974), 685–702; Don H. Doyle, "Social Theory and New Communities in Nineteenth-Century America," *Western Historical Quarterly*, 8 (April 1977), 151–65; and R. A. Burchell, "The Character and Function of a Pioneer Elite: Rural California, 1848–1880," *Journal of American Studies*, 15 (December 1981), 377–89.
2 *Ohio Constitution* (1802), art. 1, secs. 4, 7, art. 2, sec. 3, art. 4, sec. 1; Andrew W. Young, *First Lessons in Civil Government* (Cleveland: M. C. Younglove, 1846), 35; *Ohio Cultivator*, March 1, 1850; Chilton Williamson, *American Suffrage: From Property to Democracy, 1760–1860* (Princeton, N.J.: Princeton University Press, 1960), 136.
3 Thomas A. Flinn, "Continuity and Change in Ohio Politics," *Journal of Politics*, 24 (August 1962), 521–44.
4 The intensity of mid-nineteenth-century campaigns and elections, the appeal to emotional issues, and the shift in interest to the national level are all intertwined and interdependent phenomena, but studies that try to sort them out into their constituent components include William E. Gienapp, "'Politics Seem to Enter into Everything': Political Culture in the North, 1840–1860," in *Essays on American Antebellum Politics, 1840–1860*, ed. Stephen E. Maizlish and John J. Kushma (College Station: Texas A & M University Press, 1982), 14–69; Richard Jensen, *The Winning of the Midwest: Social and Political Conflict, 1888–1896* (Chicago: University of Chicago Press, 1971), 1–57; Harry L. Watson, *Jacksonian Politics and Community Conflict: The Emergence of the Second Party System in Cumberland County, North Carolina* (Baton Rouge: Louisiana State University Press, 1981); Michael F. Holt, *The Political Crisis of the 1850s* (New York: Wiley, 1978); Lee Benson, *The Concept of Jacksonian Democracy: New York as a Test*

Case (Princeton, N.J.: Princeton University Press, 1961); Ronald P. Formisano, *The Birth of Mass Political Parties: Michigan, 1827–1861* (Princeton, N.J.: Princeton University Press, 1971); Michael F. Holt, *Forging a Majority: The Formation of the Republican Party in Pittsburgh, 1848–1860* (New Haven, Conn.: Yale University Press, 1969); Donald E. Stokes, "Parties and the Nationalization of Electoral Forces," in *The American Party Systems: Stages of Political Development*, 2d ed., ed. William Nisbet Chambers and Walter Dean Burnham (New York: Oxford University Press, 1975), 182–202; and Samuel P. Hays, "Political Parties and the Community-Society Continuum," in Chambers and Burnham, ed., *American Party Systems*, 152–81.

5 Important theoretical contributions to the historical application of ecological inference include J. Morgan Kousser, "Ecological Regression and the Analysis of Past Politics," *Journal of Interdisciplinary History*, 4 (Autumn 1973), 237–62; Allan J. Lichtman, "Correlation, Regression, and the Ecological Fallacy: A Critique," *Journal of Interdisciplinary History*, 4 (Winter 1974), 417–33; and Allan J. Lichtman and Laura Irwin Langbein, "Ecological Regression versus Homogeneous Units: A Specification Analysis," *Social Science History*, 2 (Winter 1978), 172–93. Impressive historical applications of the technique include J. Morgan Kousser, *The Shaping of Southern Politics: Suffrage Restriction and the Establishment of the One-Party South* (New Haven, Conn.: Yale University Press, 1974); Dale Baum, "Know-Nothingism and the Republican Majority in Massachusetts: The Political Realignment of the 1850s," *Journal of American History*, 64 (March 1978), 959–86, and *The Civil War Party System: The Case of Massachusetts, 1848–1876* (Chapel Hill: University of North Carolina Press, 1984); Peyton McCrary, Clark Miller, and Dale Baum, "Class and Party in the Secession Crisis: Voting Behavior in the Deep South, 1856–1861," *Journal of Interdisciplinary History*, 8 (Winter 1978), 429–57; and William E. Gienapp, "Nativism and the Creation of a Republican Majority in the North before the Civil War," *Journal of American History*, 72 (December 1985), 529–59.

6 J. Morgan Kousser, "The 'New Political History': A Methodological Critique," *Reviews in American History*, 4 (March 1976), 1–14; William G. Shade, "'New Political History': Some Statistical Questions Raised," *Social Science History*, 5 (Spring 1981), 171–96; J. Morgan Kousser and Allan J. Lichtman, "'New Political History': Some Statistical Questions Answered," *Social Science History*, 7 (Summer 1983), 321–44; and Kenneth J. Winkle, "Voting Unit or Community? Ecological Inference and Community Studies," unpub. paper presented at Social Science History Association meeting, 1982. Professor Allan J. Lichtman made some of these points in his comment to my "Lincoln's Springfield Revisited: Community and Politics in the Antebellum Midwest," unpub. paper presented at Social Science History Association meeting, 1985.

7 The sometimes daunting complexity of local political life should dis-

courage historians from identifying "homogeneous units" or representative communities for study in place of examining as wide a range of voting units as possible. See, for example, Kousser, "New Political History"; Lichtman and Langbein, "Ecological Regression versus Homogeneous Units"; Shade, "New Political History"; and Winkle, "Voting Unit or Community?"

8 Salem *Antislavery Bugle*, November 28, 1845.

Bibliography

Primary sources

Government records and publications

DeBow, J. D. B. *Seventh Census of the United States, 1850.* Washington, D.C., 1853.

Statistical View of the United States, 1850: Compendium of the Seventh Census. Washington, D.C., 1854.

Kennedy, Joseph C. G. *Agriculture of the United States in 1860: Compendium of the Eighth Census.* Washington, D.C., 1864.

Population of the United States in 1860: Compendium of the Eighth Census. Washington, D.C., 1864.

Klippart, John H. "Agricultural Statistics." *Report of the Ohio Board of Agriculture, 1860,* 11–21.

Kuhne, Frederick. "History and Review of the Condition of Agriculture in Ohio." *Report of the Ohio Board of Agriculture, 1859,* 450–581.

Ohio Executive Documents, 1852–62.

Ohio House Journal, 1848–52.

Ohio Senate Journal, 1846–49.

Plat Book, Portage County, Ohio, 1859. Ravenna, Ohio: Office of the Portage County Engineer.

Plat Book, Shelby County, Ohio, 1859. Sidney, Ohio: Office of the Shelby County Engineer.

Poll Books, Auglaize County, Ohio, 1850–60. Dayton, Ohio: Wright State University Archives, Wright State University.

Poll Books, Highland County, Ohio, 1850–60. Cincinnati, Ohio: University of Cincinnati Archives, University of Cincinnati.

Poll Books, Portage County, Ohio, 1856–66. Kent, Ohio: Kent State University Archives, Kent State University.

Poll Books, Shelby County, Ohio, 1822–60. Dayton, Ohio: Wright State University Archives, Wright State University.

Quadrennial Enumerations of White Adult Males, Shelby County, Ohio, 1851, 1855, and 1859. Dayton, Ohio: Wright State University Archives, Wright State University.

Report of the Debates and Proceedings of the Convention for the Revision of the Constitution of the State of Ohio, 1850–51. Edited by Joseph V. Smith. 2 vols. Columbus: Medary, 1851.

Reports of the Ohio Board of Agriculture, 1846–60.

220

Reports of the Ohio Board of Public Works, 1849–55.
Sixth Census of the United States, 1840. Washington, D.C., 1841.
Statistics of the United States, 1860. Washington, D.C., 1866.
Statutes of Ohio and the Northwestern Territory Adopted or Enacted from 1788 to 1833 Inclusive, edited by Salmon P. Chase. 3 vols. Cincinnati, 1833.
U.S. Census of Agriculture, Manuscript Schedules for Shelby County, Ohio, 1850 and 1860. Dayton, Ohio: Wright State University Archives, Wright State University.
U.S. Census of Population, Manuscript Schedules for Highland County, Ohio, 1850 and 1860. Washington, D.C.: National Archives, microfilm.
U.S. Census of Population, Manuscript Schedules for Portage County, Ohio, 1850 and 1860. Washington, D.C., National Archives, microfilm.
U.S. Census of Population, Manuscript Schedules for Shelby County, Ohio, 1850 and 1860. Washington, D.C.: National Archives, microfilm.
U.S. Census of Population, Manuscript Schedules for Wayne County, Ohio, 1850. Washington, D.C.: National Archives, microfilm.

Books

Atwater, Caleb. *A History of the State of Ohio.* 2d ed. Cincinnati, 1838.
Caldwell, J. A. *Caldwell's Atlas of Wayne County.* Sunbury, Ohio: J. A. Caldwell, 1877.
Camp, George Sidney. *Democracy.* New York: Harper and Brothers, 1841.
Century Edition of the American Digest. 50 vols. St. Paul: West, 1900.
Combination Atlas Map of Shelby County, Ohio. Philadelphia: Page and Smith, 1875.
Curry, William L. *History of Union County, Ohio.* Indianapolis: B. F. Bowen, 1915.
Douglass, Ben. *History of Wayne County, Ohio.* Indianapolis: Robert Douglass, 1878.
Drake, Daniel. *Physician to the West: Selected Writings of Daniel Drake on Science and Society.* Edited by Henry D. Shapiro and Zane L. Miller. Lexington: University Press of Kentucky, 1970.
Gallagher, William D. *Facts and Conditions of Progress in the North-West.* Cincinnati: H. W. Derby, 1850.
Grimké, Frederick. *The Nature and Tendency of Free Institutions.* Edited by John William Ward. Cambridge, Mass.: Harvard University Press, 1968.
Hawes, George W. *Ohio State Gazetteer and Business Directory for 1859 and 1860.* Cincinnati, 1859.
History of Morgan County, Ohio. Chicago: L. H. Watkins & Co., 1886.
History of Portage County, Ohio. Chicago: Warner, Beers, 1885.

History of Ross and Highland Counties, Ohio. Cleveland: W. W. Williams, 1880.

History of Shelby County, Ohio. Philadelphia: R. Sutton & Company, 1883.

History of Wayne County, Ohio. Indianapolis: B. F. Bowen & Company, 1910.

Johnson, Crisfield. *History of Cuyahoga County, Ohio.* Cleveland: D. W. Ensign, 1879.

Jones, Samuel. *A Treatise on the Right of Suffrage.* Boston: Otis, Broaders and Company, 1842.

Kilbourn, John. *The Ohio Gazetteer or Topographical Dictionary.* 11th ed. Columbus, 1833.

Klippart, John H. *The Wheat Plant.* Cincinnati, 1860.

Norton, A. Banning. *A History of Knox County, Ohio.* Columbus: Richard Nevins, 1862.

Peck, John Mason. *A New Guide to the West.* Cincinnati, 1848.

Phelps' Travelers' Guide through the United States. New York: Horace Thayer, 1853.

Story, Joseph. *Commentaries on the Conflict of Laws.* 2d ed. London, 1841.

Taylor, William A. *Ohio Statesmen and Annals of Progress.* 2 vols. Columbus: Westbote, 1899.

de Tocqueville, Alexis. *Democracy in America.* Edited by Phillips Bradley. 2 vols. New York: Random House, 1945.

The Traveller's Directory and Emigrant's Guide. Buffalo: Steele & Faxon, 1832.

W. W. Reilly & Co.'s Ohio State Business Directory. Cincinnati: Morgan & Overend, 1853.

Young, Andrew W. *First Lessons in Civil Government.* Cleveland: M. C. Younglove, 1846.

Newspapers and periodicals

American Railroad Journal
Ashland Standard
Cincinnati Gazette
Cincinnati *Daily Gazette*
Cleveland Herald
Columbus *Daily Ohio Statesman*
Columbus *Ohio State Journal*
Columbus *Ohio Statesman*
Columbus *Semi-Weekly Ohio Statesman*
Family Visitor (Cleveland)
Marietta Intelligencer
Ohio Cultivator (Columbus)
Salem *Anti-Slavery Bugle*
Wooster Democrat
Wooster *Republican Advocate*

Private papers

Larwill Family Papers. Ohio Historical Society, Columbus, Ohio.
Lincoln, Abraham. *Collected Works*, edited by Roy P. Basler. 8 vols. New Brunswick, N.J.: Rutgers University Press, 1953.

Secondary sources

Books

Atherton, Lewis. *Main Street on the Middle Border.* Bloomington: Indiana University Press, 1954.
Barron, Hal S. *Those Who Stayed Behind: Rural Society in Nineteenth-Century New England.* Cambridge, Eng.: Cambridge University Press, 1984.
Baum, Dale. *The Civil War Party System: The Case of Massachusetts, 1848–1876.* Chapel Hill: University of North Carolina Press, 1984.
Bender, Thomas. *Community and Social Change in America.* Baltimore: Johns Hopkins University Press, 1978.
Benson, Lee. *The Concept of Jacksonian Democracy: New York as a Test Case.* Princeton, N.J.: Princeton University Press, 1961.
Benton, Josiah Henry. *Voting in the Field: A Forgotten Chapter of the Civil War.* Boston: Privately Printed, 1915.
Warning Out in New England. Boston: W. B. Clarke, 1911.
Berwanger, Eugene H. *The Frontier Against Slavery: Western Anti-Negro Prejudice and the Slavery Extension Controversy.* Urbana: University of Illinois Press, 1967.
Billington, Ray Allen, and Martin Ridge. *Westward Expansion: A History of the American Frontier.* 5th ed. New York: Macmillan, 1982.
Bishop, Yvonne M. M., Stephen E. Fienberg, and Paul W. Holland. *Discrete Multivariate Analysis: Theory and Practice.* Cambridge, Mass.: MIT Press, 1975.
Bogue, Allan G. *From Prairie to Corn Belt: Farming on the Illinois and Iowa Prairies in the Nineteenth Century.* Chicago: University of Chicago Press, 1963.
Boorstin, Daniel J. *The Americans: The National Experience.* New York: Random House, 1965.
Brown, Ralph H. *Historical Geography of the United States.* New York: Harcourt, Brace, 1948.
Bushman, Richard L. *From Puritan to Yankee: Character and the Social Order in Connecticut, 1690–1765.* New York: Norton, 1967.
Campbell, Angus, Philip E. Converse, Warren E. Miller, and Donald E. Stokes. *The American Voter.* New York: Wiley, 1960.
Capen, Edward Warren. *The Historical Development of the Poor Law of Connecticut.* New York: Columbia University Press, 1905.
Clark, John G. *The Grain Trade in the Old Northwest.* Urbana: University of Illinois Press, 1966.

Conzen, Michael P. *Frontier Farming in an Urban Shadow: The Influence of Madison's Proximity on the Agricultural Development of Blooming Grove, Wisconsin.* Madison: State Historical Society of Wisconsin, 1971.

Curti, Merle. *The Making of an American Community: A Case Study of Democracy in a Frontier County.* Stanford, Calif.: Stanford University Press, 1959.

Dahl, Robert A. *Who Governs? Democracy and Power in an American City.* New Haven, Conn.: Yale University Press, 1961.

Danhof, Clarence H. *Change in Agriculture: The Northern United States, 1820–1870.* Cambridge, Mass.: Harvard University Press, 1969.

De Grazia, Alfred. *Public and Republic: Political Representation in America.* New York: Knopf, 1951.

The Democratic Party of the State of Ohio. Edited by Thomas E. Powell. 2 vols. Columbus: Ohio Publishing Company, 1913.

Downes, Randolph C. *Frontier Ohio, 1788–1803.* Columbus: Ohio State Archaeological and Historical Society, 1935.

Dykstra, Robert R. *The Cattle Towns.* New York: Knopf, 1968.

Elkins, Stanley M. *Slavery: A Problem in American Institutional and Intellectual Life.* Chicago: University of Chicago Press, 1959.

Fehrenbacher, Don E. *The Era of Expansion, 1800–1848.* New York: Wiley, 1969.

Fienberg, Stephen E. *The Analysis of Cross-Classified Categorical Data.* Cambridge, Mass.: MIT Press, 1977.

Finkelman, Paul. *An Imperfect Union: Slavery, Federalism, and Comity.* Chapel Hill: University of North Carolina Press, 1981.

Fishlow, Albert. *American Railroads and the Transformation of the Ante-Bellum Economy.* Cambridge, Mass.: Harvard University Press, 1965.

Formisano, Ronald P. *The Birth of Mass Political Parties: Michigan, 1827–1861.* Princeton, N.J.: Princeton University Press, 1971.

Fredrickson, George M. *The Inner Civil War: Northern Intellectuals and the Crisis of the Union.* New York: Harper & Row, 1965.

Gates, Paul W. *The Farmer's Age: Agriculture, 1815–1860.* New York: Holt, Rinehart and Winston, 1960.

Gitelman, Howard M. *Workingmen of Waltham: Mobility in American Urban Industrial Development, 1850–1890.* Baltimore: Johns Hopkins University Press, 1974.

Griffen, Clyde, and Sally Griffen. *Natives and Newcomers: The Ordering of Opportunity in Mid-Nineteenth-Century Poughkeepsie.* Cambridge, Mass.: Harvard University Press, 1978.

Hammarberg, Melvyn. *The Indiana Voter: The Historical Dynamics of Party Allegiance During the 1870s.* Chicago: University of Chicago Press, 1977.

Hietala, Thomas R. *Manifest Design: Anxious Aggrandizement in Late Jacksonian America.* Ithaca, N.Y.: Cornell University Press, 1985.

Higham, John. *From Boundlessness to Consolidation: The Transformation of*

American Culture, 1848–1860. Ann Arbor, Mich.: William L. Clements Library, 1969.

Holt, Edgar Allan. *Party Politics in Ohio, 1840–1850.* Columbus: Ohio Archaeological and Historical Society, 1931.

Holt, Michael F. *Forging a Majority: The Formation of the Republican Party in Pittsburgh, 1848–1860.* New Haven, Conn.: Yale University Press, 1969.

The Political Crisis of the 1850s. New York: Wiley, 1978.

Horwitz, Morton J. *The Transformation of American Law, 1780–1860.* Cambridge, Mass.: Harvard University Press, 1977.

Howe, Daniel Walker. *The Political Culture of the American Whigs.* Chicago: University of Chicago Press, 1979.

Hudson, John C. *Plains Country Towns.* Minneapolis: University of Minnesota Press, 1985.

Hurst, James Willard. *Law and the Conditions of Freedom in the Nineteenth-Century United States.* Madison: University of Wisconsin Press, 1956.

Janowitz, Morris. *The Community Press in an Urban Setting: The Social Elements of Urbanism.* 2d ed. Chicago: University of Chicago Press, 1967.

Jensen, Richard. *The Winning of the Midwest: Social and Political Conflict, 1888–1896.* Chicago: University of Chicago Press, 1971.

Johnson, Hildegard Binder. *Order Upon the Land: The U.S. Rectangular Land Survey and the Upper Mississippi Country.* New York: Oxford University Press, 1976.

Jones, Robert Leslie. *History of Agriculture in Ohio to 1880.* Kent, Ohio: Kent State University Press, 1983.

Katz, Michael B. *The People of Hamilton, Canada West: Family and Class in a Mid-Nineteenth-Century City.* Cambridge, Mass.: Harvard University Press, 1975.

Michael J. Doucet, and Mark J. Stern. *The Social Organization of Early Industrial Capitalism.* Cambridge, Mass.: Harvard University Press, 1982.

Kennedy, Aileen Elizabeth. *The Ohio Poor Law and Its Administration.* Chicago: University of Chicago Press, 1934.

Kettner, James H. *The Development of American Citizenship, 1608–1870.* Chapel Hill: University of North Carolina Press, 1978.

Knoke, David, and Peter J. Burke. *Log-Linear Models.* Beverly Hills: Sage, 1980.

Kousser, J. Morgan. *The Shaping of Southern Politics: Suffrage Restriction and the Establishment of the One-Party South.* New Haven, Conn.: Yale University Press, 1974.

Lemon, James T. *The Best Poor Man's Country: A Geographical Study of Early Southeastern Pennsylvania.* Baltimore: Johns Hopkins University Press, 1972.

Lewis, R. W. B. *The American Adam: Innocence, Tragedy, and Tradition in the Nineteenth Century.* Chicago: University of Chicago Press, 1955.

Lindstrom, Diane. *Economic Development in the Philadelphia Region, 1810–1850*. New York: Columbia University Press, 1978.

Litwack, Leon. F. *North of Slavery: The Negro in the Free States, 1790–1860*. Chicago: University of Chicago Press, 1961.

Lockridge, Kenneth A. *A New England Town: The First Hundred Years: Dedham, Massachusetts, 1636–1736*. New York: Norton, 1970.

Lowry, Ira S. *Migration and Metropolitan Growth: Two Analytical Models*. San Francisco: Chandler Publishing Company, 1966.

Maizlish, Stephen E. *The Triumph of Sectionalism: The Transformation of Ohio Politics, 1844–1856*. Kent, Ohio: Kent State University Press, 1983.

McClelland, C. P., and C. C. Huntington. *History of the Ohio Canals: Their Construction, Cost, Use and Partial Abandonment*. Columbus: Ohio State Archaeological and Historical Society, 1905.

McClelland, Peter D., and Richard J. Zeckhauser. *Demographic Dimensions of the New Republic: American Interregional Migration, Vital Statistics, and Manumissions, 1800–1860*. Cambridge, Eng.: Cambridge University Press, 1982.

McCormick, Richard P. *The History of Voting in New Jersey: A Study of the Development of Election Machinery, 1664–1911*. New Brunswick, N.J.: Rutgers University Press, 1953.

McKinley, Albert Edward. *The Suffrage Franchise in the Thirteen English Colonies in America*. Philadelphia: University of Pennsylvania Press, 1905.

Merton, Robert K. *Social Theory and Social Structure*. Rev. ed. New York: Free Press, 1957.

Milbrath, Lester W., and M. L. Goel. *Political Participation: How and Why Do People Get Involved in Politics?* 2d ed. Chicago: Rand McNally, 1977.

Miller, Roberta Balstad. *City and Hinterland: A Case Study of Urban Growth and Regional Development*. Westport, Conn.: Greenwood, 1979.

North, Douglass C. *The Economic Growth of the United States, 1790–1860*. New York: Norton, 1966.

Owsley, Frank L. *Plain Folk of the Old South*. Baton Rouge: Louisiana State University Press, 1949.

Pessen, Edward. *Riches, Class, and Power before the Civil War*. Lexington, Mass.: Heath, 1973.

Pole, J. R. *Political Representation in England and the Origins of the American Republic*. London: Macmillan, 1966.

Pred, Allan. *Urban Growth and City-Systems in the United States, 1840–1860*. Cambridge, Mass.: Harvard University Press, 1980.

Ridgway, Whitman H. *Community Leadership in Maryland, 1790–1840: A Comparative Analysis of Power in Society*. Chapel Hill: University of North Carolina Press, 1979.

Roseboom, Eugene H. *The Civil War Era: 1850–1878*. Vol. 4 of *A History of the State of Ohio*, edited by Carl Wittke. Columbus: Ohio State Archaeological and Historical Society, 1944.

Scheiber, Harry N. *Ohio Canal Era: A Case Study of Government and the Economy, 1820–1861.* Athens: Ohio University Press, 1969.

Shade, William G. *Banks or No Banks: The Money Issue in Western Politics, 1832–1865.* Detroit: Wayne State University Press, 1972.

Sharp, James Roger. *The Jacksonians versus the Banks: Politics in the States after the Panic of 1837.* New York: Columbia University Press, 1970.

Shryock, Henry S., Jacob S. Siegel, and Associates. *The Methods and Materials of Demography.* Washington, D.C.: U.S. Department of Commerce, 1973.

Smith, Joseph P. *History of the Republican Party in Ohio.* Chicago: Lewis, 1898.

Smith, Thomas H. *The Mapping of Ohio.* Kent, Ohio: Kent State University Press, 1977.

Stover, John F. *Iron Road to the West: American Railroads in the 1850s.* New York: Columbia University Press, 1978.

Suttles, Gerald D. *The Social Construction of Communities.* Chicago: University of Chicago Press, 1972.

Taylor, George Rogers. *The Transportation Revolution, 1815–1860.* New York: Rinehart, 1951.

tenBroek, Jacobus. *The Constitution and the Right of Free Movement.* New York: National Travelers Aid Association, 1955.

Thernstrom, Stephan. *The Other Bostonians: Poverty and Progress in the American Metropolis, 1880–1970.* Cambridge, Mass.: Harvard University Press, 1973.

Poverty and Progress: Social Mobility in a Nineteenth Century City. Cambridge, Mass.: Harvard University Press, 1964.

Thrower, Norman J. W. *Original Survey and Land Subdivision: A Comparative Study of the Form and Effect of Contrasting Cadastral Surveys.* Chicago: Rand McNally, 1966.

Turner, Frederick Jackson. *The Frontier in American History.* New York: Henry Holt, 1920.

The United States, 1830–1850: The Nation and Its Sections. New York: Holt, Rinehart, and Winston, 1935.

Utter, William T. *The Frontier State: 1803–1825.* Vol. 2 of *A History of the State of Ohio,* edited by Carl Wittke. Columbus: Ohio State Archaeological and Historical Society, 1942.

Verba, Sidney, and Norman H. Nie. *Participation in America: Political Democracy and Social Equality.* New York: Harper & Row, 1972.

Vincent, J. R. *Pollbooks: How Victorians Voted.* Cambridge, Eng.: Cambridge University Press, 1967.

Ward, David. *Cities and Immigrants: A Geography of Change in Nineteenth-Century America.* New York: Oxford University Press, 1971.

Watson, Harry L. *Jacksonian Politics and Community Conflict: The Emergence of the Second Party System in Cumberland County, North Carolina.* Baton Rouge: Louisiana State University Press, 1981.

Weisenberger, Francis P. *The Passing of the Frontier, 1825–1850*. Vol. 3 of *A History of the State of Ohio*, edited by Carl Wittke. Columbus: Ohio State Archaeological and Historical Society, 1941.

Welter, Rush. *The Mind of America, 1820–1860*. New York: Columbia University Press, 1975.

Wiebe, Robert H. *The Opening of American Society: From the Adoption of the Constitution to the Eve of Disunion*. New York: Random House, 1984.

The Search for Order, 1877–1920. New York: Hill & Wang, 1967.

Williamson, Chilton. *American Suffrage: From Property to Democracy, 1760–1860*. Princeton, N.J.: Princeton University Press, 1960.

Wolfinger, Raymond E., and Steven J. Rosenstone. *Who Votes?* New Haven, Conn.: Yale University Press, 1980.

Woodson, Carter G. *A Century of Negro Migration*. Washington, D.C.: Association for the Study of Negro Life and History, 1918.

Wooster, Ralph A. *Politicians, Planters and Plain Folk: Courthouse and Statehouse in the Upper South, 1850–1860*. Knoxville: University of Tennessee Press, 1975.

Zuckerman, Michael. *Peaceable Kingdoms: New England Towns in the Eighteenth Century*. New York: Knopf, 1970.

Articles

Alcorn, Richard S. "Leadership and Stability in Mid-Nineteenth-Century America: A Case Study of an Illinois Town." *Journal of American History*, 61 (December 1974), 685–702.

Barnhart, John D. "Sources of Southern Migration into the Old Northwest." *Mississippi Valley Historical Review*, 22 (June 1935), 49–62.

"The Southern Influence in the Formation of Ohio." *Journal of Southern History*, 3 (February 1937), 28–42.

Baum, Dale. "Know-Nothingism and the Republican Majority in Massachusetts: The Political Realignment of the 1850s." *Journal of American History*, 64 (March 1978), 959–86.

Berthoff, Rowland. "The American Social Order: A Conservative Hypothesis." *American Historical Review*, 65 (April 1960), 495–514.

"Independence and Attachment, Virtue and Interest: From Republican Citizen to Free Enterpriser, 1787–1837." In *Uprooted Americans: Essays to Honor Oscar Handlin*, edited by Richard L. Bushman et al., 97–124. Boston: Little, Brown, 1979.

Bogue, Allan G. "Social Theory and the Pioneer." *Agricultural History*, 34 (January 1960), 21–34.

Bohmer, David A. "The Maryland Electorate and the Concept of a Party System in the Early National Period." In *The History of American Electoral Behavior*, edited by Joel H. Silbey, Allan G. Bogue, and William H. Flanigan, 146–73. Princeton, N.J.: Princeton University Press, 1978.

Bourke, Paul F., and Donald A. DeBats. "Identifiable Voting in Nineteenth-Century America: Toward a Comparison of Britain and the United States before the Secret Ballot." *Perspectives in American History*, 11 (1977–78), 259–88.
"Individuals and Aggregates: A Note on Historical Data and Assumptions." *Social Science History*, 4 (Spring 1980), 229–50.
Bowers, William L. "Crawford Township, 1850–1870: A Population Study of a Pioneer Community." *Iowa Journal of History*, 58 (January 1960), 1–30.
Brown, Lawrence A., John Odlund, and Reginald G. Golledge. "Migration, Functional Distance, and the Urban Hierarchy." *Economic Geography*, 46 (July 1970), 472–85.
Burchell, R. A. "The Character and Function of a Pioneer Elite: Rural California, 1848–1880." *Journal of American Studies*, 15 (December 1981), 377–89.
Campbell, Angus. "Surge and Decline: A Study of Electoral Change." In Angus Campbell, Philip E. Converse, Warren E. Miller, and Donald E. Stokes, *Elections and the Political Order*, 40–62. New York: Wiley, 1966.
Clark, Christopher. "Household Economy, Market Exchange and the Rise of Capitalism in the Connecticut Valley, 1800–1860." *Journal of Social History*, 13 (Winter 1979), 169–89.
Coleman, Peter J. "Restless Grant County: Americans on the Move." *Wisconsin Magazine of History*, 46 (Autumn 1962), 16–20.
Conzen, Michael P. "Local Migration Systems in Nineteenth-Century Iowa." *Geographical Review*, 64 (July 1974), 339–61.
Davis, Harold E. "The Economic Basis of Ohio Politics, 1820–1840." *Ohio State Archaeological and Historical Quarterly*, 47 (October 1938), 288–318.
Donald, David. "An Excess of Democracy: The American Civil War and the Social Process." In David Donald, *Lincoln Reconsidered: Essays on the Civil War Era*, 209–35. 2d ed. New York: Random House, 1956.
Downes, Randolph C. "Evolution of Ohio County Boundaries." *Ohio Archaeological and Historical Publications*, 36 (1927), 340–477.
Doyle, Don H. "The Social Functions of Voluntary Associations in a Nineteenth-Century American Town." *Social Science History*, 1 (Spring 1977), 333–55.
"Social Theory and New Communities in Nineteenth-Century America." *Western Historical Quarterly*, 8 (April 1977), 151–65.
Easterlin, Richard. "Population Change and Farm Settlement in the Northern United States." *Journal of Economic History*, 36 (March 1976), 45–75.
Elkins, Stanley, and Eric McKitrick. "A Meaning for Turner's Frontier." *Political Science Quarterly*, 69 (September and December 1954), 321–53, 565–602.

Elklit, Jorgen. "Nominal Record Linkage and the Study of Non-Secret Voting: A Danish Case." *Journal of Interdisciplinary History*, 15 (Winter 1985), 419–43.

Engerman, Stanley L. "Up or Out: Social and Geographic Mobility in the United States." *Journal of Interdisciplinary History*, 3 (Winter 1975), 469–89.

Erickson, Leonard. "Politics and Repeal of Ohio's Black Laws, 1837–1849." *Ohio History*, 82 (Summer-Autumn 1973), 154–75.

Finn, Chester E. "The Ohio Canals: Public Enterprise on the Frontier." *Ohio State Archaeological and Historical Quarterly*, 51 (January–March 1942), 1–41.

Flinn, Thomas A. "Continuity and Change in Ohio Politics." *Journal of Politics*, 24 (August 1962), 521–44.

Formisano, Ronald P. "Deferential-Participant Politics: The Early Republic's Political Culture, 1789–1840." *American Political Science Review*, 68 (June 1974), 473–87.

Gienapp, William E. "Nativism and the Creation of a Republican Majority in the North before the Civil War." *Journal of American History*, 72 (December 1985), 529–59.

"'Politics Seem to Enter into Everything': Political Culture in the North, 1840–1860." In *Essays on American Antebellum Politics, 1840–1860*, edited by Stephen E. Maizlish and John J. Kushma, 14–69. College Station: Texas A & M University Press, 1982.

Glazer, Walter S. "Participation and Power: Voluntary Associations and the Functional Organization of Cincinnati in 1840." *Historical Methods Newsletter*, 5 (September 1972), 151–68.

Grigg, D. B. "E. G. Ravenstein and the 'Laws of Migration,'" *Journal of Historical Geography*, 3 (January 1977), 41–54.

Hammack, David C. "Problems in the Historical Study of Power in the Cities and Towns of the United States, 1800–1960." *American Historical Review*, 83 (April 1978), 323–49.

Hays, Samuel P. "Political Parties and the Community-Society Continuum." In *American Party Systems: Stages of Political Development*, edited by William Nisbet Chambers and Walter Dean Burnham, 152–81. 2d ed. New York: Oxford University Press, 1975.

"The Politics of Reform in Municipal Government in the Progressive Era." *Pacific Northwest Quarterly*, 55 (October 1964), 157–69.

Henretta, James A. "Families and Farms: *Mentalité* in Pre-Industrial America." *William and Mary Quarterly*, 3d ser., 35 (January 1978), 3–32.

Hessler, Sherry O. "'The Great Disturbing Cause' and the Decline of the Queen City." *Bulletin of the Historical and Philosophical Society of Ohio*, 20 (July 1962), 169–85.

Higgs, Robert. "The Growth of Cities in a Midwestern Region, 1870–1900." *Journal of Regional Science*, 9 (December 1969), 369–75.

Hillery, George A., Jr. "Definitions of Community: Areas of Agreement." *Rural Sociology*, 20 (June 1955), 111–23.

Hopkins, Richard J. "Occupational and Geographic Mobility in Atlanta, 1870–1876." *Journal of Southern History*, 34 (May 1968), 200–13.

Hudson, John C. "Migration to an American Frontier." *Annals of the Association of American Geographers*, 66 (June 1976), 242–65.

Hulbert, Archer Butler. "The Old National Road – The Historic Highway of America." *Ohio Archaeological and Historical Publications*, 9 (1901), 405–519.

Huntington, Charles C. "A History of Banking and Currency in Ohio before the Civil War." *Ohio Archaeological and Historical Quarterly*, 24 (July 1915), 235–539.

Jones, Douglas Lamar. "The Strolling Poor: Transiency in Eighteenth Century Massachusetts." *Journal of Social History*, 8 (Spring 1975), 28–54.

Katz, Michael B., Michael J. Doucet, and Mark J. Stern. "Migration and the Social Order in Erie County, New York: 1855." *Journal of Interdisciplinary History*, 8 (Spring 1978), 669–701.

"Population Persistence and Early Industrialization in a Canadian City: Hamilton, Ontario, 1851–1871." *Social Science History*, 2 (Winter 1978), 208–29.

Kelley, Stanley, Jr., Richard E. Ayres, and William G. Bowen. "Registration and Voting: Putting First Things First." *American Political Science Review*, 61 (June 1967), 359–77.

Kirk, Gordon W., Jr., and Carol Tyirin Kirk. "Migration, Mobility and the Transformation of the Occupational Structure in an Immigrant Community: Holland, Michigan, 1850–80." *Journal of Social History*, 7 (Winter 1974), 142–64.

Kousser, J. Morgan. "Ecological Regression and the Analysis of Past Politics." *Journal of Interdisciplinary History*, 4 (Autumn 1973), 237–62.

"The 'New Political History': A Methodological Critique." *Reviews in American History*, 4 (March 1976), 1–14.

Gary W. Cox, and David W. Galenson. "Log-Linear Analysis of Contingency Tables: An Introduction for Historians with an Application to Thernstrom on the 'Floating Proletariat,'" *Historical Methods*, 15 (Fall 1982), 152–69.

and Allan J. Lichtman. "'New Political History': Some Statistical Questions Answered." *Social Science History*, 7 (Summer 1983), 321–44.

Lang, Elfrieda. "Ohioans in Northern Indiana before 1850." *Indiana Magazine of History*, 49 (December 1953), 391–404.

Lee, Everett S. "A Theory of Migration." *Demography*, 3 (Number 1, 1966), 47–57.

Lichtman, Allan J. "Correlation, Regression, and the Ecological Fallacy: A Critique." *Journal of Interdisciplinary History*, 4 (Winter 1974), 417–33.

and Laura Irwin Langbein. "Ecological Regression versus Homogeneous Units: A Specification Analysis." *Social Science History*, 2 (Winter 1978), 172–93.

Malin, James C. "The Turnover of Farm Population in Kansas." *Kansas Historical Quarterly*, 4 (November 1935), 339–72.

McCormick, Richard P. "New Perspectives on Jacksonian Politics." *American Historical Review*, 65 (January 1960), 288–301.

McCrary, Peyton, Clark Miller, and Dale Baum. "Class and Party in the Secession Crisis: Voting Behavior in the Deep South, 1856–1861." *Journal of Interdisciplinary History*, 8 (Winter 1978), 429–57.

McKitrick, Eric L. "The Study of Corruption." *Political Science Quarterly*, 72 (December 1957), 502–14.

Modell, John. "The Peopling of a Working-Class Ward: Reading, Pennsylvania, 1850." *Journal of Social History*, 5 (Fall 1971), 71–95.

Muller, Edward K. "Early Industrialization in the Ohio Valley: A Review Essay." *Historical Geography Newsletter*, 3 (Fall 1973), 19–30.

"Selective Urban Growth in the Middle Ohio Valley, 1800–1860." *Geographical Review*, 66 (April 1976), 178–99.

Porter, Eugene O. "Financing Ohio's Pre-Civil War Railroads." *Ohio State Archaeological and Historical Quarterly*, 57 (July 1948), 215–36.

Potter, J. "The Growth of Population in America, 1700–1860." In *Population in History: Essays in Historical Demography*, edited by D. V. Glass and D. E. C. Eversley, 631–88. Chicago: Aldine, 1965.

Pred, Allan. "The External Relations of Cities during 'Industrial Revolution.'" University of Chicago, Department of Geography, *Research Paper No. 76*. Chicago: University of Chicago, 1962.

Ravenstein, E. G. "The Laws of Migration." *Journal of the Royal Statistical Society*, 48 (1885), 167–227.

Rose, Gregory S. "Hoosier Origins: The Nativity of Indiana's United States-Born Population in 1850." *Indiana Magazine of History*, 81 (September 1985), 201–32.

Rowland, Ronald L. "Voter Residency Requirements in State and Local Elections." *Ohio State Law Journal*, 32 (1971), 600–17.

Scheiber, Harry N. "Urban Rivalry and Internal Improvements in the Old Northwest, 1820–1860." *Ohio History*, 71 (October 1962), 227–39.

Schmidt, Louis Bernard. "The Internal Grain Trade of the United States, 1850–1860." *Iowa Journal of History and Politics*, 18 (January 1920), 94–124.

"The Westward Movement of the Wheat Growing Industry in the United States." *Iowa Journal of History and Politics*, 18 (July 1920), 396–412.

Segal, Harvey H. "Canals and Economic Development." In *Canals and American Economic Development*, edited by Carter Goodrich, 216–48. New York: Columbia University Press, 1961.

"Cycles of Canal Construction." In *Canals and American Economic Development*, edited by Carter Goodrich, 169–215. New York: Columbia University Press, 1961.

Shade, William G. "'New Political History': Some Statistical Questions Raised." *Social Science History*, 5 (Spring 1981), 171–96.

Shankman, Arnold. "Soldier Votes and Clement L. Vallandigham in the 1863 Ohio Gubernatorial Election." *Ohio History*, 82 (Winter-Spring 1973), 88–104.

Stephenson, Charles. "A Gathering of Strangers? Mobility, Social Structure, and Political Participation in the Formation of Nineteenth-Century American Workingclass Culture." In *American Workingclass Culture: Explorations in American Labor and Social History*, edited by Milton Cantor, 31–60. Westport, Conn.: Greenwood, 1979.

Stokes, Donald E. "Parties and the Nationalization of Electoral Forces." In *The American Party Systems: Stages of Political Development*, edited by William Nisbet Chambers and Walter Dean Burnham, 182–202. 2d ed. New York: Oxford University Press, 1975.

Swierenga, Robert P. "Ethnocultural Political Analysis: A New Approach to American Ethnic Studies." *Journal of American Studies*, 5 (April 1971), 59–79.

Thernstrom, Stephan. "Socialism and Social Mobility." In *Failure of a Dream? Essays in the History of American Socialism*, edited by Peter Laslett and Seymour M. Lipset, 509–25. New York: Doubleday, 1974.

_____ and Peter R. Knights. "Men in Motion: Some Data and Speculations about Urban Population Mobility in Nineteenth-Century America." *Journal of Interdisciplinary History*, 1 (Autumn 1970), 7–35.

Throne, Mildred. "A Population Study of an Iowa County in 1850." *Iowa Journal of History*, 57 (October 1959), 305–30.

Trester, Delmer J. "David Tod and the Gubernatorial Campaign of 1844." *Ohio State Archaeological and Historical Quarterly*, 62 (April 1953), 162–78.

Vedder, Richard K., and Lowell E. Gallaway. "Migration and the Old Northwest." In *Essays in Nineteenth Century Economic History: The Old Northwest*, edited by David C. Klingaman and Richard K. Vedder, 159–76. Athens: Ohio University Press, 1975.

Walsh, Margaret. "The Spatial Evolution of the Mid-western Pork Industry, 1835–75." *Journal of Historical Geography*, 4 (January 1978), 1–22.

Weatherford, John W. "The Short Life of Manhattan, Ohio." *Ohio Historical Quarterly*, 65 (October 1956), 376–98.

Winkle, Kenneth J. "A Social Analysis of Voter Turnout in Ohio, 1850–1860." *Journal of Interdisciplinary History*, 13 (Winter 1983), 411–35.

Wood, J. S. "Elaboration of a Settlement System: The New England Village in the Federal Period." *Journal of Historical Geography*, 10 (October 1984), 331–56.

Zelinsky, Wilbur. "Changes in the Geographic Patterns of Rural Population in the United States, 1790–1960." *Geographical Review*, 52 (October 1962), 492–524.

Zimmer, Basil G. "Participation of Migrants in Urban Structures." *American Sociological Review*, 20 (April 1955), 218–24.
Zuckerman, Michael. "The Social Context of Democracy in Massachusetts." *William and Mary Quarterly*, 3d ser., 25 (October 1968), 523–44.

Dissertations and unpublished papers

Bohmer, David H. "Voting Behavior During the First American Party System: Maryland, 1796–1816." Unpublished Ph.D. diss., University of Michigan, 1974.
Bourke, Paul F., and Donald A. DeBats. "Society and Politics in a New Community: Washington County, Oregon, in the 1850s." Unpublished paper presented at Social Science History Association meeting, 1980.
Parkerson, Donald H., and Jo Ann Parkerson. "Estimating the Population Dynamics of New York State, 1845–1855." Unpublished paper presented at Social Science History Assocation meeting, 1985.
Rozett, John M. "The Social Bases of Party Conflict in the Age of Jackson: Individual Voting Behavior in Greene County, Illinois, 1838–1848." Unpublished Ph.D. dissertation, University of Michigan, 1974.
Winkle, Kenneth J. "Lincoln's Springfield Revisited: Community and Politics in the Antebellum Midwest." Unpublished paper presented at Social Science History Association meeting, 1985.
"Political Friends: Migration and Officeholding in Lincoln's Springfield." Unpublished paper presented at Social Science History Association meeting, 1986.
"The Politics of Community: Migration and Politics in Antebellum Ohio." Unpublished Ph.D. dissertation, University of Wisconsin, 1984.
"The Voters of Lincoln's Springfield: Politics and Community in the Antebellum Midwest." Unpublished paper presented at Organization of American Historians meeting, 1986.
"Voting Unit or Community? Ecological Inference and Community Studies." Unpublished paper presented at Social Science History Association meeting, 1982.

Index